Reinventing Rhetoric Scholarship

Reinventing Rhetoric Scholarship

Fifty Years of the Rhetoric Society of America

Edited by Roxanne Mountford, Dave Tell, and David Blakesley

Parlor Press
Anderson, South Carolina
www.parlorpress.com

Parlor Press LLC, Anderson, South Carolina, USA

© 2020 by The Rhetoric Society of America. Individual chapters are copyrighted by the respective authors and published under Creative Commons license, "Attribution-NonCommercial-NoDerivatives 4.0 International (CC BY-NC-ND 4.0)," subject to the standard conditions.

All rights reserved. Printed in the United States of America
SAN: 254-8879

Library of Congress Cataloging-in-Publication Data on File

Names: Mountford, Roxanne, 1962- editor. | Tell, Dave, 1976- editor. | Blakesley, David, editor.
Title: Reinventing rhetoric scholarship : fifty years of the Rhetoric Society of America / edited by Roxanne Mountford, Dave Tell, and David Blakesley.
Description: First edition. | Anderson, South Carolina : Parlor Press, 2021. | Includes bibliographical references. | Summary: "Reinventing Rhetoric Scholarship: Fifty Years of the Rhetoric Society of America collects essays reflecting on the history of the Rhetoric Society of America and the organization's 18th Biennial Conference theme, "Reinventing Rhetoric: Celebrating the Past, Building the Future," on the occasion of the Society's 50th anniversary"-- Provided by publisher.
Identifiers: LCCN 2020048492 (print) | LCCN 2020048493 (ebook) | ISBN 9781643170985 (paperback) | ISBN 9781643170992 (pdf) | ISBN 9781643171005 (epub)
Subjects: LCSH: Rhetoric. | Rhetoric--Research. | Rhetoric--Study and teaching. | Rhetoric Society of America--History.
Classification: LCC P301 .R353 2021 (print) | LCC P301 (ebook) | DDC 808--dc23
LC record available at https://lccn.loc.gov/2020048492
LC ebook record available at https://lccn.loc.gov/2020048493

Cover and interior design by David Blakesley.
Cover image by Wyron A on Unsplash. Used by permission.
RSA 2014 logo designed by Lori Klopp.
Printed on acid-free paper.

3 4 5

Parlor Press, LLC is an independent publisher of scholarly and trade titles in print and multimedia formats. This book is available in print and digital formats from Parlor Press on the World Wide Web at http://www.parlorpress.com or through online and brick-and-mortar bookstores. For submission information or to find out about Parlor Press publications, write to Parlor Press, 3015 Brackenberry Drive, Anderson, SC 29621, or e-mail editor@parlorpress.com.

Contents

Fiftieth Anniversary: Looking Back   3

RSA at Fifty: (Re)Inventing Stories   5
Andrea A. Lunsford

A History of RSA in Ten Minutes   19
Carolyn R. Miller

An RSA Fellow Remembers: The Last 25 Years   24
Jacqueline Jones Royster

Why We Named Ourselves a Society: Richard E. Young on the Origins of the RSA   28
Richard E. Young with Richard Leo Enos

Autobiography of an Accidental Rhetorician   32
James J. Murphy

The Founding of the Rhetoric Society of America   36
Victor J. Vitanza

Walker to the Rescue   38
Jack Selzer

Another Hard Look at Ourselves: The Transdisciplinary Influence of Rhetoric of Science Scholarship   44
Leah Ceccarelli

Reconsidering the "Divorce" between Speech and English: Rethinking Disciplinary History through Microhistory"   54
David Stock

Nervously Loquacious at the Edge of an Abyss   63
David Blakesley

Women, Foreigners, and the Pragmatic Origins
of Speech Communication   69
Zornitsa Keremidchieva

On Not Repeating Mistakes: The Case for a More Inclusive
Society for the Study of Catholic Rhetoric   77
Elizabethada A. Wright

Reinventing the Field: Looking Forward   87

The Other Toulmin Model: Concepts, Topoi, Evolution   88
Ben Wetherbee

A Friendly Injustice: Kenneth Burke, René Girard,
and the Rhetoric of Religion   97
Paul Lynch

Inspiration as Invention: Continuing Reflections on the
Relationship between Religion and Rhetoric   107
Joonna Smitherman Trapp

Enlivening the Rhetorical Imagination: Rorty, Vico, and
the Poetics of Rhetorical Invention   116
Scott Welsh and Laura Leavitt

Inventing in Our Own House: Theorizing Democracy
from the Standpoint of Rhetoric   123
Michelle Iten

The Mt. Oread Manifesto and the Realities of 2018   131
Joseph Good

Some Reflections on the Wideness of the Atlantic   138
Kristian Bjørkdahl

Why Do We Study Rhetoric? How Should We Do It?
Who Should We Do It for? Greetings from a Rhetorical
Cousin Living at the Edge of Europe   146
Jens E. Kjeldsen

Rhetorical Interventions   155

Do I Look Fat in this Essay?   156
Abby Knoblauch

What Happened to Hubert Humphrey?   164
David Zarefsky

What Institutional Logics Can Teach Us About Institutional Rhetorics (And Why We Should Care)   172
Ryan Skinnell

A Rhetoric of Food Justice Movements: An Exploration in Rhetorical Quilting   179
Shelley Sizemore and Ron Von Burg

Veterans Deployed to Standing Rock: The Rhetoric of Serving Country through Peaceful Protest   187
Heidi Hamilton

Reinventing *Yin-Yang* to Teach Rhetoric to Women   196
Hui Wu

Rethinking the Oxymoron: Situating Campbell's "Rhetoric of Women's Liberation" in Waves of Feminist Rhetorical Practices   205
Rachel Chapman Daugherty

The Biopolitics of Counter-Attunement: A Marxist-Foucauldian Critical Agency   214
Catherine Chaput

The Invention and Reinvention of the Outsider Persona: Jackson, Trump, and Anti-Establishment Ethos   221
Jacob W. Justice

Contributors   232

Reinventing Rhetoric Scholarship

Fiftieth Anniversary: Looking Back

RSA AT FIFTY: (RE)INVENTING STORIES

Andrea A. Lunsford

Greetings and happy fiftieth birthday to the Rhetoric Society of America. It is a pleasure and a great privilege to be with you here today in Minneapolis, the city where we first gathered half a century ago, and I am grateful to the University of Minnesota Departments of Writing Studies and Communication Studies as well as to the magnificent Weisman Art Museum and to the conference organizers for this inspiring and challenging program—and for giving me this opportunity to address you on this epideictic occasion.

Now, please take a trip with me back to the year of our founding: 1968, in the heart of the civil rights movement. *The Year that Rocked the World, The Year that Shaped a Generation, The Year that America Grew Up*—these are just a few of the many books devoted to the twelve momentous months of that year. Even if you were not around in 1968, you know a lot of the story:

> **January 23**: North Korea captures the USS Pueblo
>
> **February 27**: Walter Cronkite delivers his scathing "Report from Vietnam" speech
>
> **March 16**: The My Lai Massacre (it was commemorated this year by a brilliant opera performed by Rinde Eckert, singing the role of Hugh Thompson, Jr., who tried to stop the massacre, and the Kronos Quartet)
>
> **March 31**: Johnson announces he will not run for re-election
>
> **April 4**: Martin Luther King, Jr. is assassinated; Mahalia Jackson sings "Precious Lord, Take My Hand" at the funeral
>
> **April 11**: Civil Rights (Fair Housing) Act is passed
>
> **June 5**: Robert F. Kennedy is assassinated

August 28: Protests during the Democratic National Convention in Chicago against the Vietnam War and police brutality erupt in riots

October 16: Tommie Smith and John Carlos raise gloved fists in support of human rights at the Summer Olympic Games

October 31: Johnson announces the end of bombing in Vietnam, though "the American War" went on until 1975

November 5: Nixon is elected

December 24: Apollo 8 circles the moon and sends back the now iconic Earthrise photo

In 1968, James Baldwin published *Tell Me How Long the Train's Been Gone* along with a series of essays and a famous interview in *Esquire* called "How to Cool It." The Academy Awards were postponed until April 10th following Dr. King's murder. That year, *In the Heat of the Night, Guess Who's Coming to Dinner, Bonnie and Clyde,* and *The Graduate* won coveted nominations for best film. *In the Heat of the Night* came away with the prize, as did Rod Steiger for best actor: none for Howard Rollins, the African American actor who played Virgil Gibbs in that movie or for Sidney Poitier, who starred with Katherine Hepburn (best actress) in *Guess Who's Coming to Dinner*. The Grammy award for album of the year went to The Beatles' *Sergeant Pepper's Lonely Hearts Club Band* (record of the year was The 5th Dimension's *Up, Up and Away*) while the best-selling singles that year were The Beatles' "Hey, Jude" and Otis Redding's "Sitting on the Dock of the Bay." At the Emmys, *Mission Impossible* and *Get Smart* were big winners; the only person of color nominated seems to have been Bill Cosby for his work in *I Spy*. Bill Russell and the Celtics defeated the Lakers in the NBA championship; the Packers beat the Raiders in the second Super Bowl; the Detroit Tigers took down the reigning St. Louis Cardinals in the World Series. The number of baseball players of color made for a pretty short list. And we didn't get Title IX until 1972. In 1968, there was no WNBA and little support of any kind for women's sports.

That's a bit of a stroll down memory lane, and I haven't even mentioned Timothy Leary, who was arrested in 1968 amid the heyday of experimental drug use. Or Allen Ginsberg, who testified for the defense in the Chicago Conspiracy trial and led crowds of young people chanting on the shores of Lake Michigan. Or ever more counterculture antiwar protests, including those led by Bobbie Seale and the Chicago Seven, the enormous changes brought about by television, or Marshall McLuhan's cunning assessment of them in *The Medium is the Massage* (1967) and *War and Peace in the Global Village* (1968).

But a mere list of events, awards, and publications from this year, no matter how lengthy, doesn't begin to capture the atmosphere of the time. To me, teaching public high school in Orlando, Florida, after being discouraged from pursuing a PhD ("go home and have babies," my white male professors told me), the very air vibrated with tension and sometimes terror. The Ku Klux Klan was thriving in the South: a September 13, 1968, broadside advertised a "Public Speaking Event" at the Lonesome Pine Rodeo grounds in Blacksburg, Virginia, sponsored by the South Carolina Knights of the Klan and speeches by the Grand Dragon and the Great Titan. I sat in stunned silence as our principal announced Dr. King's assassination and watched with horror the bloody images of Bobby Kennedy's real-life death on live TV. For the first time in my life, I feared for the survival of the country and especially for the country's populations of color.

As Charles Kaiser writes in *1968 in America*, "1968 was the pivotal year of the sixties; the moment when all of a nation's impulses toward violence, idealism, diversity, and disorder peaked to produce the greatest possible hope—and the worst possible despair." He goes on to argue that

> Black people are the real heroes of this story. Before everything else that happened in the sixties, it was their rejection of the submissive roles white men had selected for them that legitimized the aspirations of every other victim of oppression. After that, the physically handicapped could insist on equal access to all public facilities—and the students of a college for the deaf could demand a deaf president—because Blacks had resolved at the beginning of the decade to demand the right to be served at every lunch counter in the land. (256)

But while these events, a cacophony of conflicting, contradictory, exhilarating, and terrifying moments were taking place, another less dramatic but potentially important movement began, what we now think of as part of the "the revival of rhetoric" in the sixties. The appearance of Richard M. Weaver's *The Ethics of Rhetoric* in 1953, Daniel Fogarty's *Roots for a New Rhetoric* in 1959, Wayne Booth's *The Rhetoric of Fiction* in 1961, Sister Miriam Joseph's *Rhetoric in Shakespeare's Time* in 1962, Karl Wallace's "The Substance of Rhetoric: Good Reasons" in 1963, Edward P. J. Corbett's *Classical Rhetoric for the Modern Student* in 1965, Kenneth Burke's *Language as Symbolic Action* in 1966, Lloyd Bitzer's "The Rhetorical Situation" in 1968, Perelman and Oldsbrecht-Tyteca's *The New Rhetoric*, written in 1958 and translated into English in 1968, and the founding of one of our field's major journals, *Philosophy and Rhetoric*, co-edited by Carroll Arnold and Henry Johnstone, are just some of the key texts that helped fuel an interest in rhetoric and a reexamination of its role in education and society. Perhaps it's not surprising, then, that in the spring of 1968, just weeks before Dr. King's death, an invitational workshop on rhetoric was held as part of the Conference on College Composition and Communication (CCCC) right here in Minneapolis. Organized by J. Carter Rowland, the workshop included Wayne Booth, William Irmscher, Ross Winterowd, John Rycenga, Henry Johnstone, Richard Larson, Corbett, and other (white) men who became members of the Board of Directors and crafted what would become the Rhetoric Society of America's mission statement, printed in the first edition of the *Rhetoric Society Newsletter*:

> The first purpose of the Rhetoric Society is to promote communication among those who are concerned with rhetoric . . . and with the use of language between man and man [sic]: rhetoricians, linguists, literary theorists, literary critics, psychologists, sociologists, teachers of English composition, and English editors from textbook publishing houses. The Rhetoric Society's second purpose will be to disseminate knowledge of rhetoric and the powers of rhetoric to those who have been previously unaware of it. In addition the Rhetoric Society will be prepared to stand sponsor to seminars in the MLA, panels and workshops in the CCCC, and to sponsor and provide participants for lectures and panels in the NCTE and for all other occasions. (1)

This beginning, however, didn't bear immediate fruit, and so some members staged an attempt to revive the Society in 1971. Larson drafted a constitution and Winterowd mailed it out to all recorded members (none of color as far as I can determine, and only a very few women, though Janice Lauer was listed), asking for their approval and inviting nominees for an eleven-member Board of Directors. Members duly complied (no dissenting votes) and proposed twenty-four members as candidates for the Board. A ballot with names and vitas of those agreeing to stand for election went out in the fall of 1971. Those elected included Dudley Bailey, Corbett, Larson, and Winterowd from English; Carroll Arnold, Donald Bryant, Leland Griffin, Lawrence Rosenfield, and Karl Wallace from communication; George Yoos from philosophy; and Ellis Page from educational psychology. The minutes note that "No students were elected to the Board because none were nominated." I presume that the same could be said for women and people of color: none were elected because none were nominated.

The group then decided that the Directors needed to meet in person to select officers, and since the CCCC and the Speech Communication Association of the Eastern States were both meeting in Boston in March, they met there, selecting Corbett as Chair of the Board and Larson as secretary; Yoos agreed to serve as Editor of the *Rhetoric Society Newsletter* beginning in the fall of 1972. The 1972 CCCC meeting was chaired by Liz McPherson (at last, a woman!) with the theme of "Reconsidering Roles: What are We About" and by a fairly odd coincidence, I was there too: it was my first conference of any kind, ever, because I had screwed my courage to the sticking point some months earlier and proposed a panel with a colleague and a young African American woman at Hillsborough Community College in Tampa, where I taught for four years. To my surprise and terror, the panel was accepted, and so the three of us drove from Tampa to Boston, straight through, since we couldn't afford to stay overnight on the way up. I held a BA and MA in English, I was teaching writing when all I knew anything about was British and American literature. But I had received—free from the publisher—a copy of the second edition of Corbett's *Classical Rhetoric for the Modern Student* in 1971, and found in that volume someone talking seriously about the teaching of writing. I was electrified, practically memorized the book, and applied not only to the CCCC but to Ohio State's PhD program, in which Corbett taught. I was not admitted right away but put on a "waiting list"—though they eventually got down to me, and I was somewhat grudgingly admitted as a "mature student" in the late spring and given a graduate teaching assistantship. I resigned my job and prepared to move to Columbus in the fall. So while the group of eminent (white male) scholars met to rekindle the Society and to relaunch the *Newsletter*, a hopeful white woman was presenting a workshop with her African American student and trying to hitch her star to rhetoric and composition.

I arrived at Ohio State in the fall of 1972 to find that Corbett didn't teach any courses on rhetoric; rather he was teaching eighteenth century poetry and the Bible as literature. But I soon found that rhetoric was taught in the speech communication department by James Goldwin, Goodwin Berquist, and others, so I set about auditing all their courses while lobbying Corbett to begin teaching in the field (he eventually taught history of rhetoric and a course on style). And to my great good fortune, Corbett was at the time editing *CCC*, so I got to learn that field by serving as his assistant for four years.

And, of course, I joined the Rhetoric Society of America and subscribed from 1972 on to the *Newsletter*, which Maureen Goggin describes as being "transformed from a practical tool for exchanging news items, descriptions of works-in-progress, and program descriptions to a sophisticated scholarly journal, . . . marked in 1976 when the journal was upgraded and renamed

Rhetoric Society Quarterly" and still edited by Yoos (630). (Goggin goes on to note that it "provides invaluable bibliographies on various topics concerning rhetoric," including a fairly early publication of my own, the 1986 "A Bibliographic Note on William Edmonstoune Aytoun's Manuscript: *Lectures on Rhetoric and Belle Lettres*," the handwritten copes of which I had read and studied at the National Library of Scotland.) And I was lucky enough to attend some of the early meetings of the RSA, organized by Charles Kneupper at the University of Texas at Arlington. The first was held in 1984, with Bitzer giving the keynote on "George Orwell's Rejection of Tyrannical Rhetoric"; the second in 1986 with Corbett delivering "Where Are the Snows of Yesteryear: Has Rhetoric Come a Long Way in the Last 25 Years?" Thus are the small ironies and coincidences of our lives that, in retrospect, begin to trace the outlines of a life's work, a life's story.

What I have been attempting to do in these remarks thus far is to suggest that out of the climactic uproar of the 1960s, a story about rhetoric began to emerge, a "new" rhetoric—one that sought to reclaim principles of classical western rhetoric, establish the role it should play in education and in public discourse, and conceive of writing and speaking as actions rather than as aesthetic artifacts. It was a story I embraced wholeheartedly when I began my graduate studies in the early 1970s.

In retrospect, as Deborah Brandt has taught us, as the cultural capital of writing grew, beginning in the age of the printing press and reaching a crescendo in the nineteenth and early twentieth centuries, the fortunes of rhetoric declined. What counted was not the eloquence of old but what could be put in writing. As a result, colleges had turned away from the "old" rhetorical tradition, which had focused on students composing and performing their own discourses, and increasingly to controlled instruction in correct writing and, primarily, to reading, to hermeneutics, and to the consumption rather than the production of discourse.

So what was also "new" in the 1960s and 1970s revival of rhetoric was, at least in part, an attempt to return to the old tradition, and, a little later, to concentrate on the actual discursive practices and products of student writers. What characterized early programs in rhetoric was not only a recognition that the ancient arts of rhetoric provided a robust theoretical and historical foundation for the teaching of writing and speaking but also a determination to achieve disciplinary status for the field, along with a deep commitment to undergraduate education and access to that education for all students (think Geneva Smitherman and Mina Shaughnessy, whose *Talkin' and Testifyin'* and *Errors and Expectations* appeared within months of each other in 1977). What is new in this story of the rhetorical tradition, then, is the very self-conscious linking of rhetoric with writing or composition.

As I noted earlier, this revival of classical rhetoric was something I took to heart: my very first publication, in fact, was a short essay titled "Let's Get Back to the Classics." So I more or less bought the story of western rhetoric's origins and powers wholesale—the golden age of Greek and Roman rhetoric, which laid down principles and theories and practices that could be taught and learned and that could guide a life worth living. Everyone here knows that story well. And everyone here knows that, eventually, some—both inside and outside the RSA—began to question it. I was teaching at the University of British Columbia in the mid-1980s when my students and I began to ask, "Where are the women? Where are people of color?" The story of western rhetoric, so crisply and elegantly told in the second edition of Corbett's *Classical Rhetoric for the Modern Student* still held power, but its omissions became more and more noticeable. As the redoubtable Kathleen Welch has pointed out repeatedly, "We in comp/rhet face a problem that confronts all our colleagues. Curricula, students, and faculty remain so white that we appear to be a blizzard" (168). Indeed, our group still seems to be predominantly blizzardish in complexion: and while seven of our eighteen presidents have been women (Win Horner was the first in 1988), no person of color has led RSA—until this year, when we are being led, brilliantly, by Kirt Wilson.

But thanks to scholars like Karlyn Kohrs Campbell (whose keynote at the 4th biennial RSA conference is the now-classic "Genre and Culture: The Test Case of Women's Rhetoric"), and Cheris Kramer and Sally Miller Gearhart in the 1970s, and Shirley Wilson Logan, Elizabeth Flynn, Sonja and Karen Foss, Cindy Griffin, Barbara Biesecker, Pat Bizzell, Jackie Royster, Susan Jarratt and many others in the 1980s and 1990s (and I could go on and on, including many feminist scholars in this room today), women began to insert themselves into the story of rhetoric. Their efforts were echoed by other African American, Latinx, Anglo, Chinese, and Indigenous writers, speakers, and rhetors.

Shortly after the turn of the new century, RSA helped spearhead an effort to bring scholars from ten organizations together to talk about forming an Alliance of Rhetoric Societies (the American Forensic Association, American Society for the History of Rhetoric, Coalition of Women Scholars in the History of Rhetoric, Canadian Society for the History of Rhetoric, CCCC, International Society for the History of Rhetoric, International Society for the Study of Argumentation, Kenneth Burke Society, National Communication Association, and RSA). Out of these meetings came plans for a working conference, which the late, much-missed Michael Leff and I co-chaired, held at Northwestern University in the fall of 2003. Those who wanted to participate submitted statements in response to one of the following questions, which I'm paraphrasing here:

1. How ought we to understand the concept of rhetorical agency?

2. Do we have a "rhetorical tradition"? Are we better advised to think of traditions rather than a single tradition? If we do recognize a tradition or several traditions, how do we identify and characterize it (or them)?

3. What should be the institutional and social goals for academic rhetoric in the twenty-first century? How can rhetoric best contribute to the social, political, and cultural environments that extend the University?

4. What does it mean to teach rhetoric? What does it mean to teach composition and performance seriously? What is the relationship between rhetoric and composition? Should they be distinguished?

(For more, see the interview with Leff and me in *Kairos*.) Plenary speakers Jerzy Axer, Royster, Karl Campbell, and Steven Mailloux, and respondents Booth, Jim Aune, Sharon Crowley, and Jeffrey Walker set us up for the major work of the conference: small group discussions of the four major questions, with each group reporting out at the end. Though the group was still predominantly white and male, white women and women of color were present, along with some scholars from beyond our shores, lending at least a bit of international perspective to the deliberations. As Leff wrote in an essay we published following the event, "At the ARS conference, the working group on tradition began with what Pat Bizzell and Susan Jarratt describe as 'a plea from one of the conference organizers to accept the pluralization of rhetoric's tradition.' They are referring, of course, to Andrea Lunsford" (6).

In spite of Leff's plug, I was certainly not the only one arguing for pluralization, for a retelling of the story of rhetoric. But there were also plenty of others arguing that we should hold to the tried and true old story of western rhetoric. Indeed, the discussions were lively, to say the very least, as we struggled over the story we would tell about rhetoric and its tradition or traditions, about who is allowed in and who is not allowed into the circle of rhetoric. Those conference discussions and struggles were directly related to a project in its inception: an anthology of rhetoric and writing that hoped to embody a much more inclusive story of rhetoric. In the early years of this century, colleagues Jarratt, Royster, Robert Hariman, Lu Ming Mao, Thomas P. Miller, Jody Enders and I proposed *The Norton Anthology of Rhetoric and Writing*, with the heady and, as it turned out, completely ridiculous idea that we could produce such a text quickly. But while it was relatively easy to come to agreement on principles (listed below), elaborating these principles, deciding on themes or what we call "throughlines" to bring coherence to the volume, choosing selections, and writing introductions, headnotes, glosses—was daunting and often paralyzing:

- To demonstrate the multivocal, multifocal, multiethnic, multimedia nature of rhetoric
- To reunite reading, writing, speaking, listening, and performing
- To honor practice as well as theory
- To define rhetoric as a global phenomenon.

Like Elizabeth Warren, however, we persevered, adding Kirt Wilson to our group of editors and, at long last, submitting the general introduction and first several parts of the anthology to Norton in recent months. We hope that the manuscript will soon be complete and that this attempt at a more inclusive and multiplicitous story of rhetoric and writing will be published with the next two years.

Why is it important to me to think of rhetorical traditions, and of the work we do as rhetoricians and rhetors, in terms of narrative, of story? In the most simple terms, because story is the universal genre (we know of no culture on earth that does not have stories), because stories lie at the base of all cultures, because our lives are attempts to tell particular stories that can guide us, because, in Anne Haas Dyson and Celia Genishi's telling book title, we have *A Need for Story*. Walter Fisher, defining people as *homo narrans*, argues that "In the beginning was the word or, more accurately, the logos. And in the beginning logos meant story" (74). Fisher goes on to posit a new perspective that "sees people as storytellers—authors and co-authors who creatively read and evaluate the texts of life" and elaborates this in what he calls the "narrative paradigm" (86).

In "Life as Narrative," Jerome Bruner argues that "the culturally-shaped cognitive and linguistic processes that guide the self-telling of life narratives achieve the power to structure perceptual experience, to organize memory, to segment and purpose-build the very events of a life." (694). And very recently, in her brilliant exploration of how writing and reading about love can help students come to voice and achieve agency, Bronwyn LaMay demonstrates how stories—the ones they tell and the ones they read—literally shape who these young people can become. LaMay's analysis, based on her two-year ethnographic study of students of color in a very tough California high school coming together (unwillingly at first) to discuss the plots and counterplots of their life stories through an intimate encounter with Toni Morrison's *Song of Solomon*, shows the students' growing awareness of how they are living out ingrained stories about who they are and what they will become, stories created and told by a society (and even a school system) that isn't interested in hearing their voices. But it also shows some of them challenging these ingrained stories and beginning to resist and to retell them.

In a book published recently, journalist and author Steve Almond presents *Bad Stories: What the Hell Just Happened to Our Country*, in which each of the seventeen chapters tells a "bad story," from "The United States is a Representative Democracy" to "What Amuses Us Can't Hurt Us," to "Give Us Your Tired, Your Poor, Your Huddled Masses." Throughout, Almond is at pains to show how these bad stories shape and limit our ability literally to "think straight" about our country and our culture, much less to "strike through the mask" of these stories and create new ones that embody the values we want to claim. Almond quotes Israeli historian Yuval Noah Harari, who in *A Brief History of Humankind* argues that "our species came to dominate the world because we learned to cooperate flexibly in large numbers. This capacity stems from our ability to believe in the imagined, to tell stories that extend our bonds beyond clan loyalties" (6).

I've been belaboring an emphasis on story throughout these remarks because I want to argue not only that it is important to understand, challenge, explore, and remake the stories we tell about rhetoric, its origins, principles, uses, and practices—but also because it is important to take on the *responsibility* for story, for narrative, and for the way stories shape our experience of the world. Along with Lyotard and scholars in many other disciplines, we have interrogated, challenged, and rejected master narratives, master stories that have held enormous power over our lives. We know in our bones what Nigerian writer Chimamanda Ngozi Adichie calls "The Danger of a Single Story," when whole groups of richly complex people are reduced to a single narrative. In her remarkable 2009 TED talk of that title, Adichie tells about her life as a child in Nigeria, growing up reading British and American stories and writing her own stories with characters that all had "fair hair and blue eyes." That was a single story that shaped her way of reading and writing. In her talk, she says it's fairly simple to create a single story: just "show people as one thing and one thing only, over and over again, and that is what they will become." Adichie notes that stories are enmeshed in structures of power, that "how they are told, when they are told, how many are told are all dependent on power, and the ultimate power is to tell the story of another person—but to make it THE definitive story of that person." Or that people. Or that culture. Perhaps all times have been defined by struggles over stories, who gets to tell them, who has the power to create and reify them. But certainly our own time is rife with the struggle over stories, over narratives. In the spring of this year, even military officials in this country were talking about a "war of narratives." And almost hourly, we can witness attempts to create a "single story" of supposed past American greatness and the draconian steps that are "necessary" to recapture it.

On a more hopeful note, of course, we have only to think of #OccupyWallSt, #BlackLivesMatter, #Metoo, #TimesUp, #enoughisenough, #neveragain, #indigenouswomenrise, #lagenteunida—and many others, to see efforts to create narratives that can displace a single story about groups of people and cultures. In a recent issue of *Anthropology News*, Anna Babel uses speech act theory to analyze the discourse of #MeToo, tracing the locutionary, illocutionary, and perlocutionary forces deployed in this discourse and showing how they work to create a story that has had effects internationally. She writes,

> #MeToo does not *create* a community; it opens an existing community to public discussion. The #MeToo hashtag asks people to open their eyes and ears to stories they may have once been able to ignore. It might be easy to ignore or dismiss one woman, but can you discount the stories of nearly every woman you know? The widespread use of #MeToo exposes or educates members of society who may not have been conscious of the ubiquity of sexual harassment and assault—precisely because whisper networks are closed or among friends, following informal channels. . . .
>
> Whisper networks educate, [she goes on] but they also confine. They make only some of us responsible for our stories. One of the difficult things about the Larry Nassar case and other recent sexual abuse scandals is the long list of people who could have, should have, were in a position to know what was going on and chose not to know. Telling a secret in public means it is no longer a secret. With that authority comes responsibility; when we all know the stories, we can't claim "I didn't know." The use of the #MeToo hashtag, then, not only opens up the closed community of whisper networks to public view, it asks the public to take responsibility for the stories they hear, to see things they may not want to see. (69-70)

As I think about the past and the future of RSA, I want our group to take on the project not only of examining and challenging narratives and stories that crush dreams, choke freedoms, and leave people voiceless but also to work hard at creating and maintaining stories that are worthy of our best vision of ourselves, our discipline, our cultures, our planet. What I want is for us to pursue what I am calling *narrative justice*. Because I don't see how we can ever achieve social justice, for example, when the narratives in which people are trapped, silenced, and harmed simply will not allow for it. Hence the need for *just narratives,* which can then lay the groundwork for and make possible social justice.

When I look at this year's RSA Program, put together by our president-elect Kirt Wilson along with Roxanne Mountford, Bill Keith, and Christa Olson, I see evidence that the work I am calling for is under way: as they say in their welcome, "RSA scholars are pursuing research into international and decolonialized forms of rhetoric, paths which represent well our collective future." I see ASHR sponsoring an entire day of discussions of "Diversity and Rhetorical Traditions." I see sessions on reinventing stories of wilderness preservation, on understanding how comics help to invent and reinvent just narratives, more just stories about indigeneity, about what's "acceptable" in academic discourse, about the meaning of "refugee" and "immigrant" and "literacy" and even "the people," about reshaping public memory, the discourse of HIV/AIDS, of (dis)ability, of the second amendment. Just narratives of "queer life," queer worldmaking, and global feminism; a close look at the stories embedded in our "key terms"; the use of textiles to create just narratives, and so much more on reinventing—our pedagogies, our journals, our methods, our discipline.

I believe this conference can stand as testimony and signpost to the future of the RSA, one in which scholars and teachers and practitioners of rhetoric will continue to broaden and deepen the scope of rhetoric and link hands and stories with rhetors around the globe to resist the dangerous and harmful single stories reiterated daily on radical right-wing media: "only guns can keep us safe," "immigrants are rapists and animals," "mainstream media delivers only 'fake' news," "historically black colleges and universities are 'pioneers of choice,'" "climate change is a hoax." Such stories, as I've argued, hold tremendous power if they go unchecked. Against them, we are already at work creating inclusive, respectful, and lovingly playful stories that reflect our best selves, our best values.

We have the tools. We have the ability. We have the strategies, from classical tropes and schemes to the powerful patterns of African American vernacular traditions. We have the methods, from Ratcliffe's rhetorical listening, to Lather's ethical ethnography, to Royster and Kirsch's critical imagination, strategic contemplation, social circulation, and globalizing perspectives.

Now I ask—do we have the WILL to use the tools and abilities and strategies and methods at our disposal to create and sustain stories that promise narrative justice for all. That's my birthday wish for RSA at Fifty—and well beyond.

Works Cited

Adiche, Chimamanda Ngozi. "The Danger of a Single Story." *TED Global* 2009. 18 April, 2016. https://www.ted.com/talks/chimamanda_adichie_the_danger_of_a_single_story. Accessed 20 June 2019.

Almond, Steve. *Bad Stories*. Red Hen Press, 2018.

Babel, Anna. "The Invisible Walls of the Whisper Network." *Anthropology News*, vol. 59, no. 3, 2019, pp. 67-72.

Booth, Wayne. *The Rhetoric of Fiction*, U Chicago P, 1983.

Brandt, Deborah. *The Rise of Writing: Redefining Mass Literacy*. Cambridge UP, 2014.

Bruner, "Life as Narrative." *Social Research*, vol. 54, no. 1, Spring 1987, pp. 11-32.

Campbell, Karlyn Kohrs. "Agency: Promiscuous and Protean." *Communication and Critical/Cultural Studies*, vol 2, no. 1, 2005, pp. 1-19.

Corbett, Edward P. J. "A New Look at Old Rhetoric." *Rhetoric: Theories for Application. Papers Presented at the 1965 Convention of the NCTE*, edited by Starr Canastraro and Robert M. Gorrell, NCTE, 1967, pp.16-22.

Corbett, Edward P. J. *Classical Rhetoric for the Modern Student*. Oxford UP, 1965.

—. "Statement from the Chairman." *Rhetoric Society Newsletter*, vol. 2, no. 1, 1972, p. 2.

—. "What Is Being Revived?" *College Composition and Communication*, vol. 18, no. 3, 1967, pp. 166-172.

Denborough, David. *Retelling the Stories of Our Lives: Everyday Narrative Therapy to Draw Inspiration and Transform Experience*. W. W. Norton, 2014.

Dyson, Anne Haas, and Celia Genishi. *The Need for Story*. NCTE, 1994.

Fisher, Walter R. "The Narrative Paradigm: In the Beginning." *Journal of Communication*, vol. 35, no. 4, 1985, pp. 74–89.

Goggin, Maureen Daly. "The Rhetoric Society of America: Origins and Contributions." *Encyclopedia of Rhetoric and Composition: Communication from Ancient Times to the Information Age*, edited by Theresa Enos, Garland, 1996, pp. 629-30.

"Interview with Professors Andrea Lunsford and Michael Leff about the Alliance of Rhetoric Societies. *Kairos*, vol. 8, no. 2, 2003 http://kairos.technorhetoric.net/8.2/interviews/arsinterview/intro.htm. Accessed 20 June 2019.

Kaiser, Charles. *1968 in America*. Grove, 1997.

Kaurman, Michael. *1968: The Year America Grew Up*. Roaring Brook, 2005.

Ku Klux Klan. "Public Speaking" Broadside. Sept. 13, 1968, U South Carolina Archives.

Kurlansky, Mark. *1968: The Year That Rocked the World*. Random House, 2005.

LaMay, Bronwyn. *Personal Narrative, Revised: Writing Love and Agency in the High School Classroom*. Teachers College Press, 2016.

Lather, Patricia. *Troubling the Angels*, Perseus, 1997.

Leff, Michael, and Andrea Lunsford, "Afterwards, a Dialogue." *Rhetoric Society Quarterly*, vol. 34, no. 3, 2004, pp. 55-67.

Lugones, Maria. "Playfulness, 'World' Traveling, and Loving Perception." *Hypatia*, vol. 2, no. 2, 1987, pp. 3-19.

Lyotard, Jean-Francois. *The Postmodern Condition: A Report on Knowledge*. U Minnesota P, 1984.

McLuhan, Marshall. *Understanding Media: The Extensions of Man*. 2nd ed., New American Library of Canada, 1966.

Ratcliffe, Krista. *Rhetorical Listening: Identification, Gender, Whiteness*. Southern Illinois UP, 2005.

Registre, Judithe. "Why Narrative Justice Is the Next Frontier for Social Change." *Inclusivus*, Feb. 27, 2018, https://inclusivus.org/inpowered-perspectives/2018/2/27/why-narrative-justice-is-the-next-frontier-for-social-change/. Accessed 20 June 2019.

Roland, J. Carter. "Announcement." *Rhetoric Society Newsletter*, vol. 1, no. 1, 1968, p. 1.

Royster, Jacqueline Jones, and Gesa Kirsch. *Feminist Rhetorical Practices*, Southern Illinois UP, 2012.

Russell, Lisa. "Promoting Responsible Storytelling in Global Health." *YouTube* Dec. 18, 2017, https://www.youtube.com/watch?v=iCTfu0CtKcU. Accessed 20 June 2019.

Spence, Donald P. *Narrative Truth and Historical Truth*. W. W. Norton, 1984.

Thomas, Susan E., editor. *What Is the New Rhetoric?* Cambridge Scholars, 2007.

Welch, Kathleen. "Technology / Writing / Identity in Composition and Rhetoric Studies: Working in the Indicative Mode." In *Living Rhetoric and Composition: Stories of the Discipline*, edited by Duane Roen, Stuart Brown, and Theresa Enos, Routledge, 1998, pp.159-70.

A History of RSA in Ten Minutes

Carolyn R. Miller

The RSA 50th anniversary planners have invented multiple ways to observe and celebrate our history. There are conference sessions: two by the RSA Fellows in which they recollect the first and second 25 years, a Supersession on Reinventing RSA's History, and others on the history and future of many aspects of rhetoric itself. There's also a special anniversary issue of *RSQ* that includes an "anecdotal history" (Halloran).[1] My task here at the 50th anniversary reception is to give you a 10-minute overview of our history. As I am neither a founder nor an historian, I offer this in a spirit of epideictic amateurism.

We date RSA to that significant year, 1968—when I graduated from Penn State with my MA in English, when some of you were serving in Vietnam or trying to get a draft deferment, and when many of you were not yet born. In that year—when MLK and RFK were assassinated; when LBJ signed the Civil Rights Act; when student demonstrations and worker strikes paralyzed France; when the Viet Cong launched the Tet offensive; when protests and violence disrupted the Chicago Democratic convention; when a manned spacecraft, Apollo 8, orbited the moon for the first time; when the film *2001: A Space Odyssey* premiered, the Broadway musical *Hair* opened, and the Beatles' "Hey Jude" was the top single—in that same year a small group of faculty met at the CCCC here in Minneapolis. Among them were people whose names you'll recognize: Wayne Booth, Donald Bryant, Edward P. J. Corbett, Henry Johnstone, Richard Larson, Janice Lauer, Ross Winterowd, George Yoos, and Richard Young ("Board of Directors"). They determined to form a rhetoric society.

The first issue of their *Newsletter*, December 1968, summarized the agreements of the group: "The first purpose of the Rhetoric Society," they said, "is

---

1. In addition to this and the other sources cited here, see Goggin (84–90).

to promote communication among those who are concerned with rhetoric. The Rhetoric Society invites to full participation all those concerned with rhetoric . . . : rhetoricians, linguists, literary theorists, literary critics, psychologists, sociologists, teachers of English composition, and English editors from textbook publishing houses."

"The Rhetoric Society's second purpose," they went on, "will be to disseminate knowledge of rhetoric and the powers of rhetoric to those who have been previously unaware of it. In addition, the Rhetoric Society will be prepared to stand sponsor to seminars in the Modern Language Association, panels and workshops in the Conference on College Composition and Communication, and to sponsor and provide participants for lectures and panels in the National Council of Teachers of English and for all other occasions. Membership in the Rhetoric Society will imply a commitment to aid in all possible ways the dissemination of the knowledge and understanding of rhetoric" ("Outline of Principles and Purposes" 1).

But there is also in the accounts of these early meetings an air of beleaguered apprehension. As newly elected Chairman of the Board Edward Corbett wrote in 1972, "Many of us have few, if any, colleagues with whom we can share our interest and enthusiasm. It is an exciting rhetorical age that we live in, but unless we can keep our own interest in rhetoric active, we are not likely to have much of an impact on the academy and the larger world." He also lamented the diminished state of the treasury but indicated that there was a waiting list of people who wanted to join and expressed confidence "that we will have no difficulty getting enough members to sustain the activities of the Society. In fact," he went on, "we worry more about growing so large that we lose the spirit of intimacy and camaraderie that have always characterized the relationships of those who share a common interest in rhetoric" (3).

As the first Constitution was being drafted in 1969, Richard Young wrote to Ross Winterowd, "The models of the society which I have in mind are the bull-session, the informed conversation, the letter of inquiry or advice, rather than the CCCC, NCTE, or MLA" (qtd. in Young 327).

* * *

How did we get from there to here? You can find many dates and names in the History section of the RSA website, but here are some major milestones:

> 1968, First issue of the *Newsletter of the Rhetoric Society of America* published, 2 pages; annual membership dues listed as $5.00 ("Outline of Principles and Purposes")

1969, Membership is 180, over half with affiliations outside English ("Board Report").

1971, First constitution adopted (Corbett); it provided explicitly for disciplinary diversity on the Board of Directors ("Constitution of the Rhetoric Society of America")

1976, *Newsletter of the RSA* became *Rhetoric Society Quarterly*

1984, First biennial conference held at University of Texas–Arlington

1989, Death of Charles Kneupper, instigator and organizer of the first four conferences, all at UT–Arlington

1991, First *RSQ* issue that was not typewritten and mimeographed on 8.5 x 11-inch paper, but typeset and printed in a standard 6 x 9-inch journal format

1992, First conference away from UT–Arlington, here in Minneapolis (the fifth conference, though the program cover announced it as the fourth, proving that rhetoricians are not mathematicians)

1992, The Kneupper Award for best *RSQ* article inaugurated

2000, George Yoos Distinguished Service Award first given

2000, RSA abandoned its all-volunteer status by contracting with an association management organization (the indispensable Kathie Cesa); membership was about 600

2004, Student chapters authorized by the Board

2004, Awards program expanded to include a dissertation award, a book award, and the Gerard A. Hauser Award for outstanding student conference paper, as well as the recognition of influential members as RSA Fellows.

2005, RSQ moved from editor's academic institution to a commercial publisher, Taylor & Francis

2005, First Summer Institute, held at Kent State University

2007, RSA became a 501(c)3 non-profit organization for tax purposes; membership about 1000

2008, RSA admitted to ACLS, a sign of full scholarly recognition

2010, Death of RSA President Michael Leff, only a month into his term; conference attendance that year was 1100

2011, Development Council established, to encourage fund-raising in support of RSA goals and activities

2012, Book series in Transdisciplinary Rhetoric established at Penn State University Press

* * *

I want to end by circling back to the beginning, to one of the very early newsletters, from July 1969 (the second one, though identified as Vol. 1, No. 1, proving that rhetoricians are not archivists). There, we find a summary of the discussions of the preliminary board of directors, under the title "What Is a 'Rhetoric Society'?"

> Two of the normal activities of a professional association are holding meetings at which exchanges of information among the membership can take place and issuing a journal presenting articles which accomplish this same kind of exchange of information. The members of the provisional board of directors . . . have twice expressed reluctance to see the Society engage in either of these two activities. They point out, quite accurately, that there are more professional meetings than any of us can attend. And that a number of people are already beginning to wonder if they really contribute anything to the profession. Similarly, it is a cliche that there are already too many journals. Here there is a two-fold objection. Not only are there more journals than one can easily, or even with difficulty, follow, but also there are more journals than there are publishable articles. Yet, somehow, these journals are being filled. Against this background comes the question that your preliminary board of directors has been informally wrestling with: what is a "rhetoric society?" ("What Is a 'Rhetoric Society'?")

RSA has answered the question raised by its founders by rejecting their opposition to meetings and journals. It has come a long way from the bull-session and the newsletter, an outcome that some may celebrate but some may regret. But most will agree that despite, or even because of, our growth, we have retained the "intimacy and camaraderie" of those early days.

Works Cited

"Board of Directors." *Newsletter: Rhetoric Society of America*, vol. 1, no. 1, 1968, 1.
"Board Report." *Newsletter: Rhetoric Society of America*, vol. 1, no. 1, 1969, 3.
"Constitution of the Rhetoric Society of America." *Newsletter: Rhetoric Society of America*, vol. 2, 1972, 1–4.
"Outline of Principles and Purposes." *Newsletter: Rhetoric Society of America*, vol. 1, no. 1, 1968, 1–2.

"What Is a 'Rhetoric Society'?" *Newsletter: Rhetoric Society of America*, vol. 1, no. 1, 1969, 3.

Corbett, Edward P. J. "Statement from the Chairman." *Newsletter: Rhetoric Society of America*, vol. 2, 1972, 2–3.

Goggin, Maureen Daly. *Authoring a Discipline: Scholarly Journals and the Post-World War II Emergence of Rhetoric and Composition*. Lawrence Erlbaum, 2000.

Halloran, S. Michael. "The Growth of the Rhetoric Society of America: An Anecdotal History." *Rhetoric Society Quarterly*, vol. 48, no. 3, 2018, 234–41.

Young, Richard. "Working on the Margins: Rhetorical Studies and the New Self-Consciousness." *Rhetoric Society Quarterly*, vol. 20, no. 4, 1990, 325–32.

An RSA Fellow Remembers: The Last 25 Years

Jacqueline Jones Royster

Good afternoon. I count it a special honor and pleasure to be included in this roundtable today and to share with you a reflection about the roles that the Rhetoric Society of America has played in my own professional life and by extension, I believe, as a premier professional organization in the lives of others of my cohort.

My engagement with the RSA started almost exactly 25 years ago. By 1993, I had been an active academic for 18 years. For 16 of those years, I had been employed at Spelman College where I had founded, directed, and developed what was then called the Comprehensive Writing Program. Because of that work, the nature of the institution as a gender-specific institution, the southern context in which we operated, and the time frame for the evolution of rhetorical studies in American colleges and universities, I had been most active in CCCC, NCTE, MLA, NCA, and NWSA. My plate was full. In 1992, however, I moved to Ohio State, the home of Edward P.J. Corbett and the largest RCL program in the nation—and at a point in the evolution of rhetorical studies when we were on the cusp of a resurgence of interest and activity. I make this point to emphasize that 1993 (25 years ago) within my operational sphere was a moment of transition. The field was changing and I was also changing.

In moving from a very small liberal arts college in the South to arguably the largest university in the nation, an institution that also had the largest RCL program in the nation, I was able, not so much to shift focus (which really isn't true) but to broaden my professional community in an amazingly satisfying way. For the first time in 1994, I actually had room in the scope of my responsibilities and in my schedule, and I had adequate funding to attend conferences that allowed me connections, not just in composition, literacy, literature, and women's studies, but quite specifically in rhetorical studies, where the core imperative for my work had always resided as evidenced by my dissertation, yeah those many years ago, entitled: "Communicating in Writing: A Rhetorical Model for Developing Composition Skills." Being at Ohio State, though, for the first time I was able to enjoy the privilege of bringing these interests to bolder relief in the company of others of complementary interests and actually the privilege of attending RSA *with* others from my *own* institution who were also participating actively in this professional community.

Needless to say, while I was already actively engaged with other organizations, my becoming more engaged with the RSA community of scholars was important to me, and I have been grateful over these last 25 years to have had the opportunity. So, why would yet another professional society be such a blessing for me? Let me point to just two basic reasons:

1. I am an archival researcher in the history of rhetoric, focused on a racialized and gendered group. In 1994, I found the RSA community to have the most diverse disciplinary perspectives and the most welcoming ear for the *kind* of work that I was doing—and with an interesting overlap with a cohort of folks that I had known from my other organizations. So, even though I had not attended RSA before the 1990s, I felt, *still* very much at home, but in some ways even more so:

    - The conference was smaller than my other conferences, which made it much easier to cross paths with a range of folks and have amazingly inspirational cross-cutting conversations.
    - Colleagues were actually interested in the research topics in which I was interested but from perspectives different from my own, and I was able to hear the work of those folks, to find my own leading edges, and to share my viewpoints with folks who didn't look at me too sideways if I exhibited a passion for the women that I study. At RSA, I didn't feel so much like an anomaly. I didn't always need to explain and justify that I was actually interested in the language use, the contexts—local and global, the conditions, and not just the impacts and consequences of these rhetorical performances, but the trajectory of these patterns over time.

2. RSA was a place, not just to speak, but to be heard, to engage, to think at the innovative edges of my work. A few examples:

- In 1998, I was asked to present a keynote address. The title of my talk was "Sarah's Story: Making a Place for Historical Ethnography in Rhetorical Studies." Even before the publication of my book *Traces of a Stream: Literacy and Social Change*, RSA made a place for my work at the center of attention and not just to the side.
- From 2004 through 2015, at the encouragement of colleagues, such as Pat Bizzell, Arabella Lyon, Lester Olson, and others, I was able to find a place for my concerns about connecting ethos and action to human rights, civil rights, and citizenship—whether in a panel presentation, keynote address, conference proceedings, a special issue of *RSQ*, or a summer institute workshop. In other words, RSA has provided a range of venues and a listening ear for topics that I cared about specifically and also deeply.
- RSA was also the first place where I got the opportunity to think out loud about Civil War women—not simply about the impact of war on women's lives, but the work and leadership of women who found themselves, like their men, at war. It was an amazing moment for me in giving a featured talk about concerns that were simultaneously old and new and to share that moment with a room full of folks who were, quite simply, just okay with that.

So, what have these last 25 years of RSA chronicled and enabled? Dare I say that for me being a member of this organization has been both inspirational and affirming, but for rhetorical studies itself, as one of our most ancient traditional areas in the academic world, RSA has been quietly declaring growth, development, and change—rather than calcification—in that this organization has been quite deliberate in encouraging participation across boundaries, by various and sundry definitions of what constitutes a boundary, boundaries that we don't treat as boundaries, but us opportunities for people like me to think, to learn, to connect, to be in our own moment without throwing away our past or compromising our sense of now or future.

So, my last point for RSA in 2018 is this: At this anniversary moment, my expectation is that we will re-dedicate ourselves, pulling out our most courageous spirit, to not being afraid of change or the people in all of our variety who might participate in these processes, and not being afraid to interrogate with the boldest critiques that we can muster what exactly it means in our places and over time to be "language using beings" twirling through space on our amazingly diverse but small and quite fragile blue planet. I think that in this field that is millennia old, we have only just begun to fashion generative theoretical and analytical paradigms, to find new potential for knowledge-making, innovation, and transformation, and to know, without a shadow of a doubt, that our best and most powerful opportunities quite clearly lie, not in our past 50 years but in our next 50 years. May we live long and prosper in our glorious and quite noble causes.

Why We Named Ourselves a Society: Richard E. Young on the Origins of the RSA

Richard E. Young with Richard Leo Enos

Introduction

Our organization, since its origins fifty years ago, has been a "society."[1] The inspiration of, and credit for, our name belongs to Richard E. Young. Young's vision was modeled after the Royal Society of England.[2] The reason for choosing "society" was deliberate. Young and the founders wished to think of themselves as a community. RSA started as a community of friends. This friendship began at conferences hosted by other

---

1. This essay was the basis for a presentation given by Richard Leo Enos at the 50th Anniversary Conference of the Rhetoric Society of America in Minneapolis, Minnesota on May 31 to June 3, 2018. Parts of this essay were used with permission by S. Michael Halloran in his essay, "The Growth of the Rhetoric Society of America: An Anecdotal History," *Rhetoric Society Quarterly*, 48.3 (2018): 234-241.

2. Richard Young and Richard Leo Enos have been colleagues for approximately forty-six years. They both taught at The University of Michigan (Ann Arbor) and again at Carnegie Mellon University where they worked with others to create the Ph.D. in Rhetoric Program that began in 1980. Young was one of the founders of RSA, the author of numerous research publications on rhetoric and (with Alton Becker and Kenneth Pike) the author of one of the most influential texts of our discipline: *Rhetoric: Discovery and Change*. Enos is a Past President of RSA, a RSA Fellow, a recipient of the George Yoos Distinguished Service Award and the Cheryl Geisler Mentorship Award. Their friendship endures and, to this day, they talk at least twice a month.

organizations, principally those in English. Hearing each others' work at established conferences, this group formed friendships based on their shared intellectual curiosity over rhetoric. Conferences became a convenient time to meet, and at these conferences, this small community of rhetoricians began to reserve rooms in convention hotels where they could gather for casual meetings. At these informal (but planned) discussion groups, colleagues were invited to talk or listen about work in rhetoric and soon developed not only a kinship but also a desire to become more organized. The following is a synthesis of several conversations between Richard E. Young and Richard Leo Enos, as well as Young's written responses to specific questions, regarding the origins of the Rhetoric Society of America. It is written in the form of an oral history. —*RLE*

Richard E. Young's Remembrance

Prior to our founding, when we were first thinking about forming a group interested in the study of rhetoric, we were all from English departments. I wrote a private letter to Edward P. J. Corbett (The Ohio State University) and Ross Winterowd (The University of Southern California), which was then shared with the group as one proposal for forming some sort of organization. This letter was subsequently published in an early *RSA Newsletter* under the title, "What is a 'Rhetoric Society'?" I had in mind creating a social and intellectual environment that would foster rhetorical knowledge, kind of a self-help group.

We found ways of sharing what we knew. Some of us, like Corbett, Richard Hughes, and James L. Kinneavy, already knew a great deal about rhetoric; some, like me, not so much. We used to set aside time at conventions, and some of us would talk about what we'd been working on. It was fifty years ago, but I remember vividly sitting in hotel rooms listening to Richard Ohmann introducing transformational generative grammar, Kinneavy discussing *kairos,* and Corbett discussing classical invention. I remember how impressed I was when "discovering" the *Quarterly Journal of Speech* and *Speech* [now *Communication*] *Monographs*; there were actually people who already were well versed in what I was trying to learn! That is one reason we insisted that those from speech communication and philosophy be included as directors of the RSA. Soon individuals such as Bruce Gronbeck (speech communication) and George Yoos (philosophy) became early members of this "society" of friends. In short, any and all who were interested in rhetoric were welcome to come and talk and listen.

Most of us had of necessity become autodidacts; most of us were teaching ourselves about rhetoric, since traditional education in English literature was silent on the subject. This effort to be inclusive was conscious and a counter-response to the way that departments of English had evolved since the early decades of the twentieth century. By the 1960s, English had stripped away many of the facets of its earlier identity, including rhetoric, to the extent that English came to mean only the study of literature. This situation was exacerbated by the fact that speech had left English and established its own organization and taken rhetoric with it.

One of the revelations of these earlier years is that rhetoric was nonetheless a feature of many departments and programs and this "Society" sought to be inclusive to all who studied rhetoric, to see themselves as welcome and central to the development of this new society, the Rhetoric Society of America. Essentially, my proposal was that we would form a community that would serve as a substitute for what those of us interested in rhetoric could not get in our own departments, the kind of informal day-to-day exchanges about new ideas, books, bibliographies, critical comments, job openings and so on; I had hoped that our society would be a replacement for the type of common, daily interactions that we ordinarily take for granted with colleagues. The trouble was we had few, in some cases no, colleagues working in rhetoric. There was little interest at the time, and often disdain, toward rhetoric in departments of English.

At the time, I did not envision a formal organization with memberships and a journal as what was needed. As mentioned above, during these early years this society was facilitated by a newsletter compiled and edited by George Yoos. An examination of early entries in the *Rhetoric Society Newsletter* is revealing by both the types and the variety of its entries. Bibliographies and reviews were complemented by informal letters, often done to ask readers questions about rhetoric. Announcements of upcoming events and informal book reviews were frequent entries. In short, the "newsletter" reflected the spirit and conversational attitude of an inclusive society that wished to share ideas about rhetoric as it had begun with the informal conference gatherings. Eventually, this modest newsletter evolved into our *Rhetoric Society Quarterly (RSQ)* with George Yoos as its founding editor.

I was of two minds about *RSQ*. Initially, I didn't think we needed a journal. There certainly wasn't a large audience for scholarly articles on rhetoric, at least in English departments. A newsletter seemed more useful and appropriate to the sort of community we had in mind. For most English teachers, freshman composition was about the only exposure they had to rhetoric, an unwelcome one for most, despite the early calls in the late fifties and early sixties by Albert Kitzhaber, Wayne Booth, Richard Braddock, Virginia Burke, Richard Hughes, Robert Gorrell and others for serious scholarly work and more effective teaching of a better rhetoric. This may be why textbooks became one of the most important means of developing the discipline, at least in English. Even so, looking back on it, I am surprised by how many of the early members of the Society published rhetoric texts. Better, more intellectually sophisticated texts were the toe in the door.

We need different things today in order to grow and refine the discipline, which accounts for *RSQ* and our organization that accompanies it. That there are quality journals to publish in now and a large audience to read them is wonderful; it is a pleasure to see something we started grow into what it is today. That said, I hope that we don't lose the excitement, curiosity, and comradeship we felt at the time of our origin as a society of friends sharing our interest in, and curiosity about, rhetoric.

Works Cited

Halloran, S. Michael. "The Growth of the Rhetoric Society of America: An Anecdotal History," *Rhetoric Society Quarterly*, vol. 48, no. 3, 2018, 234-241.

"What Is a 'Rhetoric Society'?" *Newsletter: Rhetoric Society of America*, vol. 1, no. 1, 1969, 3.

Young, Richard E., Alton L. Becker, and Kenneth L. Pike. *Rhetoric: Discovery and Change*. Houghton Mifflin Harcourt, 1970.

Autobiography of an Accidental Rhetorician

James J. Murphy

The development of my academic career as an historian of rhetoric is somewhat of a mirror of national developments.

The Educational Background

I entered Saint Mary's College of California in 1941, in what was basically a pre-rhetorical age. My liberal arts experience there was based on the Great Books curriculum, close readings of texts from Sophocles to Freud. We read five dialogues of Plato but not his *Phaedrus*, and ten books of Aristotle though not his *Rhetoric*. Our introduction to Saint Augustine was his *Confesssions* rather than *On Christian Doctrine*. Our exposure to lingual methodology was the medieval "scholastic method," the application of dialectic to philosophic problems as exemplified in the writings of Saint Thomas Aquinas.

Public speaking classes were available under the English department, using current activity-centered textbooks of the day. There was also a thriving intercollegiate debate program, in which I took part. In none of these was there a theoretical base. As with many speech and drama departments then common in American colleges and universities, there was a heavy reliance on survivals of the elocutionary movement.

After the war I returned to teach at Saint Mary's in the English department, teaching literature and speech and managing the intercollegiate forensics program during the period 1950 to 1953 after achieving an MA in English at Stanford by commuting to Palo Alto. Again, this teaching was activity-centered rather than conceptually grounded.

My rhetorical breakthrough came after 1953 when I decided to return to Stanford full time to begin work on a PhD in English. In addition to literature courses in English I learned that the separate department of Speech and Drama offered a program in the history of rhetoric. Professor James Gordon Emerson introduced me to the ideas of Plato, Aristotle, and Cicero as well as the oratory of Demosthenes and Cicero. It was a set of blinding revelations. Suddenly I could see everything I thought I knew about language in three new dimensions. (Ultimately, I took a PhD in English with a doctoral minor in rhetoric.) Almost by accident I had come across a rhetoric program that I probably would not have ever seen if I had stayed in the traditional round of colleges and universities.

I discovered also that there were huge gaps in the history of rhetoric. For example, when I went to the office of my dissertation advisor, Robert W. Ackerman, to complain that there was no history of medieval rhetoric for my work on Chaucer and rhetoric, he turned to me and said simply, "Write one."

One publication in this period may demonstrate further the tenuous state of rhetorical studies. When Ernst Curtius published his *European Literature and the Latin Middle Ages* in 1953 covering a wide range of topics, he unwittingly unleashed a flood of more than twenty journal articles effectively equating rhetoric with the tropes and figures. This development would not likely have occurred if the scholarly public had had a more balanced view of the subject.

The *PMLA* Episode

One occurrence stands out in my mind as reflecting the academic opinion of rhetoric in the early 1960s. I was then teaching at Princeton University. I submitted a manuscript to a major journal, *Publication of the Modern Language Association*. The paper dealt with rhetoric in the writing of the medieval English poet, Geoffrey Chaucer. Shortly I received an emphatic, almost angry rejection that included the statement that "Rhetoric is not a subject, and if it were it could not be studied." (Interestingly, after the same article was published later in the prestigious British journal *Review of English Studies*, I received a hand-written letter from an internationally known historian of language and literature, identifying himself as the PMLA reviewer and apologizing for being wrong in his previous judgment.)

A few years later, this same identification issue recurred on a statewide level in California. In 1965 I was recruited by the University of California at Davis to found a new department drawn from the speech section of the existing Speech and Drama department. We chose the name Department of Rhetoric. Since any new department (and any new name) required approvals through multiple committee levels all the way to the Regents of the University of California, this meant a turbulent year of proving and re-proving rhetoric not only as a subject but as a research area of humanist value. We were successful despite the opposition of several campus departments. (To our chagrin, after all our hard labor, the comparatively disorganized Department of Speech at UC Berkeley sent a two-paragraph letter to the Regents and also chose the name Rhetoric based on our lengthy application paperwork.)

Meanwhile, there was no real national forum for scholarly discussions of rhetoric and its history. The nearest equivalents were the main journal of the Speech Communication Association, *Quarterly Journal of Speech*, and its sister journal, *Speech Monographs*, devoted to "scholarly" articles. There were also four eclectic regional speech journals willing to accept a wide range of submissions. Frequent topics, though, were critiques of individual orations and biographical studies of given speakers. The Conference on College Composition and Communication (founded 1949) was primarily devoted to classroom instruction.

In 1968, for example, W. Ross Winterowd opened his book *Rhetoric: A Synthesis* with the statement that "With only a few notable exceptions, the art of rhetoric has been static for two hundred years." (Preface, v). Later in the book, he noted with approval Lane Cooper's 1960 translation of Aristotle's *Rhetoric* and Edward P.J. Corbett's 1965 *Classical Rhetoric for the Modern Student* (180).

For several years, though, a group of us managed to secure tolerance for sessions during the annual Modern Language Association meetings under the rubric of "Rhetoric and Literature," but it was some time before we could convince the MLA Research Division to publish *The Rhetorical Tradition and Modern Writing* (1982). This ground-breaking collection included essays by E.D. Hirsch Jr, James Kinneavy, Virginia N. Steinhoff, Susan Miller, S. Michael Halloran and Merrill D. Whitburn, Edward P. J. Corbett, Winifred Bryan Horner, Gerald P. Mulderig, Nan Johnson, Donald C. Stewart, Richard E. Young, and James J. Murphy.

Something else happened in 1982–1983 that pointed to a new national attitude toward rhetoric. I learned that some people were making photocopies of my out-of-print *A Synoptic History of Classical Rhetoric* (Random House, 1972) and selling them to their students. So I decided to reprint the book myself to renew the copyright and stop this trade. I soon learned that to make this work, I had to take out a business license and create a new entity; readers familiar with rhetorical history will recognize the irony of my choice of name— Hermagoras Press, named after an influential figure whose works have not survived, just as the press was initially reprinting out-of-print works. To my surprise, the *Synoptic History* immediately became a minor best-seller—and the salvation of Hermagoras Press—with sales of 1,000 to 1,500 copies per year for the next decade. Apparently, there was a hidden market.

This encouraged me to think of the press as a tool—one buyer at a conference once told me that Hermagoras Press was "not a company but a crusade." Ultimately, the press produced 31 titles before I sold it in 1995 to Lawrence Erlbaum Associates (now a part of Routledge Publishing). Hermagoras Press probably would not have been possible two decades earlier.

By the 1980s, of course, the rhetorical tide had already started to turn. The Rhetoric Society of America was founded in 1969. The American Society for the History of Rhetoric started in 1977, first as the American Branch of the new International Society for the History of Rhetoric, and then (because of American tax laws) as an independent society. The indefatigable Theresa J. Enos single-handedly initiated publication of *Rhetoric Review* in 1980.

All this was a far cry from the days when a journal reviewer could state categorically that rhetoric was not a subject.

The Founding of the Rhetoric Society of America

Victor J. Vitanza

From my several remembrances of what I experience as an Event (*Ereignis*), I will recall in a style of orality the wonders of RSA. Others, of course, will have different remembrances and approaches.

With others, I applied and received a National Endowment for Humanities Fellowship-in-Residence for nine months, 1978-1979. The fellowship gave us the opportunity to work with Richard Young, at Carnegie Mellon University, on the topic of "Rhetorical Invention and Composing Process." Other participants included Sharon Bassett, James A. Berlin, Lisa Ede, David Fractenberg, Robert P. Inkster, Charles Kneupper, Sam Watson, Jr., Vickie Winkler, and William Nelson. We were from literature (English departments), speech (communication studies), and philosophy. We were colleagues who helped each other, learned from each other.

Other participating colleagues included Alton Becker, Linda Flower and John Hayes, and especially Janice Lauer—all important figures in the field of linguistics and anthropology as well as rhetoric and composition. But wait, across the river there was the University of Pittsburgh, where William Coles taught. Yes, he visited with us for several hours one day. Thereafter, virtually all of us had to read his book the *Plural I—and After*. What a daze this book! In contrast to Richard Young, there was Alton Becker and Kenneth Pike's book, entitled: *Rhetoric: Discover and Change* (1970). But keep in mind that during the first weeks we studied, yes, Albert R. Kitzhaber's 1953 dissertation: "Rhetoric in American Colleges, 1850-1990." As you may know, the dissertation was finally published by Southern Methodist University Press, in 1990.

The opening months, we met twice a week, Mondays and Thursdays. What was so wonderful was the return to rhetorical invention. We discussed Aristotle's 28 topoi, which Cicero whittled down to 16, and before long ended up with Kenneth Burke's pentad. And yes, the event—Young, Becker, and Pike put forth the matrix of Contrast, Variation, Distribution, together opening Particle, Wave, and Field. Yes, Young *et al.* put forth Tagmemics and Heuristics. There's so much more.

After the first NEH Fall semester, we, the ten of us, began to meet once a week, in the evenings, reading and discussing, yes, Jacque Derrida's early book (*Of Grammatology*), Michel Foucault (*The Archaeology of Knowledge*), Michael Polanyi (*Personal Knowledge: Towards a Post-Critical Philosophy*), and so many more! I have to tell you, however, that during a break, Sharon Bassett, showed me this strange-looking book by Paul Feyerabend: *Against Method* (1975). She pointed to the index: "rhetoric, 1-309." What a hoot.

When we all left Pittsburgh at the end of the seminar, Charles Kneupper said he was going to start a biennial RSA national conference. At that time, he had accepted a position at the University of Texas at Arlington, where I was. He developed three conferences and was working on the fourth when he passed away. Michelle Ballif and I followed through the event. However, the first RSA conference was held in 1985 on the theme "Oldspeak/Newspeak Rhetorical Transformations" at the Flagship Inn in Arlington, Texas.

When I left Pittsburgh, I said to the seminarians, I was going to start a journal that in no time became *PRE/TEXT: A Journal of Rhetoric Theory*. All the cats said to me: "Yes, V, do it." The first volume appeared in Spring-Fall 1980, featuring articles on Paul Feyerabend. I sent him a copy. He was excited. Samuel Ijsseling, whom I met in Pittsburgh at a conference, was my European Associate Editor. He is the one who wrote *Rhetoric and Philosophy in Conflict*.

For more information about the NEH Fellowship and the collaborations it inspired, see Stephanie A. Almagno's dissertation about us: "An NEH Fellowship Examined: Social Networks and Composition History." Nedra Reynolds was her chair and John Trimbur was one of the readers. Find it at this URL: https://digitalcommons.uri.edu/oa_diss/634/.

Walker to the Rescue

Jack Selzer

In all the excitement over the fiftieth anniversary of RSA and in all the records of the Society's accomplishments, it is difficult to believe—but nevertheless true—that at its twenty-fifth anniversary, RSA was in a bit of trouble. The primary benefit of RSA membership is a quality journal, after all, and in the mid-1990s, *Rhetoric Society Quarterly* was experiencing difficulties. Fortunately, Jeffrey Walker stepped in to save and advance the franchise.

It is well known that George Yoos contributed mightily to the nascent RSA by serving generously and effectively for many years as editor of the Society's major publication. As Philip Keith documented in 1990 (323), Yoos took over as editor of the third issue of the *Newsletter of the Rhetoric Society of America* in 1972. Over the next two decades he transitioned the publication into *Rhetoric Society Quarterly* (its title after 1975), established its persistently interdisciplinary focus, and during the 1980s through great personal effort steered the journal away from its reliance on bibliographies, reviews, and invited articles and into a new status as an academic journal with an editorial board, associate editors (notably Patricia Sullivan), a book review editor, and the publication of respected manuscripts submitted without any solicitation by the editor.[1] Any review of the contents of the publications overseen by Yoos will appreciate the number of outstanding pieces that Yoos brought to the attention of the field. James Berlin, Ann Berthoff, Lloyd Bitzer, Stephen Browne, Donald Bryant, Scott Consigny, Sharon Crowley, Cheryl Geisler, Michael Halloran, Randy Harris, David Kaufer, Andrew King, Michael Leff, Donovan Ochs, Cheryl Geisler, Carolyn Miller, Keith Miller, Marie Secor: these and many other familiar names wrote for *RSQ* while Yoos was editor. And its issues dedicated to Aristotle's *Rhetoric*, Plato's *Phaedrus*, Augustine, and George Campbell still make for stimulating reading. No wonder Joshua

Gunn and Diane Davis recently described *RSQ* under Yoos's direction as "the beating heart or central organ that kept rhetorical information in circulation, making the society stronger" (4).

But as Yoos (born 1923) approached retirement and as the work associated with an increasingly ambitious journal multiplied, instabilities emerged. In anticipation of Yoos's departure, Eugene Garver of St. John's University (near to Yoos's St. Cloud State) had joined Yoos as co-editor for volume 18 (1988); and when Yoos stepped down for good as editor in 1990,[2] Garver and Keith took over as co-editors, improved the professional appearance of the journal, and put together a dream team of staff (e.g., Richard Enos as book review editor) and editorial advisors: Don Bialostosky and Larry Green, Lisa Ede and Win Horner, Michael Leff and Michael Halloran among others. More important, they published several outstanding issues—in volume 22 (1992) alone, for example, *RSQ* published a stunning, innovative number on feminist rhetorics, starring Susan Jarratt, Patricia Bizzell, Marjorie Woods, Lynn Worsham, Kay Halasek, Catherine Hobbs, Michelle Ballif, and Jan Swearingen, among others.

But Yoos, Keith, and Garver were unable to command institutional support commensurate with their ambitions.[3] After 1992 the journal was appearing in a less timely way and with some erratic contents. Issues 3 and 4 in 1993 were published together, in an effort to get the publication back on time, and Rex Veeder (also of St. Cloud State) was added as a third editor to manage the workload; but things continued to languish. Only two issues of the "quarterly" appeared in 1994, and volume 25 (1995) appeared just once, as a (very interesting) annual, and very late. Under the circumstances, *RSQ* was not always being taken seriously by tenure and promotion committees, members of RSA were growing impatient,[4] and the RSA Board began a search for a new editor.

But when Jeffrey Walker was chosen to take over *RSQ* in 1995, I was surprised. I had absolutely no reservations about Walker himself; quite the contrary. He had been my Penn State colleague since receiving his Berkeley PhD in 1985, had published his revised dissertation in 1989 (*Bardic Ethos and the American Epic Poem*), had just been (easily) tenured and promoted to associate professor, and had produced several innovative essays in top journals. On a personal level he had proven to be an excellent and affable colleague— a team player willing to serve as director of composition or play an active part putting on our annual summer conference, a pedagogical innovator who added his thinking on the enthymeme to our argument-based composition program, an active and generous intellect who was already gathering and sharing the materials that would become his magisterial *Rhetoric and Poetics in Antiquity* (Oxford, 2000). Respected and admired by most everyone in his department, and the intellectual backbone of our developing doctoral emphasis in rhetoric within the English PhD program, Jeff Walker was guiding my own thinking in fundamental, generous, patient, and good-humored ways as I was just beginning my study of Kenneth Burke's early career.

Walker, in short, definitely had the scholarly chops and the personal temperament to edit *RSQ* effectively. If he was at that time junior to Yoos, Garver, Keith and the very senior editors of *College English, College Composition and Communication, Quarterly Journal of Speech* and the other most respected rhetoric journals of the day, he was nevertheless no one's inferior as a scholar or organizer. But the journal itself had compromised some of its reputation, and it looked (to me at least) to be a "fixer-upper" that might never be fully fixed.[5] Our rhetoric group at Penn State knew that playing a larger role in the field's journals was important to our collective reputation, but I don't think I was the only one who doubted that *RSQ* was the kind of publication that would contribute to our leadership aspirations.

We needn't have worried. In the first issue of volume 26 (1996), Walker announced his ambitious vision for what *RSQ* might become. Unbeknownst to me, he had articulated that vision in his application for the job and lined up necessary institutional support from our department head and other locals—a course reduction to allow him to oversee the operation, a graduate student editorial assistant (first Kakie Urch, then Debra Hawhee), office space in Burrowes Building, and an arrangement with Penn State Press to produce each issue. That last item permitted him to "redesign the journal's cover and its page-layout," thereby creating a professional look for *RSQ* that inspired immediate confidence. Walker created "restructured manuscript review procedures . . . to give each credible submission a double-blind review," an evaluation process that would enable contributors to assure their colleagues that the contents of *RSQ* were indeed fully peer reviewed. To establish that the journal would now appear on a reliable schedule and to reach out further to likely contributors, he aspired "to complete the [peer] review and give the author a decision within eight weeks"—an aspiration that he meant to pursue with the help of a collection of distinguished Editorial Advisors and a supportive set of Editorial Associates in English and Speech Communication at Penn State. "Every contributor should be able to expect an ambitious review process, a timely resolution, and, if the work is accepted, timely publication," he promised (6), and by involving more people in the workings of the journal he was implicitly inviting them to contribute articles. Most important, in ambitious terms he laid out what he hoped to achieve: "*RSQ* is admirably positioned to become the premier journal of professional affiliation and collegial exchange for rhetoricians doing their work in different disciplinary and institutional locations. . . . At least potentially, [it can become] a central and even definitive forum for professional inquiry in rhetoric." Welcoming special issues and symposia (all of them refereed, of course) and "longer articles, consistent with the goal of publishing significant, high quality work," he promised to make *RSQ* into "an outlet for first-rate work from emerging younger scholars as well as established senior scholars . . . *RSQ* must strive to publish work that embodies the highest standards of professional scholarship in rhetoric" (5). No wonder the Board named him the new editor: Walker had thought of everything.[6]

What's more, Walker was already materializing his vision, in record time. That first issue included Deirdre McCloskey's "The Rhetoric of Liberty," Patricia Roberts's "Habermas, *Philosophes*, and Puritans," and reviews of Donovan Ochs's *Consolatory Rhetoric*, Sharon Crowley's *Ancient Rhetoric for Contemporary Students*, and Barry Brummett's *Landmark Essays on Kenneth Burke*. Within the next year there were reviews by Andrew King, Kendall Phillips, Cheryl Glenn, Gary Olson, and Tilly Warnock; a special issue on the rhetoric of science; articles by Ellen Quandahl (on Burke), Jim Jasinski (on the Federalist Papers), James Kastely (on Aristophanes), and Richard Enos and Ed Corbett (and two others, on classical oratory); and "A Conversation with James Kinneavy." I'll spare you further cataloging of the spectacular articles and reviews that followed, for the point is clear enough. Suffice it to say that *RSQ* was now publishing Henry Johnstone and Gerard Hauser, Michelle Ballif and Barbara Warnick, and articles on science and the internet, film and fashion, erotics and embodiment, African-American abolitionists and a woman's suffrage address. The final article in Walker's final issue was by Art Walzer, Marie Secor, and Alan Gross on the Earl of Spencer's funeral address honoring Princess Diana. Rescue complete.

Walker served a four-year term, ending in 1999. The new editor, Gregory Clark, honored him with space in the first issue of the new century (volume 30) for "The Outgoing Editor's Farewell: A *Propempticon*." I remember smiling when I saw that title, for Walker was always promoting to his colleagues, only half in jest, the genre of *propempticon*,[7] "the farewell address" (as he explained) offered on the occasion of heroes departing after (or before) great adventures and exploits. Walker wasn't saluting himself, though; he instead used the occasion to recall the contributions of the previous editors of *RSQ*, to wish the new editor success, and to thank those who had assisted him during his editorship. In keeping with the conventions of the *propempticon* genre, he addressed the journal itself as a kind of ship, off to confront new challenges and opportunities: "Perhaps you will enter Thrace," he told his journal, "and cross to the lands of Scythians. Perhaps you will be renowned! Perhaps you will teach rhetoric! But always I'll remember you, dear Journal, and the time we spent amid the contending schools, the libraries, the brilliant sophists orating from the *bema*, and the discourses we shared together." With that wit and a smile, he closed his term as editor.

I didn't know it then, but soon Jeff and his wife Yoko would be departing Penn State, when his *Rhetoric and Poetics in Antiquity* (2000) and the accomplishment of his term as *RSQ* editor won him a new position at Emory (from 2000–2004) and then a tremendous opportunity to join the faculty at the University of Texas. (He also would enjoy a stint as NEH Fellow in 2007–2008, among numerous other honors.) His and Yoko's departure left a major void. No more *propempticon*s at the end of every academic year. No more easy opportunities to engage with the affable superscholar down the hall. Parties not quite the same. But it all paved the path for him to produce more great work as our field's most distinguished classical rhetorician, most recently with *The Genuine Teachers of This Art: Rhetorical Education in Antiquity* (2011). Come to think of it, then, I should have written this tribute to Jeff Walker in the form of a *propempticon*, shouldn't I have? But I'm not up to that. Let's leave it at this: in the twenty-first century Greg Clark and the other outstanding editors who have succeeded since have built brilliantly on what Walker crafted to make *RSQ* what it now is. Let us raise a glass to all of those editors, and let us forever remember what, at a moment of crisis, Jeff Walker accomplished for RSA and for the study of rhetoric.

Notes

1. In this brief overview of the first quarter century of RSA's publication, I have been guided by Keith; by Goggin's authoritative study of rhetoric journals; and by my own inspection of the contents of each issue of *RSQ*. I benefited as well from consultations with Jeff Walker and Debra Hawhee. I should also add that Yoos announced at the end of 1979 that he was adding to the *RSQ* staff his St. Cloud colleagues Philip Keith and Jonathan Lawson (as associate editors) and Joseph Young (as assistant editor).

2. Yoos stayed on as Associate Editor through 1995.

3. Yoos's frustrations are apparent in the tone of several of his editor's notes, as well as in his "farewell" editor's note in *RSQ* vol. 20, no. 4 (1990).

4. Many members had stopped paying their dues to the society. Walker later disclosed that issues were being sent to about a thousand addresses but that fewer than three hundred people were paying for them through their annual dues (reported in Gunn and Davis 42).

5. This was before I had learned that just about everything is a fixer-upper.

6. I don't know who all was on the RSA Search Committee for a new editor, the committee that settled on Walker, but I do know that it included Carolyn Miller and Ed Schiappa.

7. Penn State rhetoricians at Walker's insistence would always gather for an evening together at the end of the academic year to take stock of the year, celebrate accomplishments, and look to the future—always over food and drink. The "farewell" would be in honor of graduate students in rhetoric who had just earned the PhD and who were off to take up their first academic jobs. With a huge smile (and often a speech) Walker thus proclaimed the event to be a "propempticon rhetoricae" in the tradition of ancient sophists who gathered monthly for an elaborate banquet accompanied by speeches--"A farewell banquet for rhetors."

WORKS CITED

Gunn, Joshua, and Diane Davis. "Introduction: *RSQ's* Greatest Hits." *Fifty Years of Rhetoric Society Quarterly*, edited by Joshua Gunn and Diane Davis, Routledge, 2018, pp. 1–10, 41–44.

Goggin, Maureen. *Authoring a Discipline: Scholarly Journals and the Post-World War II Emergence of Rhetoric and Composition*. Erlbaum, 2000.

Keith, Philip. "Essays in Honor of George Yoos: An Introduction." *Rhetoric Society Quarterly*, vol. 20, no. 4, 1990, p. 323.

Walker, Jeffrey. *Bardic Ethos and the American Epic Poem*. Louisiana State UP, 1989.

—. *The Genuine Teachers of This Art: Rhetorical Education in Antiquity*. U of South Carolina P, 2011.

—. *Rhetoric and Poetics in Antiquity*. Oxford UP, 2000.

Another Hard Look at Ourselves: The Transdisciplinary Influence of Rhetoric of Science Scholarship

Leah Ceccarelli

The fiftieth anniversary of the Rhetoric Society of America (RSA) is an occasion to take stock of our fortunes. The specific asset that I would like to assess is our intellectual social capital, that is, how the study of rhetoric is perceived in the broader academy. This is an especially pertinent question in our current era, when rhetorical inquiry is no longer limited to a particular kind of object that we claim as our own (such as oratory in the public forum), but extends across a dizzying array of artifacts and processes. Rhetoricians who choose to study a subject that is shared by scholars from other areas of inquiry might properly think of themselves as participating in a larger scholarly conversation about that subject. For example, digital rhetoric scholars are likely to cite human-computer interaction researchers, information scientists, and media theorists, among others. Rhetoricians who study built environments are likely to speak not only to other rhetoricians, but also to architects, art historians, design theorists, and critics of material culture in a variety of other disciplines. My primary area of study, the rhetoric of science, is part of a broader transdisciplinary field known as "science studies" that includes historians of science, philosophers of science, and various other scholars from disciplines such as anthropology and sociology.

If one thinks about the scholarly literature as Kenneth Burke imagined it, as an unending conversation, then each discipline might be understood to be adding its own voice to the exchange taking place in a large academic parlor (110-11). Our work as rhetoricians is most valuable to the progress of that larger conversation when it adds something insightful that has not yet been said, pushing the discussion in a productive new direction, or revealing something important that otherwise would be overlooked. Our work is least valuable to the broader conversation when it is not heard at all, or worse, when it is heard and rejected by our academic counterparts in related fields of study.

In 2005, I did a reception study that looked at how rhetoric of science research was being reviewed by other science studies scholars to see whether we were making a significant contribution to the larger scholarly conversation. I called it "A Hard Look at Ourselves" because what I found was disheartening. Academics whose disciplinary homes were in the history and philosophy of science were pronouncing the work of some of our most respected rhetoric of science scholars to be a "flagrant violation of etiquette" (Agassi 329), a "hatchet-job" stained with "immodesty" (Ruse 128), and marred by "wild exaggeration about the analytic scope and significance" of its claims (Durant); they pronounced the findings of rhetoricians "rather commonplace to a historian" (Turney 149), and lacking novelty for "readers familiar with the issues" (Roland 159).

My own first book, which had received an early positive review by a respected philosopher (Rorty), had also been given a thumbs down by a couple of establishment historians of science who claimed my literature review "shoehorned" historians into categories that were false but "convenient" for my "rhetorical purposes" (Smocovitis 420) and who suggested that I was a mere sophist, exhibiting the "deceptive potential" of rhetoric through a deliberate violation of academic ethics (Abir-Am 298). A friend of mine who was an insider to the history of science community told me not to despair; the individuals who wrote those reviews were notorious for offering harsh critique, even of their fellow historians. And he was right; a reading of their other reviews turned up similar rants. But there was a difference between their assessment of a historian's unsatisfactory engagement with the literature as "oversimplified" and "limited," and their critique of my book for the same putative errors. In my case, they pronounced the fault to be a sin, dishonorable in its rhetorical intent (Ceccarelli, "A Hard Look" 261).

That experience taught me that rhetoricians of science have a special burden to bear when entering conversations with other science studies scholars. Because the popular understanding of rhetoric is negative, those who are not familiar with the rhetorical tradition have a tendency to treat rhetoricians of science with an extra dose of moral critique, charging us with being deceitful rhetors when they disapprove of our work. In other words, when entering the ongoing discussion in the academic parlor, we have a stereotype to overcome before we can be charitably heard.

A few years have passed since I did that reception study, so I thought that it was time to take another hard look at ourselves, focusing on how science studies scholars from other fields are responding to some of the most recent books published by rhetoricians of science.[1] Have we discovered the means of persuasion available to get us past the constraint of our presumed sophistic ethos, so that our sister scholars can open themselves to hearing what we have to add to the broader intellectual exchange? The answer is a qualified yes.

Do not get me wrong. There are still some screeds being written about our research. Some of our most distinguished scholars continue to be savaged in the pages of *Isis*, the flagship journal of the History of Science Society. They are attacked for their "patchwork" treatment of the literature (Carusi 421), or for producing "grasshopper history" that leaps "unevenly across the past" while displaying "dated assumptions," a "lack of familiarity" with the literature, and an "almost arrogant" undeserved confidence (Fara 140-41). One recent rhetoric of science book was critiqued by a sociologist for its "distortion of the historical record" (Panofsky 208), and by an anthropologist for offering a portrayal that "comes dangerously close to a caricature," falling "behind recent debates" in the broader transdisciplinary literature "despite … quoting some of the relevant authors" (Schramm 343).

The attribution of unsavory rhetorical purposes for these faults is also present in the current crop of reviews. Rhetoricians of science are being charged with letting their preferred theories and ideologies distort the historical record. They are criticized for offering "a disturbing return to a history of science that is teleological and progressive, where various sciences are unified and simplified by a common goal to visualize the world in accordance with" a particular theory (Nasim 169), and for using case studies "to corroborate" their models and schemes, rather than using theories to explain their cases (Fara 141). They are criticized for a "reduction of complexity," for using a method that "begs the warrant" for their personal "preferences" (Panofsky 209), and for conjuring up those preferences as "a rhetorical figure" untethered to how experience "is actually shaped" by the actors involved (Schramm 345-46). In short, my demoralizing review of recent reviews suggests that some rhetoricians of science are still facing discriminatory attitudes from fellow academics who assume that scholarship in the field of rhetorical inquiry is polluted with objectionable rhetorical intent.

Ironically, the very scholars who are being censured for their illegitimate rhetorical ends are simultaneously criticized by reviewers for not being effective rhetors. According to one historian of science, a rhetoric of science scholar simply "fails to deliver her theory persuasively" (Fara 141). Other rhetoricians are judged to be offering an argument that "remains sketchy"

---

1. I would like to thank my undergraduate research assistant, Maren Anderson, for helping with this research.

and "unconvincing" (Nasim 170), or to be destroying their own ethos with a "stereotypical portrayal of natural science positivism vis-à-vis the enlightened sophistication of their own humanities approach," the hubris of which "literally takes the steam out of their critique" (Schramm 348). As one historian of science puts it, the "sort of analysis" being offered by rhetoricians adds nothing to the literature produced "by historians, philosophers, and sociologists of science in the last 25 years. ... Those seeking any distinct advance on the current literature will not find it here" (Nasim 170–71).

This is all fairly damning testimony. But as I discovered with my earlier reception study, some scholars revel in their performance of the scathing review genre. A look at citations made to these very same rhetoric of science books in the science studies literature suggests that the situation might be more encouraging than it seems. Despite the harsh reviews these books received, many scholars from outside the field of rhetoric have found them to be positively edifying. For example, Alan G. Gross and Joseph E. Harmon's book on scientific visuals, critiqued by a reviewer for being too tied to theory, is cited approvingly in a psychologist's article for the way its deployment of theory "analyzed systematically" the graphs and tables of scientists (Paivio 149), and a couple of sociologists use a major theoretical frame of the Gross and Harmon book to ground their own article's analysis of another text (Boersma and Schinkel 1052–54). Lynda Walsh's book on scientists as prophets, critiqued in a review for its superficial and unorganized history, is considered solid enough to be made into textbook knowledge by a professor of cultural geography who describes in some detail the "fascinating history" it documents (Hulme 111-12). A philosophy professor seems to agree, referring to Walsh's book multiple times in one of his articles and judging her argument to be "insightful," appreciatively pointing readers to it (Yeo 413, 415-17). Likewise, historians marshal Walsh's book as a resource multiple times in their research to support their general arguments (Heymann et al. 33, Navarro 187). Kelly Happe's award-winning book on rhetorics of race, gender and genetics, which a couple of reviewers rejected for its ideological bias, was taken up enthusiastically by an anthropologist, who claims that he wrote his book to be "in dialogue" with Happe's book and a number of other "important works" on the subject (Inda 5). Happe's argument is also described favorably by other anthropologists (Manderson et al. 314), geographers (Mansfield and Guthman 19), and a sociologist who seeks to extend Happe's point to a new context (Keval 172).

In addition to this evidence of the uptake of rhetoric of science books in other fields, I also found a number of book reviews by science studies scholars that are positively glowing with their recommendation that rhetoricians' voices be heard in the academic parlor. For example, one professor emerita of the history of science begins her review, in *Isis*, of Jordynn Jack's *Science on the Home Front* by warning her readers that the book is not a "traditional history"; but then she goes on to judge it according to the standards of that field, and she does so positively. She is especially impressed that so much of Jack's book uses "unpublished material, some of it only recently declassified or made available." This historian also recognizes the transdisciplinary potential of Jack's book, saying it "adds to the history of science some useful concepts and vocabulary," such as epideictic, kairos, and akairos (Rossiter 899).

Another distinguished professor of history wrote a similarly themed review in *Isis* of Robin Jensen's award-winning *Infertility: Tracing the History of a Transformative Term*. That reviewer judges Jensen's book useful for historians, despite the fact that the book's author is "a communications scholar" [sic].

> As a historian, I have explored the medical, social, and cultural significance of these changes in terminology; Jensen, however, has a different point to make. The distinctive contribution of this book is its examination of the rhetorical constructions used over time to define infertility. . . . Historians, whose work allows and sometimes even requires them to examine the findings of researchers in fields well beyond their own, are regularly reminded of the profound impact that disciplinary training has on the ways in which a scholar interprets evidence, frames an argument, or evaluates the context in which discoveries occur and historical processes unfold. Jensen's book, which will likely have the greatest appeal for historians with an interest in theory and method, further demonstrates the significance and value of cross-disciplinary inquiry to the history of science and medicine. (Marsh, 149-50)

The fact that a historian can see special value in the vocabulary and perspectives that a rhetorician brings to bear on the history of science demonstrates that given the right conditions, rhetoricians can be heard not just within our own professional organizations, but in other disciplinary communities as well.

Another historian of science makes a similar point about my second book (*On the Frontier of Science*). Regarding the subject of my research, he says that "scholars have debated the concept's merits" for years. "One might think that that debate would have run its course long ago, and yet the present volume offers analysis that is at once original, thoughtful, and sophisticated" (Gibson 78). A religious studies scholar proclaims my book to be "fascinating," praising especially its "etymological and philosophical development of the concepts of pioneer and frontier" and endorsing the book's "powerful lessons," such as the point that science does not have to be a competitive endeavor (Newell). In each case, it appears that I was able to speak in a tone that could be recognized as meeting scholarly standards and advancing the learned conversation, at least with this audience. We might not be reaching all of our potential interlocutors in the ongoing scholarly exchange, but we seem to be reaching at least some of them.

Eighteen years ago, Alan Gross hypothesized that as "latecomers" to the science studies party, rhetoricians of science "have been regarded, understandably, as interlopers rather than as contributors to the conversation" (449). My most recent look at how we are being received by scholars in the multidisciplinary parlor of science studies suggests that some of the other partygoers are starting to warm up to us. We are beginning to do what it takes to make our voices heard in the transdisciplinary spaces of science studies, and we are persuading scholars from those fields of the value of listening to what we have to say.

RSA is an organization with a charge "to disseminate among its members, current knowledge of rhetoric, broadly construed." But the association also has an interest in seeing its work recognized outside its membership. A few years ago, it began sponsoring a book series on "Transdisciplinary Rhetoric" with Penn State University Press to help further this end, and I became a co-editor of that series. One of the things we ask of prospective books in the series is that they make a contribution not only to rhetorical inquiry as a field of study, but to at least one other discipline as well. We believe that the potential of rhetoric to build transdisciplinary knowledge requires that rhetoricians not only borrow ideas from the literature of other disciplines, but that we give back to those other conversations something of value from our own traditions. Preliminary feedback suggests that the book series is beginning to accomplish that goal. Jensen's book on infertility is one of the books in the series, and is a case in point. In addition to receiving the glowing review in *Isis* that I excerpted above, it got an endorsement from a Harvard history and philosophy of science professor in the *Bulletin of the History of Medicine*, who said "*Infertility* will be of particular interest to feminist historians of gender and reproductive medicine," and this is not despite, but because of its rhetorical perspective; the book succeeds at "[b]ringing the history of rhetoric to bear on popular and scientific texts and images in the infertility literature" (Richardson 818).

Similar comments are coming in for other books in the series too, including work on the rhetoric of medicine, rhetoric of economics, and rhetoric of museums. Nate Stormer's book about medical rhetoric on abortion received an encouraging blurb from a sociologist, who called it "a stunning book, beautifully illustrating how rhetorical struggles over and through abortion have long been about situating ourselves—and pregnant women—in time and place. . . . Stormer's elegant genealogy, both diagnostic and gently prognostic, has the capacity to shift how we see human reproduction and our place in it" (Casper). A political scientist reviewing Mark Longaker's *Rhetorical Style and Bourgeois Virtue* endorsed the book both because it is "rhetorically gifted" and because it offers "illuminating historical analyses." Of particular note, Longaker's book got the political scientist thinking about a "possible point of connection and fruitful collaboration between students of rhetoric and students of politics." He also predicted that "[w]ith more and more political theorists taking up the 'rhetorical turn' within the study of ideas, this book will certainly find an appreciative audience among students of political thought" (Button 149, 151). Liz Weiser's book in the series, *Museum Rhetoric*, was similarly praised by a historian who specializes in national museums: "M. Elizabeth Weiser crosses more national and disciplinary borders than any previous scholar in the search for unifying analyses of the identity work of museums. . . . The result is a complex, innovative, and yet clear and elegantly presented analysis of the work done by and through museums in placing their orchestrated and authorized rhetoric in dialogue with the experiences of visiting citizens" (Aronsson). Reviews of books in the series from scholars who do not identify themselves as rhetoricians are just beginning to trickle in. But preliminary assessments are favorable.

There most certainly will be reviews that critically challenge our attempts to do transdisciplinary work, and some that reject it out of hand as *rhetorical*, employing only the most superficial, negative meaning of that term. But the fact that some researchers who otherwise would be unfamiliar with scholarship being done under the aegis of RSA are beginning to be introduced to that work, and the fact that some are saying that they are excited to engage us in conversation, is an encouraging sign. The intellectual social capital of RSA researchers is on the upswing, and that is a heartening thing to report on the fiftieth anniversary of the founding of the organization.

Works Cited

Aronsson, Peter. Cover endorsement. *Museum Rhetoric: Building Civic Identity in National Spaces*, by M. Elizabeth Weiser, The Pennsylvania State UP, 2017.

Abir-Am, Pnina. Review of *Shaping Science with Rhetoric: The Cases of Dobzhansky, Schrödinger, and Wilson*, by Leah Ceccarelli. *History and Philosophy of the Life Sciences*, vol. 24, no. 2, 2002, pp. 295-98.

"About RSA." Rhetoric Society of America, https://www.rhetoricsociety.org/aws/RSA/pt/sp/about.

Agassi, Joseph. Review of *The Rhetoric of Science*, by Alan G. Gross. *Philosophy of the Social Sciences*, vol. 29, no. 2, 1999, pp. 329-35.

Boersma, Sanne, and Willem Schinkel. "Imagining Society: Logics of Visualization in Images of Immigrant Integration." *Environment and Planning D: Society and Space*, vol. 33, no. 6, 2015, pp. 1043-62.

Burke, Kenneth. *The Philosophy of Literary Form*. U of California P, 1973.

Button, Mark E. Review of *Rhetorical Style and Bourgeois Virtue: Capitalism and Civil Society in the British Enlightenment*, by Mark Garrett Longaker. *The Review of Politics*, vol. 79, no. 1, 2017, pp. 149-51.

Carusi, Annamarie. Review of *Science from Sight to Insight: How Scientists Illustrate Meaning*, by Alan G. Gross and Joseph E. Harmon. *Isis*, vol. 106, no. 2, 2015, pp. 420-21.

Casper, Monica J. Cover endorsement. *Signs of Pathology: U.S. Medical Rhetoric on Abortion, 1800s-1960s*, by Nathan Stormer, The Pennsylvania State UP, 2015.

Ceccarelli, Leah. "A Hard Look at Ourselves: A Reception Study of Rhetoric of Science." *Technical Communication Quarterly*, vol. 14, no. 3, 2005, pp. 257-65.

—. *On the Frontier of Science: An American Rhetoric of Exploration and Exploitation*. Michigan State UP, 2013.

—. *Shaping Science with Rhetoric: The Cases of Dobzhansky, Schrödinger, and Wilson*. U of Chicago P, 2001.

Durant, John. "Is Science Only a Social Invention?" Review of *The Rhetoric of Science*, by Alan G. Gross. *Times Literary Supplement*, 15 Mar. 1991, p. 19.

Fara, Patricia. Review of *Scientists as Prophets: A Rhetorical Genealogy*, by Lynda Walsh. *Isis*, vol. 107, no. 1, 2016, pp. 140-41.

Gibson, Abraham H. Review of *On the Frontier of Science: An American Rhetoric of Exploration and Exploitation*, by Leah Ceccarelli. *Quarterly Review of Biology*, vol. 90, no. 1, 2015, pp. 78-79.

Gross, Alan G. "The Science Wars and the Ethics of Book Reviewing." *Philosophy of the Social Sciences*, vol. 30, no. 3, 2000, pp. 445-50.

Gross, Alan G., and Joseph E. Harmon. *Science from Sight to Insight: How Scientists Illustrate Meaning*. U of Chicago P, 2014.

Happe, Kelly. *The Material Gene: Gender, Race, and Heredity after the Human Genome Project*. New York UP, 2013.

Heymann, Matthias et al. "Key Characteristics of Cultures of Prediction." *Cultures of Prediction in Atmospheric and Climate Science Epistemic and Cultural Shifts in Computer-based Modelling and Simulation*, edited by Matthias Heymann et al., Routledge, 2018, pp. 18-42.

Hulme, Mike. *Weathered: Cultures of Climate*. Sage, 2017.

Inda, Jonathan Xavier. *Racial Prescriptions: Pharmaceuticals, Difference, and the Politics of Life*. Routledge, 2014.

Jack, Jordynn. *Science on the Home Front: American Women Scientists in World War II*. U of Illinois P, 2009.

Jensen, Robin. *Infertility: Tracing the History of a Transformative Term*. The Pennsylvania State UP, 2016.

Keval, Harshad. *Health, Ethnicity and Diabetes: Racialised Constructions of 'Risky' South Asian Bodies*. Palgrave Macmillan, 2016.

Longaker, Mark Garrett. *Rhetorical Style and Bourgeois Virtue: Capitalism and Civil Society in the British Enlightenment*. The Pennsylvania State UP, 2015.

Manderson, Lenore, et al., editors. *The Routledge Handbook of Medical Anthropology*. Routledge, 2016.

Mansfield, Becky, and Julie Guthman. "Epigenetic Life: Biological Plasticity, Abnormality, and New Configurations of Race and Reproduction." *Cultural Geographies*, vol. 22, no. 1, 2015, pp. 3-20.

Marsh, Margaret. Review of *Infertility: Tracing the History of a Transformative Term*, by Robin E. Jensen. *Isis*, vol. 109, no. 1, 2018, pp. 149-50.

Nasim, Omar W. Review of *Science from Sight to Insight: How Scientists Illustrate Meaning*, by Alan G. Gross and Joseph E. Harmon. *HOPOS: The Journal of the International Society for the History of Philosophy of Science*, vol. 6, no. 1, 2016, pp. 168-71.

Navarro, Jaume. "Promising Redemption. Science at the Service of Secular and Religious Agendas." *Centaurus*, vol. 59, 2017, pp. 173-88.

Newell, Catherine L. Review of *On the Frontier of Science: An American Rhetoric of Exploration and Exploitation*, by Leah Ceccarelli. *Science*, vol. 343, no. 6173, 2014, p. 841.

Paivio, Allan. "Intelligence, Dual Coding Theory, and the Brain." *Intelligence*, vol. 47, 2014, pp. 141-58.

Panofsky, Aaron. Review of *The Material Gene: Gender, Race, and Heredity after the Human Genome Project*, by Kelly Happe. *Contemporary Sociology*, vol. 44, no. 2, 2015, pp. 207-209.

Richardson, Sarah S. Review of *Infertility: Tracing the History of a Transformative Term*, by Robin E. Jensen. *Bulletin of the History of Medicine*, vol. 91, no. 4, 2017, pp. 817-19.

Roland, Alex. Review of *Strategic Deception: Rhetoric, Science, and Politics in Missile Defense Advocacy*, by Gordon R. Mitchell. *Isis*, vol. 93, no. 1, 2002, pp. 159-60.

Rorty, Richard. "Studied Ambiguity." Review of *Shaping Science with Rhetoric: The Cases of Dobzhansky, Schrödinger, and Wilson*, by Leah Ceccarelli. *Science*, vol. 293, no. 5539, 2001, pp. 2399-2400.

Rossiter, Margaret W. Review of *Science on the Home Front: American Women Scientists in World War II*, by Jordynn Jack. *Isis*, vol. 101, no. 4, 2010, pp. 898-900.

Ruse, Michael. "Booknotes." *Biology and Philosophy*, vol. 8, no. 1, 1993, pp. 125-29.

Schramm, Katharina. "Enacting Differences, Articulating Critique: Recent Approaches to Race in the Social Analysis of Science and Technology." Review of *Breathing Race into the Machine: The Surprising Career of the Spirometer from Plantation to Genetics*, by Lundy Braun; *The Material Gene: Gender, Race, and Heredity after the Human Genome Project*, by Kelly Happe; *When Biometrics Fail: Gender, Race, and the Technology of Identity*, by Shoshana Amielle Magnet; and *Medicating Race: Heart Disease and Durable Preoccupations with Difference* by Anne Pollock. *Science as Culture*, vol. 24, no. 3, 2015, pp. 340-50.

Smocovitis, Vassiliki Betty. Review of *Shaping Science with Rhetoric: The Cases of Dobzhansky, Schrödinger, and Wilson*, by Leah Ceccarelli. *Journal of the History of Biology*, vol. 35, no. 2, 2002, pp. 418-20.

Stormer, Nathan. *Signs of Pathology: U.S. Medical Rhetoric on Abortion, 1800s-1960s*. The Pennsylvania State UP, 2015.

Turney, Jon. Review of *The Meanings of the Gene: Public Debates about Human Heredity*, by Celeste Condit. *Public Understanding of Science*, vol. 10, no. 1, 2001, pp. 149-50.

Walsh, Lynda. *Scientists as Prophets: A Rhetorical Genealogy*. Oxford UP, 2013.

Weiser, M. Elizabeth. *Museum Rhetoric: Building Civic Identity in National Spaces*. The Pennsylvania State UP, 2017.

Yeo, Michael. "Fault Lines at the Interface of Science and Policy: Interpretive Responses to the Trial of Scientists in L'Aquila." *Earth-Science Reviews*, vol. 139, 2014, pp. 406-19.

Reconsidering the "Divorce" between Speech and English: Rethinking Disciplinary History through Microhistory"

David Stock

Whether in rhetoric and composition or speech communication, historians understand the power of disciplinary histories to forge disciplinary identity. Historians in rhetoric and composition are especially aware of how foundational histories can produce grand narratives that dominate the discipline's identity, values, and practices. In recent decades, revisionist historiography in rhetoric and composition has thoroughly challenged the dominance of early grand narratives by examining overlooked sites, locations, or individuals of rhetoric and writing instruction in the nineteenth and twentieth centuries (see Enoch, Gold, Logan). A methodological approach for conducting such revisionist work, one increasingly common in composition studies and emerging in communication studies, is microhistory. Bruce McComiskey describes microhistory as a "methodological middle ground" that positions historians to generate work that negotiates "the hegemonic grand narratives of [positivist, abstract] social history and the anecdotal descriptions of [relativist, insular] cultural history" (14). Pat Gehrke notes that microhistory's strong recuperative emphasis helps to preserve localized histories that challenge scholars to see themselves and their discipline differently (2).

    I see microhistory as vital in advancing efforts sponsored by the Rhetoric Society of America (RSA) to promote greater cross-disciplinary collaborations among rhetoricians in English and speech communication. Richard E. Young notes that, from the organization's beginning, RSA members were keenly aware that "'work in rhetoric was of necessity cross-disciplinary,'" and they consciously promoted that awareness (qtd. in Halloran 235). The formation of the short-lived but influential Alliance of Rhetorical Societies (ARS) reflected RSA's sustained interest in promoting dialogue among "'theorists, critics, historians, and teachers of rhetoric'" across disciplines (qtd. in Halloran 239). Recent efforts promoting collaboration have focused on the pedagogic tradition of rhetoric (see Keith and Mountford). However, a grand narrative complicating such collaboration is how "disciplinary estrangement" between English and speech communication (Mountford 408) is written into the disciplines' histories. Much like those in rhetoric and composition, early disciplinary histories of speech communication produced grand narratives that, while advancing the field's disciplinary legitimacy and professional identity, have constrained subsequent interpretations of these early historical events and participants. For instance, the dominant origins story of speech communication casts public speaking teachers as protagonists who valiantly vanquished their oppressive English teacher counterparts; one consequence of this simplified narrative on subsequent historical work is evident in the various use of such tropes as rebellion, divorce, and war to characterize the 1914 founding of the National Association of Academic Teachers of Public Speaking (NAATPS) as a national organization independent from the National Council of Teachers of English (NCTE), the national organization formed by English teachers in 1911. If, as Michael Leff and Roxanne Mountford have argued, productive cross-disciplinary collaborations between rhetoricians in English and speech communication require listening carefully to and learning about each other's histories, theories, and practices (Mountford 419), then we would do well to ensure that our histories are not unduly constrained by grand narratives or problematic tropes.

Microhistory is an apt methodology for reexamining the shared disciplinary histories of English and speech communication. Extending the goals and methods of revisionist historiography, microhistory aims to account for the "dialectical interaction of local and general historical forces" amid the varying and contexts in which disciplinary formation and development occur (McComiskey 25); it encourages multiscopic levels of analysis that "equally value and dialectically employ . . . abstract narrative and concrete description in the service of historical arguments" (17); it reduces the scale of analysis to overlooked or misinterpreted individuals, sites, or events in order to recuperate concrete detail and nuance. Microhistorical inquiry enables historians in both disciplines to complicate grand narratives of estrangement and divorce and generate more nuanced accounts that can result in alternative, even conciliatory, perspectives on our shared history.

Because a full microhistorical analysis is beyond the scope of this paper, I focus instead on highlighting the problem microhistory is positioned to address: the prevalence of problematic tropes (e.g., estrangement, rebellion, divorce, or war) in selected disciplinary histories in speech communication and English. As Cara Finnegan and Melissa Wallace note, terms such as "'divorce,' 'affairs,' and 'splits,' and subsequent interest in 'rapprochement' and 'reuniting' . . . may not fully reflect the histories we seek to write" (423). I highlight evidence of these tropes in histories from both disciplines and suggest that a central impetus stems from treatment of arguably the most prominent figure in the disciplinary emergence of speech communication: James M. O'Neill. I identify two microhistorical methods that, applied to O'Neill and the grand narrative of NAATPS's origins, invite more nuanced interpretations of the early relationship between speech communication and English. I then identify other disciplinary histories in speech that support or provide alternative interpretations. For rhetoricians in English, this paper invites attentive listening to histories of speech communication in order to counteract the erasure of public speaking teachers in composition's history (Mountford 414); for rhetoricians in speech communication, it seeks to complicate commonplace notions of speech's disciplinary origins. For both audiences, this project proposes a different orientation toward our shared history that may facilitate clearer disciplinary identities and stronger cross-disciplinary collaborations.

Grand Narratives in Early Speech Communication Histories

In his co-authored account of the formation of the NAATPS, Frank Rarig, one of the organization's founding members, describes two "revolts" in 1911 and 1913, respectively: English teachers who "rebelled" against the norms of scholarship and teaching espoused by the Modern Language Association by creating the NCTE; and public speaking teachers who, discontent with their subordinate status in English departments and in NCTE, lobbied for the creation of "the Public Speaking Section of NCTE, the *first* mechanism, *national* in scope, to bring together teachers of public speaking" (497–98). Rarig briefly reviews subsequent events leading to the creation of the NAATPS: growing complaints about the professional status of public speaking teachers in English departments; O'Neill and Frederick Robinson's drafting of a "declaration of independence" arguing for separate departments of public speaking; O'Neill's 1913 arguments about the dividing line between public speaking and English; the 1914 Public Speaking Section meeting in which attendees discussed survey results about forming a national organization; the protracted debate about affiliation with or independence from NCTE; a follow-up meeting and subsequent decision by "seventeen survivors" from that debate to organize the NAATPS. Rarig passively concludes, "Thus the issue over separation from English was settled" (499). Although their purpose is not to provide an exhaustive account of the organization's founding, Rarig and Greaves's account indicates the general contours of the grand narrative that shapes subsequent histories.

A dramatic example of this narrative is Eugene Covelli's 1961 dissertation, *James Milton O'Neill—Pioneer in Speech Education*, a six-hundred-plus page overview of O'Neill's life, work, and writing that bears the marks of a lengthy encomium. O'Neill is described as "the father of modern speech movement"; because of him, "public speaking became a distinct academic discipline independent of English" (1). One of his most important contributions was "his daring leadership in effecting the separation of public speaking from English," which stemmed from "unbelievable clairvoyance" of the dissimilarities between "oral Speech and written English" (75–76). The hero-villain dichotomy is clearly invoked, and the struggle between speech and English is characterized as a "'great rebellion'" (73). Similar to Rarig and Greaves's account, Covelli provides cursory treatment of two of O'Neill's early and significant addresses on relations between public speaking and English. With the first, O'Neill's March 1913 address on the "dividing line" between public speaking and English departments, Covelli notes, "The English people, needless to say, emphatically opposed [this] position and refused to recognize public speaking as anything more than a part of English" (78–79). With the second, O'Neill's November 1913 address to the public speaking section of NCTE, Covelli writes, "Most of the teachers of public speaking . . . hailed the address. Most of the teachers of English, on the other hand, became offended" (79–80). This cursory treatment reinforces a simplistic representation of uniform animosity between speech and English. Also similar to Rarig and Greaves's account, Covelli's brief description of the formation of the NAATPS reinforces the outcome rather than the process: "After considerable debate . . . , on Saturday morning, November 18, 1914, the teachers of public speaking voted in favor of an independent organization" (80–81). He adds, "The English people did not take kindly to the philosophy of the new public speaking association" (82). While Covelli acknowledges that the vote included full cooperation of the NAATPS with NCTE, his characterization of the events suggests a unanimous decision to form the new organization, when that was not the case.

A modest version of this grand narrative is evident in *Democracy as Discussion: Civic Education and the American Forum Movement*, where William Keith, in summarizing the formation of the NAATPS, uses the trope of oppression to characterize the relationship between English teachers and public speaking teachers. Unlike prior accounts, Keith's provides more thorough treatment of primary and secondary materials to illustrate that many speech teachers experienced friction within English departments. Keith suggests near universal agreement among public speaking teachers that "their problems all stemmed from being housed in English departments" (39) and that the founders of the NAATPS were united in their "animosity toward English departments" and "by their beefs with the NCTE [more] than any common vision of the field" (49). The narrative of oppression results in some imprecision in Keith's identification of the oppressor: sometimes English, sometimes NCTE, sometimes elocutionists. This imprecision suggests limits in the explanatory power of grand narratives and general histories, thereby underscoring the need to use microhistorical methods to render more concrete, nuanced accounts.

Problematic Tropes in Composition and Rhetoric Histories of Speech Communication

Although disciplinary histories in composition and rhetoric that address speech communication are infrequent, they also invoke antagonistic metaphors when describing historical relationships between speech communication and English. Mountford argues that the long history of "disciplinary estrangement" between speech communication and English has been perpetuated by English teachers, whose work has been "the more powerful and privileged of the two" (408) and whose "ambivalence over work in speech communication . . . suggests the ongoing legacy of domination that forced the exit of speech teachers from English in 1914" (409). In Mountford's account, the narrative of oppression generates sympathy for public speaking teachers and reinforces the appropriateness of the divorce metaphor. After briefly referencing the foundation of the NAATPS, Mountford writes, "Separated by divorce, the arts of rhetoric moved into disciplinary homes that focused on only one modality of reception and production—oral discourse in speech communication, written discourse in English," that caused them to grow "separate identities and interests" (409).

This divorce metaphor, informed by Sharon Crowley's use of "rapprochement" in her historical work, is linked to Diana George and John Trimbur's characterization of the failed relationship between communication and composition in the 1950s: "a brief affair, characterized by mutual attractions and misgivings, that proved unable to imagine a future for itself" (407). George and Trimbur's invocation of a war metaphor—the "communication battle"—stems from a publication by the outgoing editor of *College Composition and Communication* (648); yet, the authors' use of such terms (e.g., terms of engagement, battle lines, winners and losers) to structure their argument reinforces and perpetuates a grand narrative of antagonism that circulates in early disciplinary histories in speech communication.

Reconsidering James M. O'Neill

I suggest that the circulation of these narratives and tropes stems from one of the most influential figures in speech communication's early history: James O'Neill. During his tenure as a professor of public speaking at UW-Madison from 1913 to 1927, O'Neill built a modern speech department by recruiting specialists to teach courses and conduct research in their respective areas; he built the first graduate program (MA and PhD) in speech in the United States. He was one of the seventeen founding members of the NAATPS and its first president. He was the founding editor of the *Quarterly Journal of Public Speaking* (now *Quarterly Journal of Speech*); in this capacity, he was the nascent field's "disciplinographer" (Goggin xviii) in that he both authored many early publications in *QJPS* and authorized the work of others. His reputation was one who led "the movement" away from English and toward an independent organization (Covelli 66). Additionally, O'Neill's personality was charismatic, dynamic, outspoken, and controversial. While these characteristics allowed him to provide strong leadership during the NAATPS's early years, they also resulted in impatience and insensitivity, which triggered resentment among and opposition from others.

O'Neill's resulting prominence and often-honorific treatment in early disciplinary histories of speech make him a suitable candidate for critical reexaminiation via microhistorical methods. Two related methods could produce more contextualized accounts of his actions and influence: first, using a "method of clues" to identify evidence that seems odd or out of place in the historical record and that can support new generalizations; second, using "multiscopic analysis" to capture and integrate evidence from many levels, ranging from concrete to abstract, that can produce more richly layered, complex accounts (McComiskey 22, 18). McComiskey notes that searching for such clues among "a plurality of sources" often begins in the archives (21). To illustrate, when reviewing O'Neill's archived correspondence at both Northwestern and UW-Madison, I saw evidence of both hostile and conciliatory attitudes towards English, NCTE, and its leadership. I also saw evidence of O'Neill's and other public speaking teachers' efforts to collaborate with NCTE, as well as conflicting accounts and divergent attitudes among public speaking teachers regarding the formation of the NAATPS and its relationship to NCTE. These clues caused me to rethink the abstracted narrative of O'Neill as heroic liberator of speech communication and of English/NCTE as uniform oppressor, which in turn prompted me to consider more complicated, even conciliatory views of speech's relationship to English—views that are supported by other disciplinary histories (see below). The microhistorical process of dialectically situating local clues and cases with larger contexts and narratives generates more evidence for more nuanced interpretations of historical events, which produces new histories.

More Disciplinary Histories of Speech Communication

Other disciplinary histories provide nuanced or alternative accounts of speech communication's early disciplinary emergence, which support more complex views of and alternative tropes for the early relationship between speech and English. Prefacing his account of the NAATPS's formation, Herman Cohen writes, "The formal establishment of a national association of teachers of public speaking did not occur in a revolutionary setting. Rather, the founding . . . was marked by ambiguity and a measure of parliamentary uncertainty" as well as "considerable political . . . maneuvering" (30, 32). Cohen draws extensively on O'Neill's own account of the organization's formation to support this interpretation: an impromptu meeting of public speaking teachers at NCTE to discuss the creation of a national organzation for public speaking teachers; a decision to survey public speaking teachers nationwide about forming a new association; a subsequent NCTE conference meeting to discuss survey results and subsequent action; repeatedly split opinion on the organization's relationship to NCTE, followed by a "'rump session'" in which "a dissident group of 17 members of NCTE" voted to organize the national association (32–35). Cohen describes the formation of the NAATPS as "far from revolutionary" because most survey respondents favored a new association and taught at institutions with "autonomous Departments of Public Speaking" (34). Cohen also characterizes the NAATPS's attitude towards NCTE as complex: on the one hand, members of the new association expressed a desire for cordial cooperation; on the other hand, there was clear ambivalence about affiliation. Cohen thus concludes, "The association's attitude toward the discipline of English, and specifically toward the NCTE, was reminiscent of the child who ran away from home but, nevertheless, wanted to retain the respect of his parents. The break from the parent group was clothed in ambiguity and was not really a clean break" (35). In ensuing years, Cohen suggests that, with some exceptions, the general attitude among the NAATPS toward English "continued to be ambivalent" rather than antagonistic (59). While the parent-child metaphor introduces its own limitations, it does prompt a less antagonistic way of thinking about the historical relationship between speech communication and English; interestingly, this metaphor was suggested by a University of Illinois speech faculty member in 1946 as a corrective to the divorce metaphor (Finnegan and Wallace 423).

Though not as exhaustive in their treatment of speech communication's early history, Pat Gehrke and William Keith reiterate Cohen's interpretation about the ambiguity and uncertainty marking the founding of the organization (6). They describe O'Neill's 1913 NCTE speech as "deliberately provocative" in pushing back against reports that public speaking instruction should occur under the umbrella of English (5). Unlike Rarig or Covelli, Gehrke and Keith note that reception was mixed. They further note that the decision in the 1914 NCTE public speaking section meeting to vote on either independence or affiliation with NCTE resulted not only because of the split vote but also "because the plurality had not produced the desired result" (5). The authors lastly note that the new organization reflected "a bias favoring college and university teachers" despite its investment in primary and secondary schools (6).

These histories support more nuanced interpretations of early disciplinary relationships between speech and English than the narratives or tropes of other histories would suggest. And recent historical work by speech communication scholars clearly challenges the accuracy of these tropes (see Finnegan and Wallace). As Keith explains, microhistories provide a multiplicity of viewpoints needed to "challenge the elisions and occlusions in our collective self-perceptions" that stem from grand narratives and abstract histories (192). Rhetoricians in English and speech communication who engage in microhistory, both independently and collaboratively, can continue the process of reinventing their histories and disciplinary identities in ways that facilitate greater cross-disciplinary listening, understanding, and collaboration.

Works Cited

Cohen, Herman. *The History of Speech Communication: The Emergence of a Discipline, 1914-1945*. National Communication Association, 1994.

Covelli, Eugene Francis. *James Milton O'Neill—Pioneer in Speech Education*. 1961. University of Wisconsin-Madison, PhD dissertation.

Crowley, Sharon. "Communications Skills and a Brief Rapprochement of Rhetoricians." *Rhetoric Society Quarterly*, vol. 32, no. 1, Winter 2004, pp. 89–103.

Enoch, Jessica. *Refiguring Rhetorical Education: Women Teaching African American, Native American, and Chicano/a Students, 1865-1911*. Southern Illinois UP, 2008.

Finnegan, Cara A., and Marissa Lowe Wallace. "Origin Stories and Dreams of Collaboration: Rethinking Histories of the Communications Course and the Relationships Between Speech and English." *Rhetoric Society Quarterly*, vol. 44, no. 5, 2014, pp. 401–26.

Gehrke, Pat J., editor. *Microhistories of Communication Studies: Mapping the Future of Communication through Local Narratives.* Routledge, 2017.

—. "Introduction." Gehrke, pp. 1–4.

Gehrke, Pat J., and William Keith, editors. *A Century of Communication Studies: The Unfinished Conversation.* Routledge, 2015.

—. "Introduction: A Brief History of the National Communication Association." Gehrke and Keith, pp. 1–25.

George, Diana, and John Trimbur. "The 'Communication Battle,' or Whatever Happened to the 4th C?" *A Usable Past: CCC at 50: Part 2*, special issue of *College Composition and Communication*, vol. 50, no. 4, June 1999, pp. 682–98.

Goggin, Maureen Daly. *Authoring a Discipline: Scholarly Journals and the Post-World War II Emergence of Rhetoric and Composition.* Lawrence Erlbaum Associates, 2000.

Gold, David. *Rhetoric at the Margins: Revising the History of Writing Instruction in American Colleges, 1873-1947.* Southern Illinois UP, 2008.

Halloran, S. Michael. "The Growth of the Rhetoric Society of America: An Anecdotal History." *Rhetoric Society Quarterly*, vol. 48, no. 3, 2018, pp. 234–41.

Keith, William M. *Democracy as Discussion: Civic Education and the American Forum Movement.* Lexington Books, 2007.

—. "Micro-histories: A Coda." Gehrke, pp. 191–92.

Keith, William, and Roxanne Mountford. "Rhetorical Education in/between Communication and Writing: Sharing a Vision, Building a Plan." Rhetoric Society of America 6th Biennial Summer Institute, 5 June 2015, UW-Madison Union South Building, Madison, WI. Keynote Address.

—. "The Mt. Oread Manifesto on Rhetorical Education 2013." *Rhetoric Society Quarterly*, vol. 44, no. 1, 2014, pp. 1–5.

Logan, Shirley Wilson. *Liberating Language: Sites of Rhetorical Education in Nineteenth-Century Black America.* Southern Illinois UP, 2008.

McComiskey, Bruce, editor. *Microhistories of Composition.* Utah State UP, 2016.

—. "Introduction." McComiskey, pp. 3–38.

Mountford, Roxanne. "A Century After the Divorce: Challenges to a Rapprochement Between Speech Communication and English." *Sage Handbook of Rhetorical Studies*, edited by Andrea A. Lunsford, Kirt H. Wilson, and Rosa A. Eberly, Sage Publications, 2009, pp. 407–22.

O'Neill, James M. "The Dividing Line Between Departments of English and Public Speaking." *Public Speaking Review*, vol. 2, 1913, pp. 231-37.

—. "Public Speaking and English." *Public Speaking Review*, vol. 3, 1914, pp. 130-35.

Rarig, Frank M., and Halbert S. Greaves. "National Speech Organizations and Speech Education." *A History of Speech Education in America*, edited by Karl R. Wallace, Appleton-Century-Crofts, 1954, pp. 490–517.

Nervously Loquacious at the Edge of an Abyss

David Blakesley

With much of my career thrown from the molten center that is Kenneth Burke, I thought I would reflect on RSA without Burke, who left the parlor with the discussion still vigorously in progress twenty-five years ago back in 1993, at the age of 96. He was at his long-time family farm in Andover, New Jersey. He died of respiratory failure on a cold November evening, having spent it watching the *MacNeil-Lehrer Newshour*, *Washington Week in Review* and a Bill Moyers report on the "holy war" between conservative Christian values and homosexual rights in Colorado ("The New Holy War"). He had Chinese shrimp. According to his caregiver, Ginny Brand, his "future cookie" read, "To affect the quality of the day is no small achievement." Indeed.

History is not just events, trends, the record of progress, change, or devolution, accomplishments, failures, natural and unnatural disasters, and so on. RSA's recent history is the story of people, people speaking and writing, people being social, sometimes arguing, knowing, making, and doing together. We cannot know the character of our past without knowing its characters, the people who lived and live it. Like the characters here on stage with me this afternoon. Or at this conference. Or the ones who have departed, leaving us to carry on the unending conversation of history. And so we carry on. We try.

In my short talk today, I originally intended to make some startling point about how rhetoric has changed so dramatically in the past twenty-five years, how it has progressed from its rich theoretical traditions in new directions, ones that will provide a solid conceptual foundation for rhetorical studies for years to come. But has it? Will it?

In many of our theoretical models of rhetoric there appear two types: the use of persuasive resources or strategies (*rhetorica utens* or performance) and the study of rhetoric itself as an art of inquiry, of invention, or of the many ways that language and symbol systems shape human relations (*rhetorica docens*). Rhetoric elaborates ambiguity (theory, invention) but it also exploits it (practice, application).

Here we are now, clearly in an age when rhetoric is applied to everything because so much needs to be understood, particularly in our political lives. It is an age of applied rhetoric and civic engagement, when the exigencies of the moment draw the attention constantly. That's not a bad thing, especially when it's drawn to those social-political problems that have been perpetuated for too long by those with the power to sustain the status quo that supports them. Nevertheless, we also have the responsibility to understand how we got here, what we should have seen coming but didn't. Rhetorical theory, which theorizes generative principles and elaborates ambiguity, can help us unravel these mysteries and perhaps help us guard against our tendencies to be mistaken or led astray by our terms or by those who would use them against us, or be caught up in the moment and lose perspective on where we've been, where we're going.

Totalitarian v. Democratic Patriotism

In the midst of war, it would seem foolish to shout too loudly for too long in the wide open about the reasons for the predicament. When push comes to shove, it's usually time to act. In the months leading up to the bombing of Pearl Harbor, Burke wrote two short essays for *Direction* magazine. *Direction* was the journal of the Marxist antifascist coalition of the Popular Front (Weiser 288). In the first essay published in February, 1941, "Americanism: Patriotism in General, Americanism in Particular, Interspersed with Pauses," he discusses the nature of patriotism and what it means in particular contexts. In totalitarian and nationalist schemes, patriotism functions rhetorically to shut down inquiry by viewing alternative perspectives *in terms of* a doctrinal core, the "image of the nation" (2). Democratic patriotism, alternatively, functions rhetorically to open inquiry and value alternative perspectives in dialectic:

> The "total" or "totalitarian" patriot would make nationalism the very center of his thinking, with all else deduced from it. The "democratic" patriot would consider his national identity as one in a hierarchy or graded series of many identities, all of them requiring their full consideration when he is confronting issues and making decisions. (2)

Burke argues for a principled rhetoric that would elaborate ambiguity and, thus, create the necessary conditions for rhetoric. There is no need for rhetoric if everyone agrees with everyone else. Nationalism in this respect would be the end of rhetoric; in its rise to power, nationalism erases opportunities for rhetorical inquiry. Its common form is the encomium, which focuses on the present and reinforces communal unity (sometimes using a scapegoat). Democratic patriotism sees unity in difference and distinction, the full consideration of alternatives:

> And such full consideration is possible only when the issues are confronted and the decisions weighed in a dialectic that has a fully developed series of terms whereby the national interests many be seen as taking their proper place along a whole sliding scale of interests. ("Americanism" 2)

When we're tightly bound by instruments and conditions of our own making, the path of least resistance is to relent, go with the flow, sacrifice our differences for the sake of the common good. However, such moments are rare and usually only occur when the enemy is at the door.

Burke published the second essay in *Direction*, "Where Are We Now," in December, 1941. That essay ranges widely but briefly over a range of topics, most of them related to the function of capitalism and its conflicts with collectivist culture. He does focus for a time on the pamphleteering and sloganizing of political leaders, journalists, and others who sought to unify people around nationalist ideals. For Burke, "A democratic leader has as strong a motive for the coaching of factionalism as the dictator has for suppressing factionalism" (4). The discordant voices of democracy reveal multiple interpretations of the current political and economic crises, a rhetoric of inquiry we need when alternative courses of action are open or possible.

Burke recognized that his call for a full consideration of alternatives rang hollow in the immediate aftermath of the bombing of Pearl Harbor because, suddenly, the time for inquiry had passed and the need for immediate action was paramount. His short follow up to the first two essays in *Direction* was "When 'Now' Became 'Then,'" consisting of just 375 words and published in February-March 1942. Burke sounds uncharacteristically nationalistic but unflinchingly pragmatic: "But absolutely every utterance should be put forward and considered only in ways that contribute, most exactingly, towards unity of action—unity of action among ourselves, and unity of action with our international allies" ("When 'Now' Became 'Then' 5). Peace makes inquiry, even reverie, possible. War requires absolute cooperation.

Eventually, in *A Rhetoric of Motives* (1950), Burke will call war a "*special case of peace*" (19) and the ultimate disease of cooperation (22). War is a perversion, in other words, and functions as a motive that sows rhetorics of scapegoating, demonization, hierarchy, and erasure. The threat of annihilation is the purest of these rhetorical gestures. All are uplifted by a nostalgia for a bogus past, a time when homegrown values were not threatened on all sides by the enemy, an other that, with the power of language to name and rename, can be identified with evil. The celebration of each side's values reveals a deeply felt anxiety about a hypothetical future. When sides are divided and we boast of human grandeur, there's no time for introspection or wide-ranging debate about our motives. The rhetoric is applied, a living, breathing utterance, or as George Kennedy put it, a "hoot in the dark," an energy inherent in communication that is especially powerful in times of crisis, as it was in 1941, as it is now.

At moments like then, or like now, we need rhetoric more than ever to help us expose if not speak truth to power, to reveal what has been repressed in the interest of nationalism and its offshoots or cousins like fascism, what has been lost in our detachment from humanity. To start, we need more than ever the widest ranging elaboration of rhetoric as it is applied, its *praxis*, so that we can all be aware of its machinations and magic. To understand how rhetoric is applied, what theoretical foundations these applications or performances stand on, we need to work backward to their generative principles, which will help us see how we got to now. We must work backward through our terms, tracing them to their sources, discovering them in the processes of being and becoming, hoping that these revelations can teach us how we got here and prophesy where we'll end up if we're not careful.

When Burke introduces the pentad a few years later in 1945 in *A Grammar of Motives*, he illustrates its principles with reference to a large photographic mural he saw on display at the Museum of Modern Art's "The Road to Victory" exhibition, which ran from May through October, 1942. "[T]here was an aerial photograph of two launches, proceeding side by side on a tranquil sea," he writes. "[O]ne could quickly perceive the generating principle of its design" (xvi). Pentadic or dramatistic analysis becomes Burke's equipment for elaborating the attribution of motives and revealing "*terms that clearly reveal the strategic spots at which ambiguities necessarily arise*" (xviii). The "Road to Victory" exhibition, the text of which was written by Carl Sandburg, was a rallying cry couched in a narrative celebrating American values, courage, ideals, and power. One quotation sums up the spirit of the overall message. It's spoken by a farmer: "War—they asked for it—now, by the living God, they'll get it" (10).

War and Cultural Life

Burke discusses the "Road to Victory" in substantial depth in his 1942 essay "War and Cultural Life," published in the *American Journal of Sociology*. There, he wonders whether it's possible to see in the "Road to Victory" narrative the genesis of our predicament. For Burke, it's not simply a rallying cry for patriotism. It also beckons us as critics and rhetoricians to analyze this cultural rhetoric, to elaborate the many ways it assigns motive to human action. For Burke, it's the primary function of rhetoric, as *rhetorica docens*, to bring the terminologies that define and contain our lives into the light. We can't postpone this sort of reflection for more peaceful times, nor should we rely on the simplistic (and extra-linguistic) predictions of behaviorist psychology:

> What one might now most avidly look for, in the cultural sphere, is some evidence of a whole intellectual movement designed thus to "frame" the conception of our exigencies, resources, weaknesses, and intentions. The need to think of global war and of its counterpart, global peace, invites us to seek also a truly global attitude toward all mankind, with its expressions ranging from the austere down to the foibles of the human barnyard. The study of war aims should thus be grounded in the most searching consideration of human motives. So far, however, it seems that war aims are being treated as something of a cross between anticipatory or retrospective ideals and cameralistic proposals designed to enlist or appease various economic interests. And more basic inquiries into human motives seem to have been postponed, as a luxury that the moment cannot afford, precisely at a time when the need for such a search is all the more urgent. The temper of the times is revealed, perhaps, in the fact that our psychiatric experts, imbued with the spirit of total war, periodically do their mite for the cause by issuing news releases in which they prophesy the mental collapse of fascist leaders (thus automatically revealing a wish, not to *re*moralize the enemy, but to *de*moralize the enemy). (409)

I see at least two approaches to rhetoric—applied and theoretical—playing out here at RSA 2018, in the pages of *Rhetoric Society Quarterly*, at our institutes and local chapters. We need more rhetorical theory, I believe, because our contexts are always changing, even if the principles that generate them are permanent. Turning our attention to the theoretical rhetorics that might guide our analysis of present circumstances doesn't require suspending our lives as public intellectuals/citizens, teachers and activists. We can be politically engaged, social justice advocates AND theorists. We have in our moments the actualization of theories, or if not, then we need to return to them, re-theorize our rhetorics for the next time so we can see what we have not seen. We are in the midst of divisions that have (finally) been exposed in the glaring and harsh light of awareness too long suppressed. How we got to now, to borrow the title from Steven Johnson's book, is a story worth retelling, even as we might feel, with Burke, that we huddle together "nervously loquacious at the edge of an abyss" (*Permanence and Change* 272).

Burke was a theorist, most would agree. And yet there he was at the end, watching the holy wars play out in Colorado, talking to the TV, nervously loquacious. And here we are. Such moments seem more common now, 25 years later. If there's a lesson here for rhetoricians, or at least Burke scholars, it's that Burke remained engaged to the end. Or, as my good friend Diane Davis (author of a book on the rhetoric of laughter) said to me one day, maybe the lesson is that the political will kill ya. Burke would get a chuckle out of that.

Works Cited

Burke, Kenneth. *Permanence and Change: An Anatomy of Purpose*. Third edition, U of California P, 1984.
—. *A Grammar of Motives*. 1945. U of California P, 1969.
—. *A Rhetoric of Motives*. 1950. U of California P, 1969.
—. "Americanism: Patriotism in General, Americanism in Particular, Interspersed with Pauses." *Direction*, vol. 4, no. 2, Feb. 1941, pp. 2–3.
—. "Where Are We Now?" *Direction*, vol. 4, n. 12, Dec. 1941, pp. 2–3
—. "When 'Now' Becomes 'Then.'" *Direction*, vol. 5, no. 2–3, Feb.-Mar. 1942, p. 5.
—. "War and Cultural Life." *American Journal of Sociology*, vol. 48, 1942, pp. 404–10
Johnson, Steven. *How We Got to Now: Six Innovations That Made the Modern World*. Reprint edition. Riverhead Books, 2015.
Kennedy George. "A Hoot in the Dark: The Evolution of General Rhetoric." *Philosophy and Rhetoric* vol. 25, no. 1, 1992, pp. 1–21.
Moyers, Bill. "The New Holy War." BillMoyers.com, 19 Nov. 1993. https://billmoyers.com/content/the-new-holy-war/. Accessed 30 Dec. 2019.
Museum of Modern Art. "Road to Victory, a Procession of Photographs of the Nation at War." Dir. by Comdr. Edward Steichen, U.S.N.R. Text by Carl Sandburg. Museum of Modern Art, 1942.
Weiser, Elizabeth. "Burke and War: Rhetoricizing the Theory of Dramatism." *Rhetoric Review*, vol. 26, no. 3, 2007, pp. 286–302.

Women, Foreigners, and the Pragmatic Origins of Speech Communication

Zornitsa Keremidchieva

A pragmatist revival appears to be in full bloom in rhetorical and communication studies. Across our journals the tradition is explored as a philosophical orientation, a pedagogical set of principles, and a theory of communicative action (Bergman; Crick; Dascal and Gross; Greene; Jones; Stob; Stroud). With few exceptions (Tonn), strangely missing from these accounts are women's substantive contributions to pragmatism as a social field of action. With that omission, a larger story is obscured. It is a story about the way speech communication emerged with and through a pragmatic engagement with the problematics of difference and diversity. It is also a story that holds valuable insights for our ongoing challenges of reconciling our conceptions of rhetoric and communication with our commitments to shared democratic living. Hence, the goal of this paper is to recover, reflect on, and reorient our engagement with pragmatism from the past and into the future.

Pragmatism, Communication, and the (Gendered) Fields of Social Action

Pragmatism is foundational to communication studies and not only rhetoric. In 1999, Robert T. Craig identified the rhetorical, semiotic, phenomenological, cybernetic, sociopsychological, sociocultural and critical paradigms as the core orientations of our field. Based on this "constitutive metamodel," Craig argued that despite its open-ended diversity, communication theory, writ large, could be "a coherent field, and useful too" (128). In 2007, after a gentle nudge by Chris Russill, Craig agreed to add pragmatism as an eighth tradition. He couldn't help but point out, however, that the very project of developing a constitutive metamodel was in the first place an expression of pragmatism.

One can imagine that Craig's comment referenced not so much the interplay between theory and practice that pragmatism and communication studies share, but more so their common commitment to pluralism. Ironically, perhaps, Jason Hannan's review of recent books about pragmatist philosophy suggests that scholarship in the pragmatist tradition has been rich and generative to the point of yielding practically incompatible positions. Such developments, however, need not dispel our desire to keep mining the treasure trove. Neither should they reduce our discussions to definitional debates about what is or isn't proper pragmatism.

In a different sense, Craig might be referencing the shared origin story of pragmatism and speech communication as a joint and mutually reinforcing embrace of the practical art of civic engagement. A quick visit to the earliest issues of the *Quarterly Journal of Speech* reveals studies of speech pathology appearing next to articles about public speaking pedagogy, oratory, dramatics and more. What held all these interests together? In a way that radiated a pragmatist creed, writing in 1918 J. P. Ryan explained this cacophony with one word: speech. As he put it, "[t]he word speech is old, short, simple, stable, well-known, accurate, common, learned, definite, extensive, and academically acceptable for it connotes the art and denotes the science, or just as well it denotes the art, and connotes the science" (9). For Ryan, the concept of speech was not simply a transcendent term encompassing a variety of practices, forms, contexts, or performances. Rather, an interest in speech was an interest in what he called "speech culture," which entailed "the ability to think in terms of social life and social culture, to train men and women to play their part in a democracy" (10). In this view, speech was not a slice of human activity dissected from the social body but a performative mechanism for constituting common existence. Speech was theory and practice. Speech communication was pragmatism personified.

Yet, the same elements that have made pragmatism tower toward the light in our field as in others, I would argue, also throw its biggest and strangest shadow. It might be the case, as some feminist philosophers have argued, that pragmatism often disguises "a masculine perspective as a neutral, human one" (Seigfried, *The Missing Perspective* 406). This critique addresses the way in which pragmatism is continuously canonized as a primarily male philosophical tradition that is somehow detached from the intensities of women's work and experiences. It is not a simple matter to protest the secondary exclusion of women thinkers among the founders of this intellectual movement, an absence as persistent in communication studies as it is in the philosophical cannon. The evidence of women's contributions to pragmatism is in plain view. In addition to the troves of records of women's independent statements that were very much part of the movement, there is plenty of evidence that the very men whom we identify as the faces of pragmatism developed their thinking in conversation with and on the basis of the activities, speeches and writing of influential women. For example, John Dewey marked the celebration of his 70th birthday with the following statement: "I have learned many things from Jane Addams. I notice that with her usual modesty she attributed to me some of the things in Chicago which she and her colleagues in Hull House did" (Seigfried, *Shared Communities of Interest* 5).

What is the fallout of our blind spots? Besides delimiting the intellectual depth and scope of pragmatism, they also curtail our ability to assess its full range of social and theoretical potential. One underappreciated area is pragmatism's encounter with feminism as the other significant philosophical movement of the period. The historiographic and theoretical archive documenting the early interactions between pragmatism and feminism is only growing (Seigfried, *Pragmatism and Feminism*) and it points to at least two possibilities. One is that strands of feminism and pragmatism developed side by side but somewhat independently, while the second suggests that they fueled each other. Either way, discovering the intellectual and political proximity of these perspectives should not be surprising. Feminism and pragmatism share an impulse for social and political analysis. Also, they both eschew dogmatic, universalist propositions favoring instead the possibility of creative human action, adaptiveness, and situatedness.

Still, in the early 1990s the feminist rapprochement with pragmatism began with a reproach for the latter's blind spot for women's experiences. With that a debate has been reignited over how best to approach the apparent tension between commitments to diversity and the value of unity at the heart of the pragmatist notion of democratic community. Some feminists, noting the difficulty of sharing experiences across difference, have urged vigilance in assessing pragmatism's conceptions of cooperation and community, notions that otherwise appeal to feminist ethics of being-with-others. In Charlene Seigfried's view, for example, "pragmatism naturalized the transcendental search for eternal truths about reality by reflecting on the various ways that members of a community come to agree on the explanations that best join the funded character of experiences with the goals sought and then critically revise their conclusions in light of further developments" (*Shared Communities of Interest* 2).

My concern is that our main motives and strategy for engaging with pragmatism, our tendency to recover its tenets from a particular corner of the archive of philosophical conversation, are inadvertently distancing us from pragmatism's core value as a field of socially embodied reflective practice. I offer, therefore, an approach to pragmatism as grounded theory. Pragmatism is what pragmatism does. My suggestion is that an appreciation for pragmatism as a value orientation, conceptual innovation, lived experience, and ethos for democratic living can be better developed through engagement with the practitioners of pragmatism. As it happens, many of them were women and many of them were in the field, doing the work of association across difference (that the men were talking about). For me engaging with the records of these women's experiences and reflections, particularly those concerning the dynamic powers and vagaries of communication is more a matter of enriching our imagination about the possibilities of meaningful life in common than a self-contained project of recovery or restitution. So next I braid together elements from the archives and emergent stories of pragmatism, feminism, and speech communication to highlight the role of gender and otherness in these formations' shared empirical and analytical modes of becoming. I find that at the turn of the twentieth century, the confluence of three developments—first, the communicative work of women who created the material cultural imprint of pragmatism; second, philosophical conversations around communication and civic engagement; and lastly, our field's theorization and participation in the task of imagining and managing a diverse democratic society—brought forth the immigrant as the figure par excellence of pragmatism's promise and frustration. It is important to note, furthermore, that this haunting immigrant was not without gender.

Engaging Communication's Foreignness

As commonly told, the late nineteenth century in the United States, the period that gave rise to pragmatism, was a time of great social transformation. A large scale shift from rural to urban living, significant rates of immigration, and a transformation of modes of production from the relative autonomy of artisanal work to the streamlined group processes of the industrial setting prompted a rethinking of the bases of social organization. Meliorism, the belief that the world can be made better, emerged in this milieu, propelling explorations into social reform. Melioristic sensibilities found expression in a vast array of intellectual perspectives: from those of social Darwinism, economic and political institutionalism, to various strands of pragmatism and feminism. Such meliorism also fueled a vast array of social activities and organization strategies: from unionization and other forms of labor organizing, professional, recreational and mutual aid societies, social reform movements such as those for women's rights, temperance, peace and others. Theda Skocpol, like many others, has noted this period for its high rates of social engagement and social entrepreneurship. This period was really the heyday of associated living in the United States with a significant number of adults being members of at least one voluntary organization, regardless of social status.

These incredible rates of social engagement came together in various organizational forms that should also be noted for their diverse membership. Not surprisingly, pluralism emerged as a key concept of interest in public discourse as well as in pragmatist theorizations that often centered on certain conceptions of cultural diversity. Rhetorical scholars of this period have attested that the public and academic responses to the so called "problem of immigration" created a rich field of arguments and theories about the proper way to manage diversity and pluralism in the American polity (Dorsey). The Americanization campaigns that are the subject of Leslie Hahner's recent book *To Become an American* were not just a rhetorical response to the problem of managing public sentiments about immigrants. Instead, the field of Americanization work was a terrain for experimentation, a social laboratory, a testing ground for investigating the practical and theoretical value of various models and strategies for the democratic (or not so democratic) management of diversity and pluralism (Keremidchieva).

All hands were on deck. Across academic, social and institutional spaces, the immigrant figured as an object of theorization and the key to self-understanding. Rummaging through the earliest issues of our journals, it wasn't hard for me to find the immigrant wandering among the pillars of our discipline's formation. No one seemed to embody more strikingly the connection between speech education, national identity, and commitments to progress than the immigrant. The *Quarterly Journal of Speech* published articles which specifically inquired how speech and speech pedagogy could work as techniques of Americanization. For J. P. Ryan the call for attention to speech culture and the role of speech in social relationships was a response to "the rising interest in the improvement of American speech" (10). Soon enough, however, a less egalitarian and more instrumental, explicitly male-centered approach to speech education began to take hold. W. Palmer Smith argued in 1921 that "a foreigner's interest in learning to speak English and the use he makes of his acquirements in the language of American are self-manifestive indices of his attitude toward and his progress in Americanization" (370). In defending "the potency of English speech as an Americanizing agent," Smith pointed to the chain of effects that should be triggered when immigrants took classes in English speech:

> learning the truth about our country, thinking about it and talking about it, will have a tendency to develop patriotic feeling and patriotic conduct. And these patriotic thoughts and feelings when

reflected in conduct develop good citizens. It follows, therefore, that the type of assignments in the speech class will determine to a large extent the scope of its contribution to Americanization. (371)

Statements like these mark the field's abandonment of pragmatism and genuine investment in lived and shared democratic theory. Speech gave way to a more instrumental mode of rhetoric and a concept of communication that for at least a period policed strict gender, racial, and ethnic lines.

Our field's departure from the pragmatist creed at that time, however, did not mean that the work of exploring the lived associative potential of speech communication was never done. On the contrary, it persisted. It persisted in the work of women's organizations such as the YWCA. It blossomed in the work of the International Institutes that the YWCA created to provide space for immigrant women and their families to seek common bonds of humanity and understanding. For leaders in those membership organizations such as Terry Bremer of the YWCA, who should readily be added to the list of foremost voices of pragmatism, speech and association went hand in hand. Democratic life and the cultivation of a democratic ethos required "venues of acquaintance, opportunities for social contacts, occasions for exchange of thoughts" (Bremer). Katherine Gerwick, a member of the American YWCA National Board wrote that "[w]omen must see in citizenship an opportunity to set in motion an ever-widening circle of friendship which shall reach from the women in a small Ohio village to an isolated group in an Indian purdah" (69). From these premises, the organization developed all sorts of techniques and strategies aimed at overcoming the sources of alienation in modernity and in the process developed rigorous empirical methodologies for socialization, peace building, and democratic living some of which are still in use to this day (Keremidchieva).

The reflexive experiences that these women's organizations amassed in their outreach to immigrants and families across the strata of American society were hardly matched by the budding interests of their contemporary scholars in communication and other cognate fields. Yet they certainly straddled that distance between tragedy and hope that Gregory J. Shepherd identifies as the "battlefield" story of pragmatism and communication (253). They are also a reminder for something important that might be getting a bit lost in our present moment. They are a reminder that all human action is *inter*-action. They are a reminder that life demands care, and that care entails communication. They are also a reminder that life demands spirit, and that spirit is always an *other* to our selves. Fifty years into the organizational life of the Rhetorical Society of America, committing to such *other*-orientedness, with all its trials and travails, joys and rewards, I believe, remains the challenge and promise of our field.

Works Cited

Bergman, Mats. "Beyond the Interaction Paradigm? Radical Constructivism, Universal Pragmatics, and Peircean Pragmatism." *The Communication Review*, vol. 14, no. 2, 2011, pp. 96–122.

Bremer, Edith Terry. "The International Institute: A Re-Analysis of Our Foundations." Conference on International Institute Work Preceding National Conference of Social Work, Washington DC, May 14 to May 16, 1923. YWCA International Institute, St. Louis, Box 2, Folder 1:A24. Immigration History Research Center Archive. University of Minnesota.

Craig, Robert. "Communication Theory as a Field." *Communication Theory*, vol. 9, no. 2, 1999, pp. 119-61.

—. "Pragmatism in the Field of Communication Theory." *Communication Theory*, vol. 17, no. 2, 2007, pp. 125–45.

Crick, Nathan. "Rhetoric and Events." *Philosophy & Rhetoric*, vol. 47, no. 3, 2014, pp. 251–72.

Dascal, Marcelo, and Alan G. Gross. "The Marriage of Pragmatics and Rhetoric." *Philosophy & Rhetoric*, vol. 32, no. 2, 1999, pp. 107–30.

Dorsey, Leroy G. *"We are All Americans, Pure and Simple": Theodore Roosevelt and the Myth of Americanism*. Tuscaloosa, AL: University of Alabama Press, 2007.

Gerwick, Katherine. "Women's Citizenship." *Women and Leadership*, edited by Mary S. Sims and Rhoda E. McCullogh. New York: Woman's Press, 1920/1938, pp. 68-69.

Greene, Ronald Walter. "John Dewey's Eloquent Citizen: Communication, Judgment, and Postmodern Capitalism." *Argumentation and Advocacy*, vol. 39, no. 3, 2003, pp. 189–200.

Hahner, Leslie. *To Become an American: Immigrants and Americanization Campaigns of the Early Twentieth Century*. East Lansing, MI: Michigan University Press, 2017.

Hannan, Jason. "Pragmatism, Democracy, and Communication: Three Rival Perspectives." *Review of Communication*, vol. 11, no. 2, 2011, pp. 107–21.

Jones, Donald C. "John Dewey and Peter Elbow: A Pragmatist Revision of Social Theory and Practice." *Rhetoric Review*, vol. 21, no. 3, 2002, pp. 264–81.

Keremidchieva, Zornitsa. "From National to International Engagement and Back: The YWCA's Communicative Techniques of Americanization in the Aftermath of World War I." *Women's History Review*, vol. 26, no. 2, 2017, pp. 280-295.

Ryan, J. P. "Terminology: The Department of Speech." *Quarterly Journal of Speech*, vol. 4, no. 1, 1918, pp. 1-11.

Seigfried, Charlene Haddock. "The Missing Perspective: Feminist Pragmatism." *Transactions of the Charles S. Peirce Society*, vol. 27, no. 4, 1991, pp. 405-416.

—. "Shared Communities of Interest: Feminism and Pragmatism." *Hypatia*, vol. 8, no. 2, 1993, pp. 1-14.

— (1996). *Pragmatism and feminism: Reweaving the social fabric.* Chicago: University of Chicago Press.

Shepherd, Gregory J. "Pragmatism and Tragedy, Communication and Hope: A Summary Story." *American Pragmatism and Communication Research,* edited by David K. Perry. Mahwah, NJ: Lawrence Erblaum Associates, 2001, pp. 241-254.

Skocpol, Theda. *Diminished Democracy: From Membership to Management in American Civic Life.* Norman, OK: University of Oklahoma Press, 2003.

Smith, W. Palmer. "Americanization through Speech in Our High Schools." *Quarterly Journal of Speech,* vol. 7, no. 4, 1921, pp. 370-374.

Stob, Paul. "Pragmatism, Experience, and William James's Politics of Blindness." *Philosophy & Rhetoric,* vol. 44, no. 3, 2011, pp. 227–49.

Stroud, Scott R. "Comprehensive Rhetorical Pluralism and the Demands of Democratic Discourse: Partisan Perfect Reasoning, Pragmatism, and the Freeing Solvent of Jaina Logic." *Philosophy & Rhetoric,* vol. 47, no. 3, 2014, pp. 297–322.

Tonn, Mari Boor. "Jane Addams: Spirit in Action." *Rhetoric & Public Affairs,* vol. 14, no. 3, 2011, pp. 552–55.

On Not Repeating Mistakes: The Case for a More Inclusive Society for the Study of Catholic Rhetoric

Elizabethada A. Wright

I

In 2001, Joy Ritchie and Kate Ronald observed that "male contexts have come to stand for Rhetoric itself" (xxvi) and a year later in an issue of *RSQ*, Christine Ross noted that "Rhetorical theory has been a male prerogative since its inception among the Greeks" (85). Both observations were not exactly new; over a decade earlier, Karlyn Kohrs Campbell made similar comments as she worked to rectify that situation, work that hundreds (maybe thousands) of other rhetoricians have been continuing since, as Ritchie and Ronald state, to "consider…the gendered nature of rhetorical contexts, communicative strategies and epistemology" (xxiv). More recently, Julie Enszer recounted a similar situation: the field of literature had supposedly addressed the problem of exclusionary scholarship with increases in the numbers of women receiving grants and being represented in literary anthologies. However, Enszer notes that while in some areas women are represented fairly, in other areas, such as in Norton anthologies, the gains in representation of women have been quietly decreasing. Recounting a phrase from a letter of protest regarding the marginalization of women's work in the 1970s, Enszer titles her article, "She who shouts gets heard."

In this collection marking the fiftieth anniversary of the founding of the RSA, I want to shout a little. This article is part activism, part scholarship. While in 2018 there is a rich body of rhetorical theory and history that increasingly makes sure rhetoric is no longer a "white male prerogative," our gains could be chipped away with the creation of rhetorical organizations that by definition exclude or marginalize women. In particular, this paper briefly focuses on why our field should not marginalize the study of rhetorical education and theory developed by Catholic women religious (commonly known as nuns).

Carol Mattingly's *Secret Habits* provides a fabulous springboard for such scholarly study as it discusses various Catholic women's orders, the schools they ran, and the practices of reading and writing that made up the schools' curriculum. Mattingly's work seems to match well with recent studies regarding the influence of Jesuit education on rhetorical studies, as twenty-first century rhetoricians go beyond the prejudices of previous centuries to recognize the significance of the Catholic religion on rhetoric.

However, as this paper suggests, last summer's creation of ISSJR, the International Society for the Study of Jesuit Rhetoric, by ISHR, International Society of the History of Rhetoric, may be leading rhetoric down the same path that Enszer observes: by definition, this new organization excludes study of the rhetoric of Catholic Sisters. Though individuals within the ISSJR have promised to make room for the sisters' rhetoric in conferences, panels and journals, such marginalization does not help our field gain the rich perspective on rhetoric that we have been moving toward.

This paper argues that while the study of the Jesuit rhetoric is extremely important, in the twenty-teens--a time when we increasingly recognize the need for inclusiveness—such study should not marginalize the contributions of other Catholic orders—especially women's. Instead, we need societies that are inclusive as they recognize how various rhetorical contributions are intertwined. When influential people create new societies studying rhetoric that by definition exclude or (at best marginalize), the progress of our field's past fifty years is undermined.

II

The Catholic Church consists of lay people and the clergy, but overlapping both groups are members of Catholic religious communities, men and women who take religious vows to dedicate themselves to God and the Church. These communities, or orders, have existed since the dawn of Christianity, cited in literature, histories, and other texts. Members of these communities do not belong to one collective group; they live in various orders, established by different individuals and subscribing to specific missions such as teaching, a mission fulfilled by both men and women religious for centuries

(Vermeersch).[1] Some orders contain both men and women; others are exclusive to one gender. Despite their separateness, various orders often work together in efforts to achieve their missions. One such order that has frequently collaborated with others and is exclusive to one gender is the Society of Jesus, or the Jesuits, founded in 1540.

In North America, the focus of this article, Catholic women religious contributed to a large portion of education. For example, the Ursuline Sisters were among the first to teach girls in North America, creating schools first in Quebec in 1639 (Lindsay, Fidelis) and in New Orleans in 1727 (Keenan 7; Woody 329). By the end of the eighteenth century, the confluence of the new United States' freedom of religion and the French Revolution's prohibitions on Catholicism brought innumerable European female and male Catholic religious to the young country. In the United States, these members of religious orders began establishing schools for all students, including the daughters of many of the United States' earliest leaders such as Thomas Jefferson and the Adams (Ewens 26-28).[2] According to Carol Coburn and Martha Smith, by 1820, there were ten schools for girls run by women religious; by 1840, 40; by 1880, over 500 (161). When, in 1893 the American Catholic Church held its Educational Exhibit at the World's Columbian Exposition, the exhibit displayed examples from 1,376 schools, and this number represented only a portion of the Catholic schools in America (Maurelian, Spaulding and Milanis). Though these exhibited schools were run by male as well as female orders, a majority of the Catholic schools in the United States were run by women religious, as almost all narratives of Catholic education acknowledge (e.g., White, Ewens, Thompson). Additionally, various scholars (Coburn and Smith, Mahoney) observe that in the nineteenth- and early twentieth-centuries, more women attended secondary schools in the United States than did men, mostly because of the Sisters' schools for young women (Coburn and Smith 162).

Religious sisters also provided college educations to women: though there were not American Catholic colleges for women until the School Sisters of Notre Dame became the College of Notre Dame of Maryland (Mahoney 25), many institutes offered college level programs; for example, both St.

---

1. For more regarding women religious and the mission of teaching, see, for example, Rapley, McLaughlin and Fiorenza.

2. I reference Ewens's much cited "fact" that Jefferson's daughters received a Catholic education in the United States though I cannot find any reference to that fact elsewhere. A letter of Jefferson's in the National Archives, however, makes clear that not only did his daughter Polly attend a Catholic school in Paris but also contemplated joining the religious life.

Mary's College of South Bend and St. Elizabeth's College began such courses in the 1870s (Mahoney 361, McEniry). Then, at the turn of the twentieth century, there were six Catholic colleges for women, while in 1968, there were 170 (as well as 70 additional ones strictly for Sisters) (Mahoney). Counting schools that did not succeed to 1968, Thomas Landy notes women religious "established 190 four-year and junior colleges for laywomen, outstripping the number of Protestant and nonsectarian colleges of women" (65). In sum, Landy estimates the number of students went from 38,000 in 1947 to 101,000 in 1968. This number shows how influential women religious were.

III

These numbers, however, do not illustrate that women religious were teaching rhetoric or had any influence on modern rhetorical studies. Certainly, the scholarship demonstrating this influence is paltry; however, Mattingly's research addresses this dearth. Within her scholarship, Mattingly challenges many of our field's narratives regarding "the overwhelming influence of the British on US education." Looking at the influence of French sisters, she calls for more research on French Sisters' influence on American rhetoric.

Not specifically responding to the focus on French Sisters, increasing numbers of scholars have been doing so. Nan Johnson recently published on the rhetorical curriculum presented at three Ohio colleges run by women religious, and Erin Wecker on the rhetorical use of silence in the problematic Magdalen Laundries. At the Feminisms and Rhetorics conference in 2013, Amy Ferdinandt Stolley presented on rhetoric of Mother McAuley, the founder of the Sisters of Mercy, and in 2017, Laura Davies presented the feminist rhetoric of lay women involved in the Catholic Church and Jennifer Burgess on Catholic women's means of situating ethos in their business writing.

When one begins to look for rhetoric at Catholic Sisters' schools, it begins to appear in various forms. For example, just as scholars of Jesuit rhetoric note the existence of a rhetoric curriculum in Jesuit schools via these schools' demands that students develop competence in Latin, engage in active learning techniques, and combine knowledge and wisdom with virtue, so could the existence of such a rhetorical curriculum be observed at the Sisters of Providence's St. Mary-of-the-Woods in Indiana. The school's first prospectus, in 1841, announced that students would study "reading, writing, arithmetic, geography, and History, both Ancient and Modern, English Composition, Natural Philosophy" as well as various sciences and domestic skills ("Philosophy"). Not included in the initial curriculum, Latin was added by at least 1854 in a SMW's curriculum that promised "The course of instruction [that] embraces all the studies which constitute a thorough English education." With a school motto "Virtue and Knowledge Combined" from its inception to the present day, SMW not only promised this curriculum but delivered. In 1892 an alumna wrote "The object of education is to fit man for completeness in life, to make him grow in knowledge and virtue to train his facilities and develop his endowments, and thus lead him to his eternal destiny. ("Philosophy"). And Alumna from the nineteenth century to the twenty-first have gone on to use their rhetorical education in various ways, including serving as chancellor of my own university from 1996 to 2010.

If we follow Andrea Lunsford's advice to "listen hard" to find rhetorical theory (6), we can see it all over the place in curricula at many Catholic women's schools. Articles from the student periodical at the school of the Sisters of St. Joseph in St. Augustine suggest women religious encouraged their students to use language to become leaders. Oblate Sisters of Providence comprised another group of Sisters with an educational mission. Despite Diane Batts Morrow's excellent work on the Oblate Sisters of Providence, one of the few orders open for African American women, her work focuses on elements relevant to her field of history and little explores the rhetorical education provided in their Sunday school and daily classes. Although one could argue such classes need not necessarily have provided any rhetorical education of note, listening hard to this curriculum might reveal how it encouraged rhetorical excellence.

IV

We have little understanding of how Catholic rhetorical education has shaped our discipline, though the founding of ISSJR works to rectify that lack. Yet there is so much beyond Jesuit education, and so much intertwined with, dependent on and sustaining Jesuit education. For example, though there were many Jesuit schools founded in early North America, these schools were taken over by other orders because of bans imposed on the Jesuits by various countries as well as the Vatican during the eighteenth and nineteenth centuries.[3] Many Sisters were among those picking up where the Jesuits had left off or dared not go. One such order was the Ursulines. According to James Burns's 1908 study, Louisiana's governor wanted Jesuits to develop

---

3. See, for example, Roehner and Hughes. Throughout their history, the Jesuits have garnered dislike for a variety of reasons and have been prohibited from teaching or promoting their religion in various countries. In 1773, Pope Clement XIV prohibited them from actively preaching or teaching; following this, the Jesuits were prohibited in most of what is now the United States until they were reinstated by the Vatican in 1814.

schooling in New Orleans but when the Jesuits felt they did not have the means to support a college, they recruited and accompanied the Ursulines from France 1727 (17). The Ursulines certainly did not have monetary means, but they had staying power, remaining when Spanish control of the city ceded to the French, again remaining when New Orleans became part of the United States, and still remaining today. The Congregation of the Sisters of St. Joseph, the founding order for the Sisters of St. Joseph in St. Augustine--as well as in many Sisters of St. Joseph in fifteen other states--was founded in mid seventeenth-century France by a Jesuit priest (Dougherty et al. 3-50). The Sisters of Providence who founded SMW began working with the Jesuits in 1849 (Brown 595), and their relationship with the Jesuits continues to the present day in various ways, including collaboration with the Christo Rey Network, an organization providing education for economically disadvantaged inner-city students (Ryan).

While the Jesuits influenced and assisted many orders of Sisters, Mattingly makes clear the influence and assistance went both ways. For example, Mattingly notes that many sisters helped Jesuits with their English, managed much of their housekeeping, assisted financially, and—at least in one case--influenced their educational curriculum (121–122). While language instruction, housekeeping, and financial assistance might not seem sufficient to merit close study of Catholic sisters' interconnections with Jesuit rhetoric, with so little understanding of the Sisters there will never be any understanding of their rhetoric. That lack of study needs to change.

V

In their argument for the importance of Jesuit rhetorical education, Cinthia Gannett and John Brereton list the many "'Jesuit-trained' public figures, included people ranging from Clarence Thomas and Michel de Certeau, as well as many individuals who are members of RSA (15). Though I have not conducted such a survey, I believe the count of "'Catholic Sister-trained' public figures" would be just as large, or significantly larger—even though a majority of those individuals would be women, a group discouraged from being public figures.

In the fifty years since the founding of the RSA, the field of rhetoric has evolved enormously. No longer do books on rhetoric include nary a woman. The field has changed because many individuals have labored to make sure "male contexts" no longer "stand for Rhetoric itself" and that rhetorical theory is no longer a "male prerogative." Yet, as Alison Booth in 2009 repeated what Judith Fetterley had stated in 1994 regarding the influence of her earlier work, "10 years later the scene has changed far less than I anticipated"

(15). It is now 2018, and I again modify Fetterley's refrain: "Fifty years later the scene may not have changed as much as we all believe it has." The entirely male order of the Society of Jesus is important to the history of rhetorical education, certainly. However, this exclusively male order should not be representative of all Catholic rhetorical education, especially when women were so crucial to much of that education in North America. Just as female rhetoricians, both ancient and modern, are no longer peripheral to rhetorical study, Catholic women religious integral to the development of much modern day rhetoric and rhetorical education should not be on the outer edges of new societies, created by important rhetoricians among us, that begin to examine understudied areas of rhetoric. We can do better.

We do need to study the rhetoric of Jesuits, but so too do we need to study the rhetoric of the thousands of women religious who educated hundreds of thousands of students all over the world to read and write. To invest in the scholarship of one while marginalizing the other repeats mistakes many of us thought were left in the past. So in this part scholarly, part activist article, I am shouting to be heard: on the fiftieth anniversary of this important organization, let RSA encourage the formations of organizations that study the rhetoric of all Catholic orders.

Works Cited

Booth, Alison. "Recovery 2.0: Beginning the Collective Biographies of Women Project." *Tulsa Studies in Women's Literature*, vol. 28, no. 1 (Spring 2009), pp. 15–36. JStor. https://www.jstor.org/stable/40783472

Brown, Mary Borromeo. *The History of the Sisters of Providence of Saint Mary-of-the-Woods*. Vol I. Benziger Bros, 1949.

Burgess, Jennifer. "'Extend[ing] a welcome hand to the stranger coming to our shores': Catholic Women's Use of Business Writing to Maintain an Ethos of Professionalization and Outreach" Feminisms and Rhetorics Conference, 2017.

Burns, James Aloysius. *The Principles, Origin, and Establishment of the Catholic School System in the United States*. Benzinger Bros., 1908. Reprint by General Books, Memphis.

Campbell, Karlyn Kohrs. *Man Cannot Speak for Her: A Critical Study of Early Feminist Rhetoric*. Volumes 1 and 2. Praeger,1989.

Coburn, Carol K., and Martha Smith. *Spirited Lives: How Nuns Shaped Catholic Culture and Daily Life, 1836–1920*. University of North Carolina Press, 1999.

Davies, Laura. "Who Owns this Church: Feminist Methods of Protest and Lay Catholic Activism." Feminisms and Rhetorics Conference, 2017.

Dougherty, Dolorita Marie, Helen Angela Hurley, Emily Joseph Daly, St. Claire Coyne and others. *Sisters of St. Joseph of Carondelet*. Herder, 1966.

Enszer, Julie R. "'She Who Shouts Gets Heard!': Counting and Accounting for Women Writers in Literary Grants and Norton Anthologies." *Feminist Studies*. vol. 42, no. 3, 2016, pp. 720–37. JStor, doi:10.15767/feministstudies.42.3.0720.

Ewens, Mary. "The Role of the Nun in Nineteenth-Century America: Variations on the International Theme." PhD dissertation, University of Minnesota, 1971.

Fetterley, Judith. "Commentary: Nineteenth-Century American Women Writers and the Politics of Recovery," *American Literary History*, vol. 6, no. 3, 1994, pp. 600–11. JStor, https://www.jstor.org/stable/489830.

Fidelis, Mother Mary. "The Ursulines". *Catholic Encyclopedia*, Ed. Charles Herbermann. Vol. 15. Robert Appleton Company, 1912, pp. 228–29. Haithi Trust, https://babel.hathitrust.org/cgi/pt?id=nyp.33433070780394;view=1up;seq=1.

Fiorenza, Elisabeth Schussler. "Word, Spirit, and Power: Women in Early Christian Communities." *Women of Spirit: Female Leadership in the Jewish and Christian Traditions*, edited by Rosemary Radford and Eleanor McLauglin, Wipf and Stock, 1998, pp. 29–70.

Gannett, Cinthia and John C. Brereton. "Introduction: The Jesuits and Rhetorical Studies—Looking Backward, Moving Forward." *Traditions in Eloquence: The Jesuits & Modern Rhetorical Studies*. Ed. Gannett and Brereton. Fordham UP, 2016, pp. 1-38.

Hughes, Thomas. *History of the Society of Jesus in North America Colonial and Federal*. Vol 1. Longmans, Green, and Co., 1910. Forgotten Books.

Jefferson, Thomas. "To Elizabeth Wayles Eppes." 15 December 1788. *Founders Online*. National Archives. http://founders.archives/gov.

Johnson, Nan. "Rhetorical Education at Catholic Colleges for Women in Ohio; 1925-1940." *Rhetoric and Writing Studies in the New Century: Historiography, Pedagogy, and Politics*, edited by Cheryl Glenn and Roxanne Mountford. Southern Illinois UP, 2017. pp. 214–29.

Keenan, Mary Ellen. "French Teaching Communities and Early Convent Education in the United States 1727–1850. Diss. Catholic University of America. 1934.

Landy, Thomas. "The Colleges in Context." *Catholic Women's College in America*. Ed. Tracy Schier and Cynthia Russett. Johns Hopkins UP, 2002, pp. 55 97.

Lindsay, Lionel. "Ursulines of Quebec". *Catholic Encyclopedia*, Ed. Charles Herbermann, vol. 15. New York: Robert Appleton Company, 1912, pp. 229–30. Haithi Trust, https://babel.hathitrust.org/cgi/pt?id=nyp.33433070780394;view=1up;seq=1.

Lunsford, Andrea. "On Reclaiming Rhetorica." *Reclaiming Rhetorica: Women in the Rhetorical Tradition*, edited by Andrea Lunsford. University of Pittsburg Press, 1995, pp. 3-8.

Mahoney, Kathleen A. "American Catholic Colleges for Women: Historical Origins." *Catholic Women's College in America*, edited by Tracy Schier and Cynthia Russett. Johns Hopkins UP, 2002, pp. 25–54

Mattingly, Carol. *Secret Habits: Catholic Literacy Education for Women in the Early Nineteenth Century*. Southern Illinois UP, 2016.

Maurelian, Brother, John Lancaster Spaulding [and Carola Milanis]. *The Catholic Educational Exhibit at the World's Columbian Exposition, 1893. Illustrative and Descriptive*. Chicago: J.S. Hyland, 1895.

McEniry, Blanch Marie. *Three Score and Ten: A History, 1899-1969*. College of St. Elizabeth, 1969.

McLaughlin, Eleanor. "Women, Power, and the Pursuit of Holiness in Medieval Christianity." *Women of Spirit: Female Leadership in the Jewish and Christian Traditions*, edited by Rosemary Radford and Eleanor McLauglin, Wipf and Stock, 1998, pp. 99–130.

Morrow, Diane Batts. *Persons of Color and Religious at the Same Time*. University of North Carolina Press, 2002.

"Philosophy the Basis of True Education." *The Signal*, vol. 2, no. 1, 1892.

Rapley, Elizabeth. *The Devotees: Women and Church in Seventeenth-Century France*. McGill-Queens UP, 1990.

Ritchie, Joy, and Kate Ronald. "Introduction." *Available Means: An Anthology of Women's Rhetoric(s)*, edited by Joy Ritchie and Kate Ronald. University of Pittsburgh Press, 2001.

Roehner, Bertrand. "Jesuits and the State: A Comparative Study of their Expulsions (1590–1990)," *Religion*, vol. 27, no., 2, 1997, pp. 165–82. DOI: 10.1006/reli.1996.0048

Ross, Christine. "Logic, Rhetoric, and Discourse in the Literary Texts of Nineteenth-Century Women." *RSQ*, vol. 32, no.2, 2002, pp. 85-109. JStor, DOI: 10.1080/02773940209391229

Ryan, Mary. Conversation at SMW. 5 July 2017.

Stolley, Amy Ferdinandt Stolley. "'Plain, Simple, Durable': The Feminist Rhetorical Strategies of Mother Catherine McAuley. 2013 Feminisms and Rhetorics Conference.

Thompson, Margaret Susan. Discovering Foremothers: Sisters, Society, and the American Catholic Experience." *U.S. Catholic Historian*, vol. 5, nos. 3–4, 1986, pp. 273–90.

Vermeersch, Arthur. "Nuns." *The Catholic Encyclopedia*, vol. 11. Robert Appleton Company, 1911. 28 Dec. 2018 <http://www.newadvent.org/cathen/11164a.htm>.

Wecker, Erin. "Reclaiming Magdalenism or Washing Away Sin: Magdalen Laundries and the Rhetorics of Feminine Silence. *Women's Studies*, vol. 44, no. 5, pp. 264--79. Taylor & Francis Online, doi:10.1080/00497878.2015.988513.

White, Joseph M. "Introduction." *The American Catholic Religious Life: Selected Historical Essays*, edited by Joseph M. White, Garland, 1985, n.p.

Woody, Thomas. *A History of Women's Education in the United States*, vol. 1, Octagon Books, 1980.

REINVENTING THE FIELD: LOOKING FORWARD

The Other Toulmin Model:
Concepts, Topoi, Evolution

Ben Wetherbee

The analytic philosopher Stephen Edelston Toulmin—author of some 22 books between 1950 and 2001 on topics from moral reasoning to the philosophy of science to philosophical history—is most famous among rhetoricians for his 1958 title *The Uses of Argument* and its so-named "Toulmin model" of partitioning and diagramming arguments into claims, data, warrants, qualifiers, rebuttals, and backing (*Uses* 89-105). Teachers and scholars in communication and composition have found this schema—a sort of exploded view of the cultural syllogism—useful in the systematic analysis of argumentative structure for some time, dating back to Wayne Brockriede and Douglas Ehninger's 1960 *Quarterly Journal of Speech* article "Toulmin on Argument: An Interpretation and Application" and, years later, Charles W. Kneupper's parallel "Teaching Argument: An Introduction to the Toulmin Model" from a 1978 issue of *College Composition and Communication*. Both articles, alongside a formidable body of subsequent work, posit Toulmin's schematic terminology as a handy toolbox for speech communication and writing pedagogy.[1] None of this, ironically enough, was Toulmin's intention. His self-professed interest in writing *Uses* and dismantling syllogistic structure was not to systematize argument, but to rebuke analytic philosophy's rigid, pseudo-Euclidian epistemology itself (*Uses* vii).

In this essay, I am unconcerned with explicating, lauding, or criticizing the Toulmin model, apart from highlighting its rather constrictive magnetism among rhetoricians. I am not the first to suggest that rhetorical studies

---

1. For useful bibliography syntheses of how rhetoricians have appropriated and applied the Toulmin model, as well as this model's relationship to similar disciplinary ideas, see Jasinski 24-55; Bizup.

has appropriated Toulmin a bit myopically. More than anyone, I owe this observation to Joseph Bizup, whose meticulous 2009 essay "The Uses of Toulmin in Composition Studies" charts the historically selective use of Toulmin by compositionists and their frequent misunderstanding of Toulmin's larger commitments (an occasional myopia rhetorical studies in general no doubt shares).[2] As Bizup documents, compositionists through the years have approached the Toulmin model both approvingly and reproachfully, as either a useful heuristic or an oversimplistic, quasi-positivist relic. They have also cited Toulmin's 1972 book *Human Understanding: The Collective Use and Evolution of Concepts* to theorize the disciplinary formation of rhetoric and composition itself, while constructivist compositionists leaned on Toulmin (alongside Foucault, Geertz, Rorty, and others) during their debates with the cognitivists in the 1980s (Bizup W5-W10). More recently, though, books like *Human Understanding* have waned from composition and rhetorical scholarship; the Toulmin of composition studies has again more or less flattened into his so-called "model" from *The Uses of Argument*, often deployed as a foil to introduce alternative models of argumentation friendlier to the conditions of postmodernity (W15-W17).

Like Bizup, I urge rhetoricians to broaden their view of Toulmin to include his more recent, comparatively neglected works. I will, in particular, draw from *Human Understanding* and Toulmin's 1991 title *Cosmopolis: The Hidden Agenda of Modernity* to forward what I'll call, at least for now, the *other* Toulmin model—this one less a model of argumentative structure than organic rhetorical invention and evolution. In addition to advancing a useful heuristic framework, I hope this essay exemplifies the sort of Janus-faced inquiry rhetoricians might pursue on the occasion of RSA's 50th anniversary, the sort that looks to thinkers from our scholarly past while also gazing forward toward future challenges. Toulmin's work, which, as Bizup notes, one might assume to have "run its course" within rhetorical studies (W14), can be resuscitated and reinterpreted through the refractive lens of rhetorical postmodernity: we can return to Toulmin's past, motivated by the present and the modern demands of increasingly rapid, fragmented rhetorical practice.

This model I'm working toward begins with *Human Understanding*, which is most obviously a work in the philosophy of science—a thick, richly-textured study that shares Toulmin's antipathy toward positivistic certainty in *The Uses of Argument* and theorizes how disciplines change through the

---

2. Fulkerson's article on Toulmin in *The Encyclopedia of Rhetoric and Composition*, for instance, is itself an article on the Toulmin model and says close to nothing about the author's other works. My observation is not an indictment of this article itself, but rather an illustration of how the Toulmin model has, in rhetorical studies, eclipsed the rest of Toulmin's scholarly corpus.

gradual process of conceptual evolution. Concepts, for Toulmin, are particulate units of human intellectual development (*Human* 41-130). In what Toulmin calls "compact disciplines," or those with well-defined collective ideals or goals (like curing leukemia or verifying the Higgs boson), well-defined loci of discussion (universities, professional associations), and well-defined fora for discussion (journals, conferences), concepts circulate in association with each other but also with some particulate autonomy (145-73, 378-95). This perspective puts Toulmin at odds with, for example, Thomas Kuhn's lauded model of punctuated equilibrium through paradigm shifts that bring about new rules of "normal" scientific thought (see Kuhn 10-51; Toulmin, *Human* 98-117). Contra Kuhn's "revolutionary" model of scientific change, Toulmin envisions an *evolutionary* model:

> Instead of being introduced at one and the same time, and all of a piece, as a single logical system with a single scientific purpose, different concepts and theories are introduced into science interdependently, at different times and for different purposes. If they still survive today, this may be because they are still serving their original intellectual functions, or else because they have since acquired other, different functions .... This means recognizing that an entire science comprises an "historical population" of logically independent concepts and theories, each with its own separate history, structure, and implications. (130)

Toulmin's talk of populational differentiation, of course, stems deliberately from the theory of evolution via differential fitness pioneered in *On the Origin of Species* by Charles Darwin, who himself, in *The Descent of Man*, characterizes competition among words as itself a form of natural selection (ch. 3; 445-46). Toulmin's engagement with Darwin leads to perhaps the single boldest, most compelling insight from *Human Understanding*: evolution as Darwin described it, through variation, transmission, and differential fitness, is not exclusively a matter of biology. As Toulmin puts it, "Darwin's populational theory of 'variation and natural selection' is one illustration of a more general form of historical explanation; and ... this same pattern is applicable also, on appropriate conditions, to historical entities and populations of other kinds" (135). These other kinds include—for Toulmin's purposes—scientific concepts, of which "evolution" is, ironically or fittingly, one particularly good example. Concepts like "evolution" undergo processes of innovation and selection, the demands of which, as Toulmin tells it, "comprise both the immediate issues that each conceptual variant is designed to deal with, and also other entrenched concepts with which it must coexist" (140). Being true or otherwise scientifically demonstrable might help a concept's fitness, but these qualities do not guarantee fitness insofar as disciplines are cultural, ideological formations that impose *their own* conditions of fitness—though these, too, can evolve.

To be clear, then, Toulmin is no biological determinist. He is not repeating the canard that human culture—and here, humankind's creation of scientific concepts—is finally reducible to its effects in the arena of biological sexual selection. Toulmin is, in fact, flipping the script to suggest this argument would commit a category mistake: that is, animal, biological selection by reproductive fitness is not itself synonymous with evolution itself but *only one example* of a larger evolutionary phenomenon. I'll say more about other evolutionary units soon.

Toulmin's also differs, notably, from the approach to evolutionary epistemology espoused by Karl Popper, who suggests the evolution of knowledge is convergent rather than divergent. For Popper, the systematic criticism of theories leads to their refinement and, eventually, their unification, like thickets of bramble collapsing into a single, smooth stem (261-63). Toulmin's disciplinary focus allows more epistemological plurality. Efforts toward knowledge-making, for Toulmin, are *rational* (as opposed to positivistically *logical*) insofar as they advance to the needs, goals, and ideals of their disciplines; this rationality is internal and *contextual*, and therefore not quite synonymous with the quest for Truth one detects in Popper's epistemological vision (Toulmin, *Human* 83-86). As Toulmin puts it, "Questions of rationality are concerned . . . with *the conditions on which, and the manner in which, [people are] prepared to change [disciplinary] doctrine as time goes on*" (84; italics in original). Rationality, in other words, means responsiveness to change; it is the capacity for disciplines to evolve based on conceptual innovation and shared ideals.

At this juncture, it is reasonable (or rational!—I write, after all, for a disciplinary audience of rhetoricians) to ask what any of this has to do with rhetoric. In some sense, no doubt, Toulmin is speaking about the rhetoric of disciplines, about what we might call specific discourse communities and their rhetorical commitments and conventions. But this is a tame, sanitized rhetoric, especially when contrasted with the unmoored fracas of postmodern, public, political deliberation in the age of trending, Twitter, and Trump. Toulmin acknowledges this limitation in passing; he notes that, for example, that a politician's speech might prove significant for numerous factors—its advancement of an idea, its display of the speaker's oratorical skill, its reflection on the speaker's party—or precipitate any number of effects in the speaker's own personal life (401-02). Some of these factors—for instance, calling into question what we mean by "border security" or "estate tax"— mirror the process of conceptual change in compact disciplines, albeit within a much larger, messier sphere of terminological circulation. But here, it's worth noting that, say, Ted Cruz berating estate taxes in a stump speech will qualitatively differ from a consortium of economists deliberating the merits of that same term at an academic conference. The latter process reflects Toulmin's understanding of conceptual evolution. The term "estate tax" (or its dyslogistic cousin "death tax") in a politician's hands, I will now argue, better resembles a rhetorical *topos* than a Toulminian *concept*—though the relationship between this pair of terms proves valuable.

So, here is one thesis: topoi in public rhetoric are analogous to concepts in disciplinary rhetoric. Like concepts, topoi—or "places" of argument, which I understand as charged discursive nodes of cultural and rhetorical connectivity[3]—retain some individual autonomy, but also derive contextual significance in relation to each other. Like concepts, I would argue, topoi are also evolutionary units. A topos like "fake news," for better or worse, derives fitness from its provocative relevance to current political conversation and displays a historically variant meaning depending on how it's used, by whom, before what audiences, in what purposes, and so on. For better or worse, the circulation of terms like "fake news" also contribute incrementally to *cultural* evolution on a broader scale, inasmuch as American culture, for instance, is constituted in no small part from its manifestation in language and semiotics via the pens, tongues, and smartphones of American politicians and celebrities and at least one notable celebrity-turned-politician. Topoi circulate as part of rhetorical culture, and their use, reuse, and arguable misuse contribute to the evolution of rhetorical culture. We might pose one further analogy: compact disciplines and their conceptual evolutionary processes resemble something like a climate-controlled biome; rhetorical culture and its topical evolutionary process resemble the ecology of the wild.

I am, of course, not the first to associate rhetorical topoi with Toulmin's work. In a 1961 review of *The Uses of Argument*, Otto Bird labels Toulmin's project a "rediscovery of the topics," noting similarities between Toulmin's claim-data-warrant schema and the topical system of the Roman logician Boethius (Bird 536-38). This is an ironic alignment because Boethius, as Michael Leff has astutely noted, sought to convert topics into a consistent, logical, philosophical system and, in doing so, collapse rhetoric into philosophy (Leff 38; see Boethius, *De topicis differentiis* bk. 4, 79-95), while Toulmin's self-professed goal in *Uses* and beyond was to unyoke language, argument,

---

3. I elaborate on this understanding of topoi, which takes inspiration from Burke's sense of rhetorical "orientation," or location among "a bundle of judgments" in ideological space (*Permanence* 14), in Wetherbee, "*Dystopoi*" 120–22, "Picking Up." Similar conceptions of rhetorical topoi appear in Miller, "Aristotelian"; Muckelbauer 123–41.

and other cultural particularities from the strictures of formal logic. In his preface to the 2003 updated edition of *Uses*, the amused (and perhaps still bemused) author confesses that he had "never set out to expound a theory of rhetoric or argumentation," but reflects, "If I were rewriting this book today, I would point to Aristotle's contrast between 'general' and 'special' topics as a way of throwing clearer light on the kinds of 'backing' relied on in different fields of practice and argument" (viii).

Let's dwell on this distinction for a moment. Aristotle's *koinoi topoi* are ostensibly universal heuristics or avenues of argument that rhetors can deploy in diverse circumstances (*Rhetoric* 2.23 1397a-1400b). The *idia* or "special topics," by contrast, are particulate bits of information about Athenian culture, politics, and psychology that the rhetor internalizes and which Aristotle catalogues at great length in books 1 and 2 of the *Rhetoric*.[4] Toulmin notes this distinction, I assume, because it corresponds to a major thread in his work: the tension between the universal and the particular. Toulmin's preference, especially in *Cosmopolis* and his other late work, has been for the sort of epistemology evoked by the special topics: the specific, the contingent, the human (c.f. Miller, "Aristotle's").

If rhetoric discovered Toulmin in the 1960s, Toulmin finally and fully discovered rhetoric in the 1990s with *Cosmopolis*. In this book, he traces Western human thought back to the crossroads of Modernity where the Renaissance and Enlightenment met, where Rene Descartes, as Toulmin tells it, begat what Toulmin calls a "'theory-centered' style of philosophy" concerned with permanent, classifiable, and immutable knowledge (11). The moniker "cosmopolis"—the combination of "cosmos," which connotes universal cosmic order, and "polis," or the social city-state—is Toulmin's shorthand for the mistaken idea that human life, culture, and politics can be forged in the mold of universal order (67-69). Toulmin contrasts Descartes with Michel de Montaigne, the prolific essayist whose works, in Toulmin's view, represent a sustained, multipronged effort to get at the manifold strange, messy, and seemingly contradictory facets of human being—not to synthesize them all into one theory, but to appreciate and understand their very diversity and individuality (36-42). Taking inspiration from Montaigne, Toulmin aligns rhetoric with what he calls practical philosophy, linking both with the quest

---

4. In *The Abuse of Casuistry*, Albert R. Jonsen and Toulmin persuasively attempt to recover Aristotle as a sort of proto-pragmatist centrally concerned with the contingent problems of *phronesis* (36-37, 63-74). Had they covered the *Rhetoric* in more detail, the authors might have noted that Aristotle devotes far more space to discipline-specific and culturally contingent *idia* (1.4-15 1359a-1377b, 2.2-19 1378a-1393a) that he does detailing the *koinoi topoi*, which are predominately condensed into a single chapter (2.23 1397a-1400b).

not for what is *stable* but what is *adaptable* (186-88; see also Jonsen and Toulmin 73-74, 83-88, 257-58). He notes four criteria of focus: (1) not the written (or simply recorded) but the oral (or discursive, performative); (2) not the universal but the particular; (3) not to the global but the local; and (4) not the timeless but the timely (*Cosmopolis* 186-92). Returning to the arena of public rhetoric and the circulation of individual topoi, we find, I think, that Toulmin's four criteria of good practical philosophy are equally apt criteria of topical assessment.

Regarding topoi as adaptive, evolutionary units—wild cousins to Toulmin's disciplined concepts—we can ask how individual topoi are replicated through discursive performance; how they stand out, apart from, but in relation to, other pertinent topoi; what localities or specific audiences these topoi speak to; and how these topoi become timely or kairotic. In these schema, topical fitness means rhetorical utility in context. So, I am finally poised to pin down what I'm calling the *other* Toulmin model. This model describes topoi as

(A) particulate, replicable discursive units that circulate within and help shape rhetorical culture and as

(B) devices one can analyze and assess according to
   (i) their ease of replication through discursive performance,
   (ii) how they stand out as individual units but adhere to their contexts,
   (iii) how they affect specific audiences and localities, and
   (iv) how they function in a timely (kairotic) fashion.

Examples of such topoi might include "binders full of women," "fake news," "the free market," the Obama "hope" poster, "covfefe," "stable genius," and countless other bite-size but rhetorically potent fragments of discourse. In a sense, we are describing what Kenneth Burke, in *A Rhetoric of Motives*, calls a "*timely topic*," or "commonplaces of a transitory nature" such as one would assemble into a political cartoon (62; italics in original). Toulmin's criteria, though, equip us to analyze such an idea in considerably more detail than Burke's provocative but brief sketch provides.

I'll wrap up with one more terminological comparison. Readers might characterize my description above as a mere iteration of a preexisting concept: the meme. Those readers would be right—sort of. In *The Selfish Gene*, we ought to remember, Richard Dawkins coins *meme* to refer to particulate "unit[s] of cultural transmission," analogous to but significantly different from genes (192). Philosophers like Daniel Dennett have pushed the concept further, arriving at a position similar to Toulmin's when he expands evolution into something bigger than biology (see Dennett, *From Bacteria* 205-47; *Darwin's* 335-69; Blackmore); and scholars in rhetoric and communication have begun to probe the frankly persuasive and inventive functions of memes (Shifman 122-27; Jenkins; Huntington; Hill; Wetherbee, "Picking Up"). I enjoy the comparison between memes and topoi, which highlights both the pseudo-organic proliferation of textual fragments across media ecosystems and the rhetorical utility those fragments might hold for human rhetors, and I think this terminological intersection proves exceedingly useful as we approach the increasingly fragmentary mediascape that Michael Calvin McGee famously identifies with postmodernity. However, we should cautiously avoid collapsing one term into the other. Rather, if we are to describe topoi as memes, or vice versa, we should do so in an intellectually robust way that highlights how rhetorical utility itself creates important conditions of cultural fitness; in other words, we should cautiously infuse "meme" with a rhetorical sensibility while preserving its connotations in the area of cultural evolution. Toulmin's work in evolutionary epistemology and the "other model" of topical evolution I describe here should help bring such a terminological intersection into relief.

Works Cited

Aristotle. *On Rhetoric: A Theory of Public Discourse*. Translated and edited by George A. Kennedy, 2nd ed., Oxford UP, 2007.
Bird, Otto. "The Re-Discovery of the Topics." *Mind*, vol. 70, no. 280, 1961, pp. 534–39.
Bizup, Joseph. "The Uses of Toulmin in Composition Studies." *College Composition and Communication*, vol. 61, no. 1, 2009, pp. W1–W23.
Blackmore, Susan. *The Meme Machine*. Oxford UP, 1999.
Boethius. *De topicis differentiis*. Translated and edited by Eleonore Stump, Cornell UP, 2004.
Brockriede, Wayne, and Douglas Ehninger. "Toulmin on Argument: An Interpretation and Application." *Quarterly Journal of Speech*, vol. 64, no. 1, 1960, 44–53.
Burke, Kenneth. *Permanence and Change: An Anatomy of Purpose*. 3rd ed, U of California P, 1987.
—. *A Rhetoric of Motives*. U of California P, 1969.
Darwin, Charles. *The Descent of Man and Selection in Relation to Sex*. 1871. *The Origin of Species and The Descent of Man*, Modern Library, 1940, pp. 387–924.
Dawkins, Richard. *The Selfish Gene*. 30th anniversary ed., Oxford UP, 2006.
Dennett, Daniel. *Darwin's Dangerous Idea: Evolution and the Meaning of Life*. Simon & Schuster, 1996.
—. *From Bacteria to Bach and Back: The Evolution of Minds*. Norton, 2017.

Fulkerson, Richard. "Toulmin, Stephen (b. 1922)." *The Encyclopedia of Rhetoric and Composition: Communication from Ancient Times to the Information Age*, edited by Theresa Enos, Routledge, 2010, pp. 726–27.

Hill, Ian E. J. "Memes, Munitions, and Collective Copia: The Durability of the Perpetual Peace Weapons Snowclone." *Quarterly Journal of Speech*, vol. 104, no. 4, 2018, pp. 422–43.

Huntington, Heidi E. "Pepper Spray Cop and the American Dream: Using Synecdoche and Metaphor to Unlock Internet Memes' Visual Political Rhetoric." *Communication Studies*, vol. 67, no. 1, 2016, pp. 77–93.

Jasinski, James L. *Sourcebook on Rhetoric: Key Concepts in Contemporary Rhetorical Studies*, Sage, 2001.

Jenkins, Eric S. "The Modes of Visual Rhetoric: Circulating Memes as Expressions." *Quarterly Journal of Speech*, vol. 100, no. 4, 2014, pp. 442–66.

Jonsen, Albert R., and Stephen Toulmin. *The Abuse of Casuistry: A History of Moral Reasoning*. U of California P, 1988.

Kneupper, Charles W. "Teaching Argument: An Introduction to the Toulmin Model." *College Composition and Communication*, vol. 29, no. 3, 1978, pp. 237–41.

Kuhn, Thomas S. *The Structure of Scientific Revolutions*. 50th anniversary ed., U of Chicago P, 2012.

Leff, Michael C. "The Topics of Argumentative Invention in Latin Rhetorical Theory from Cicero to Boethius." *Rhetorica: A Journal of the History of Rhetoric*, vol. 1, no. 1, 1983, pp. 23–44.

McGee, Michael Calvin. "Text, Context, and the Fragmentation of Contemporary Culture." *Western Journal of Speech Communication*, vol. 54, no. 3, 1990, pp. 274–89.

Miller, Carolyn R. "The Aristotelian *Topos*: Hunting for Novelty." *Rereading Aristotle's Rhetoric*, edited by Alan G. Goss and Arthur E. Walzer. Southern Illinois UP, 2000, pp. 130–46.

—. "Aristotle's 'Special Topics' in Rhetorical Practice and Pedagogy." *Rhetoric Society Quarterly*, vol. 17, no. 1, 1987, pp. 61–70.

Muckelbauer, John. *The Future of Invention: Rhetoric, Postmodernism, and the Problem of Change*, SUNY P, 2008.

Popper, Karl R. *Objective Knowledge: An Evolutionary Approach*. Rev. ed., Oxford UP, 1979.

Shifman, Limor. *Memes in Digital Culture*. MIT P, 2014.

Toulmin, Stephen E. *Cosmopolis: The Hidden Agenda of Modernity*. U of Chicago P, 1993.

—. *Human Understanding: The Collective Use and Evolution of Concepts*. Princeton UP, 1977.

—. *The Uses of Argument*. Updated ed., Cambridge UP, 2003.

Wetherbee, Ben. "*Dystopoi* of Memory and Invention: The Rhetorical 'Places' of Postmodern Dystopian Film." *Journal of Multimodal Rhetorics*, vol. 2, no. 2, 2018, pp. 116–34.

—. "Picking Up the Fragments of the 2012 Election: Memes, *Topoi*, and Political Rhetoric." *Present Tense: A Journal of Rhetoric in Society*, vol. 5, no. 1, 2015.

A Friendly Injustice: Kenneth Burke, René Girard, and the Rhetoric of Religion

Paul Lynch

"*The whole problem of the scapegoat, I submit, is still not charted thoroughly enough....*"

—Kenneth Burke, *The Philosophy of Literary Form*

In a 2005 address to the International Society for the History of Rhetoric, Laurent Pernot observed that, because religion has returned as a public force, it is "the duty of us academics and intellectuals . . . to find new ways of thinking about religion in a world where unthinking and depraved uses of religion can be dangerous" (236). He also offered a warning: "Scholars who take this approach may be suspected of adopting a rationalist attitude and misunderstanding the very basis of religion, namely, belief in the transcendental" (236). If this call and caution seem uncontroversial, even less controversial is Pernot's title: "The Rhetoric of Religion," a homage to the enduring influence of Kenneth Burke's 1961 book. Certainly, *The Rhetoric of Religion* has made a significant contribution to our understanding religious discourse. Nevertheless, I want to suggest that Burke's approach is limited by the hermeneutics of suspicion from which it proceeds. That hermeneutics results in just what Pernot fears: a rationalist attitude that misunderstands the very basis of the religion with which Burke is concerned, or at least misunderstands or ignores alternative theologies within that religion. In effect, I want to extend a criticism first offered by Celeste Michelle Condit, who observed that *Religion* isn't so much about "religion" as it is about Christianity.

My version of this argument is that *Religion* often focuses on a particular—and contested—understanding of Christianity.

An alternative understanding can be drawn from the work of René Girard (1923-2015), the last century's other great theorist of scapegoating. Like Burke, Girard built his project on literary study, which led to a wider interest in culture and eventually religion. Unlike Burke, however, Girard finds the most compelling critique of scapegoating within the religion that structures Burke's logology. For Girard, the death of Jesus is not simply the latest expression of religious and sacrificial violence. Rather, it is the announcement that the divine sanction of scapegoating—already challenged throughout the Hebrew scriptures—is decisively ended. If the scriptures offer an argument, it is this: "it is love that I desire, not sacrifice" (Hos. 6.6; Matt. 12.7). Contrary to initial appearances, this argument passes through Pernot's needle with its riches intact: in addition to rejecting unthinking and depraved uses of religion, Girard's claim can be grasped with a rational attitude while also being compatible with belief.

* * *

For Burke, scapegoating was an enduring preoccupation (Jasinski 503-08), perhaps most succinctly expressed in the "Iron Law of History," which, Burke tells us, "welds Order and Sacrifice." Because we cannot keep commandments, order leads to guilt, guilt to the desire for redemption, redemption to a redeemer, who becomes a victim (RR 4-5).[1] The negative, which is fundamental to human symbol systems, also sets the stage for sacrificial violence (295). Burke was particularly concerned with the way scapegoating structured Nazism, which he examines in "Hitler's 'Battle'" (*Philosophy* 191-220), *Attitudes Toward History* (167-169), and *Grammar of Motives* (406-408). But there many other contexts in which Burke analyzes this seemingly unavoidable "error in interpretation" (*Permanence* 14), which he called a mistake of synecdoche, the "'basic' figure of speech" (*Philosophy* 26). Meanwhile, Burke suggests that irony was the best trope for resisting scapegoating, since irony is "based upon a sense of fundamental kinship with the enemy, as one *needs* him, is *indebted* to him" (*Grammar* 514). (If the Yankees did not exist, the Red Sox would have to invent them.) But while comic irony can momentarily defuse scapegoating, it can fully never dismantle it, even in a "post-religious" society:

> With a culture formed about the idea of redemption by the sacrifice of a Crucified Christ, just what does happen in an era of post-Christian science, when the ways of socialization have been secularized? Does the need for the vicarage of this Sacrificial King merely

dwindle away? Or must some other person or persons, individual or corporate, real or fictive, take over the redemptive role? (*RM* 31)[2]

Burke's ongoing concern with this problem suggests that his answer to the last question was yes. Yet he also believed that religion offers the ultimate expression of this socialization. He discusses this problem most explicitly in *The Rhetoric of Religion*, particularly in the book's closing "satyr-play" (5). As the Lord explains to Satan, one person can pay for another's guilt only through the "friendly injustice" of "mercy," which forgives the debtor his debt. But then, asks Satan, is there no way to right the balance? Only through a "perfect" sacrifice, says the Lord. Humans "will conceive of a sacrifice so perfect that it could cancel off all their guilt." But, reasons Satan, only a god could be that perfect. "Yes," replies the Lord. "And finally a cult will arise which holds that I, in my infinite mercy, will send my only begotten Son as the perfect sacrifice for the Earth-People's redemption" (295).

Burke's account echoes the theology of substitutionary atonement as articulated by St. Anselm of Canterbury (1033-1109).[3] According to Anselm, humanity's fall had incurred a debt that must be repaid but that was too large to be repaid. "So," explains theologian James Alison, "God came up with the idea of sending his Son into the world as a human, so that his Son could pay the price as a human, which, since he was also God, would be infinite and thus would effect the necessary satisfaction." Not surprisingly, Burke's Satan is scandalized. "How perfectly revolting!" (RR 295). Yet this revolting idea made some sense in Anselm's feudal context, in which lawbreaking threatened the lord's honor and, by extension, social order. Honor, writes theologian Elizabeth Johnson, was not simply some "egoistic self-regard," but a "beneficent authority" (7). It was "the linchpin that functioned to make an orderly civic life possible" (7). Within this context, it made sense to understand God as jealous of his reputation, just as it made sense to see the Crucifixion as a generous solution to a complex problem. Outside that context, however, God's exacting demand for recompense can appear brutal. "In sum," writes Johnson, "the satisfaction theory makes God morally repulsive" (16). Unfortunately, she also notes that Anselm "may well be the most successful theologian of all time" (xiii). His particular theology has become a synecdoche for Christianity. "No doubt," observes René Girard, "this line of reasoning has done more than anything else to discredit Christianity in the eyes of people of goodwill" (*Things* 182).

Burke's version of penal substitution is a rereading of Anselm through the psychology of form. If satisfaction is a social necessity for Anselm, it is a psychological and symbolic necessity for Burke. To his credit, Burke imagines a God who is slow to anger and rich in the comic frame. "This issue," he reminds his pupil, "cannot be solved by a hothead" (295). Yet it's also unclear that the Lord is trying to "solve" the issue, for He is not so much a rhetorician as a dialectician, at least if we follow Timothy Cursus's definition of Burkean dialectic: "Dialectic for Burke is the study of verbal universes, the disinterested pursuit of a vocabulary's implications," while rhetoric seeks "the overcoming of estrangement" (24). By those definitions, Burke's book might better be called *The Dialectic of Religion*: its purpose is to chart the structure of estrangement more than to invent responses to it. This orientation becomes clear when the Lord makes an explicit claim about Christianity:

> For sheerly logological perfection, few religions will be able to rival the religion (with its close variants) that names itself after my son. Considered even as sheer form it will be quite miraculous. Its merger of monotheism with the circumambient rites of pagan polytheism will be a major dialectical triumph. (*RR* 314)

This passage invites a number of interpretations. Burke seems to believe that the dialectic reconciliation between the monotheistic and the pagan should have been harder. Otherwise, why call it a "triumph"? That further suggests that Burke recognizes that the sacrificial equipment for living should somehow not have endured. Likely he saw its endurance as evidence of the negative's fundamental role in shaping attitudes and culture. Hence the pursuit of logology as an attempt to map the dialectic that maintains the cult of the kill (RR 5). But the very idea of a triumph also suggests that other interpretive possibilities had to be overcome. René Girard offers one such possibility.

Unfortunately, Girard has only occasionally attracted the interest of rhetoricians, though it easy to imagine why. Insisting that he had divined the capital-M metanarrative, Girard can sound like "one of the last of that race of Titans who dominated the nineteenth and twentieth centuries with their grand, synthetic theories" (Harrison). Because he saw the implications of his insight early on, he rushed to express the full sweep of his conclusions, sometimes opening himself to the charge of imprecision and haste (Haven 112-13). His colleague Michel Serres once warned that the problem with Girard's theory is that it could be understood by an eleven-year-old (Kirwan 6), a remark seemingly offered a warning that the clarity of Girard's ideas would make them academically unpopular. Most importantly for the present discussion, Girard's narrative may seem insufficiently distinct from Burke's to warrant further attention.[4] Given the space available here, my treatment of Girard may be vulnerable to similar objections. Nevertheless, I will argue that Girard's reading of the Jewish and Christian scriptures offers a plausible alternative hermeneutic that suggests that Burke's Law may not be made of Iron after all.

Girard's theory begins with the claim that desire is mimetic rather than individualistic. When humans desire, Girard argues, they desire according to the desire of the other. A person's desires do not emanate directly from within, but are rather occasioned by and articulated through "mediators." If I find myself wanting what my neighbor Jones has, it is because my desires are being sparked and enflamed by Jones himself. As this example suggests, mimetic desire is primarily acquisitive, not simply stylistic. Jones's desires tell me what to want. In some situations, acquisitive mimesis is not a problem. If I covet Jones's car, I can dream of getting my own version of the same model, all the while believing my desires are entirely original. If, however, I begin coveting Jones's wife, then I have a different kind of problem. The very mediator who animates my desire blocks me from consummating it. When one person's desire thus becomes a "replica" of another's, Girard writes, "it invariably leads to rivalry; and rivalry in turn transforms desire into violence" (*Violence* 169).

Desire becomes violence when, instead of confronting the true nature of the problem, Jones and I scapegoat some third party. Girard uses "scapegoat" in the modern sense: someone who is saddled with a blame he doesn't deserve. Perhaps another neighbor becomes the butt of inside jokes and snide derision. Through the symbolic violence of our mutual disdain, Jones and I can paper over our rivalry and keep the peace.

But the violence is not always symbolic. Sophocles' *Antigone*, for example, opens with the mutual and simultaneous slaughter of the brothers Eteocles and Polynices. Each is the other's mediator (each desires the throne because the other does) and then rival (each cannot have the throne because the other has it). This doubling collapses the distinctions that maintain cultural order, the differences through which individuals establish identity and relationship (*Violence* 49). When those differences begin to collapse, and the rivals begin to double each other, the situation devolves into what Girard calls a "sacrificial crisis" (52). A crisis becomes "sacrificial" when a community in crisis turns its attention toward a scapegoat. In this innocent party, society finds a victim whose expulsion or death offers the community a new unity. Of course, the community does not know that it is doing this. The Thebans really believe that the blame for their troubles lies first with Oedipus, then with Polynices' corpse, and finally with Antigone. The sacrifice of these victims "serves to protect the entire community from its own violence; it prompts the entire community to choose victims outside itself" (*Violence* 8; emphasis in original). (The succession of victims suggests that Sophocles himself senses the futility of the mechanism.) The sacrificers do not see themselves as butchers, the guilty in need of redemption. Rather, they transfer their guilt on to a victim who, unbeknownst to all, takes the load for all.

At this point in his research into ancient myth and ritual, Girard observes a strange paradox. After the scapegoat is expelled or killed and calm seems to return, the community comes to believe that the alleged source of the original crisis is also the source of the new peace: "the community, awed first by the raging conflict and then by its resolution, assumes that both events must have the same cause, the hapless victim, who now passes for an all-powerful peacemaker as well as a troublemaker" (*Theatre* 204). Girard argues that the pattern repeats itself again and again: the foundational victim is transformed into the foundational deity. "Such," writes Girard, "is the mimetic genesis of divine ancestors, sacred legislators, full-fledged divinities" (204). The "aggressive transference" is almost always followed by the "reconciliatory transference," which "sacralizes the victim" (*Things Hidden* 37). This is why Girard insists that scapegoating is "the heart and secret soul of the sacred" (*Violence* 31). Like Burke, Girard seems to believe that religion's redeemers are actually its victims.

Early in his research, many of Girard's readers assumed he was making a case against religion, the same sort of case made by Freud and Frazier. But Girard was in fact clearing the ground for the startling claim that Christianity (and the Judaism from which it springs) do not operate on scapegoating, but unmask it. The Jewish and Christian scriptures repeatedly show the guilty are actually innocent. "The Bible," Girard observes, "refuses to demonize or deify the victims of violent crowds" (*I See* 115). Abel is innocent when he is struck down by Cain, who, as Girard's theory would predict, goes on to found a city (Gen. 4.17). (Community is built upon victimization.) In the story of Joseph (Gen. 37-45), meanwhile, there is no doubt that the protagonist is the victim of his brothers' envy, just as there is no doubt he is innocent of the accusations of Potiphar's wife. In addition, Joseph can forgive only when Judah offers to stand in his brother Benjamin's place, thus reversing the scapegoating equation (Gen. 44:33). The Gospels also reveal the folly of the scapegoat. When Jesus sends the demons of Gerasa out of a poor wretch and into a herd of swine, the locals beg him to leave the neighborhood (Mark 5:1-17). Why do they not ask this miracle worker to stick around? Because in healing the demoniac, Jesus has deprived the community of its scapegoat. "Mark's text," writes Girard, "suggests that the Gerasenes and their demoniac have been settled for some time in a sort of cyclical pathology" (*Scapegoat* 168). But the community can no longer secure its identity around and against the madman roaming the tombs. (It's something of a credit to the Gerasenes that they realize the significance of what has happened and thus ask the healer to leave.)

Regarding Jesus himself, the Gospels make clear that, like his forebears Abel and Joseph, he is innocent. When Pilate and Herod cement their friendship over Jesus's death (Luke 23:12), when Caiaphas observes that it's better than one die than the whole nation (John 11:50), they are all resolving their conflicts through a scapegoat. The form of Jesus's death may look like yet another instance of the Iron Law of History: the victim, the death, the (temporarily) restored peace. In Burke's "Epilogue: Prologue," the Lord's eager and excitable pupil would see Jesus's death as the familiar and revolting perfection of guilt alleviation. But the Gospels' awareness of Jesus's innocence suggests that the form is being rehearsed only to reveal its futility.[5] The divinity of Jesus does not come as a result of his execution, which would be the usual mythical process (*Things* 233).

At this point, some caveats may be in order. First, we may note that one does not need to believe in Jesus's divinity as a matter of personal faith to recognize that the Gospel writers believe in both his divinity and his innocence prior to his death. In addition, Girard acknowledges that the revelation and concomitant rejection of scapegoating is not a linear process. He describes the Bible, which of course contains a great deal of violence, as a "text in travail," "not a chronologically progressive process, but a struggle that advances and retreats" (Smith, et al. 141). That is to say, the authors of the Biblical texts are often struggling with their own sacrificial equipment for living. And that struggle continues for much of the history of Christianity, in which the dialectical triumph has prevailed, thus giving the religion that names itself after God's son a "persecutory character" (*Things* 225). Essentially, historical Christianity "resacralized" the story. Christianity's greatest historical error, Girard suggests, was "to found something that in principle it ought never to have founded: a culture" (249). Culture, argues Girard, is founded on scapegoating. Insofar as the Christian faith founds a Christian culture, that culture must also rely on scapegoating. (Christian antisemitism is the oldest and most shameful example of this enduring need for scapegoats.) But the true significance of the Gospels is their attempt to refuse scapegoating. Thus, the most important critique of Christian culture comes from its own central texts.

If we entertain Girard's reading, two questions arise: First, what might result from what Pernot describes as our academic and intellectual duty? We should begin by observing that Girard's implied theology exonerates God. Like Burke, Girard recognizes that substitutionary atonement is a human product rather than a divine one. Notably different, however, is that Girard's critique emanates within the religious texts rather than outside them. We therefore have some resources for an approach to the rhetoric of religion that meets Pernot's parameters: an approach that resists "unthinking and depraved uses," that can be grasped with a "rationalist attitude," but that does not necessarily stand outside "belief in the transcendental." Ultimately, Girard's theology grows from his anthropology: because we are mimetic creatures—prone to acquisitive desire, to rivalry, and to violence—we have understood the divine as part of our own scapegoating impulse. Yet the scriptures suggest that the true religious impulse (i.e., the one best fitted to the anthropology of mimetic desire) is to resist that bloody economy.[6]

Second, how might we reconsider Burke's enduring influence on "the rhetoric of religion"? As a preliminary answer, I would begin by returning to Crusius's distinction between dialectic, "the disinterested pursuit of a vocabulary's implications," and rhetoric, "the overcoming of estrangement" (24). Burke's book charts the (perversely) perfect triumph that sewed a new wineskin onto an old one. If Burke becomes the dialectician, perhaps Girard becomes the rhetorician, who sees the possibility of repurposing the dialectic in order to overcome estrangement. The project of the religion that names itself after the Lord's son is to untangle the religious impulse from the circumambient rites of sacrifice. Its vocation is not a dialectical reconciliation of opposites but rather a rhetorical reconciliation of opponents, of victims and their persecutors. Girard senses this, but he can only gesture toward what comes next. Throughout *Things Hidden Since the Foundation of the World*, Girard acknowledges the need for new language to express the new wine. Religious language remains "contaminated by the symbolism of violence" (191), the word "sacred" is no longer viable (233), and neither is "sacrificial" (241). If Girard is right, and the old economy is a lie, then we are left with "no words or categories" or "appropriate language" (241-42) to articulate the forms of a non-sacrificial religious impulse. Our first duty as academics and intellectuals, particularly as rhetoricians, is to embark on a process of invention.

My purpose in making this argument is not somehow to say that Burke is wrong. He is quite right that historical Christianity (its theology, its liturgy, its attitudes) has often been structured by the sacrificial impulse. Burke's Lord senses the irony of this with his comic observation of the dialectical triumph. For his part, Girard pursues the implications of that irony. If the Lord recognizes that the perfection of Christianity is perverse, then perhaps some more wholesome imperfection must be invented. The irony of Girard's project is to find the available means of that new invention within the oldest of discourses. "Did you never read the scriptures?" asks Jesus. "'The stone the builders rejected/has become the cornerstone'" (Mt. 21:42). This question is a challenge both to Christians who have yet to recognize their own sacrificial equipment for living and to rhetoricians who are searching for new ways of thinking about religion without misunderstanding its very basis: the belief that final rejection of rivalry, violence, and scapegoating is possible.

Notes

1. This essay will use RR for *The Rhetoric of Religion* and RM for *A Rhetoric of Motives*.

2. In "Toward Hellhaven," Burke suggests that even our post-apocalyptic future will be structured by scapegoating, as those who escape environmental collapse in the lunar Culture-Bubble will enjoy the "Super-Lookout," in which they can look back at those left on earth (63).

3. There are many alternate theories of atonement and sacrifice even within Christian and Jewish traditions. For more on this, see the entries in Oxford and Westminster.

4. For the few exceptions among rhetoricians, see Carter, Desilet, and Worsham.

5. While Girard believes that the Gospels offer a unique revelation, he also acknowledges that it is revelation based in the Hebrew scriptures. That is to say, Jesus's life can be understood only through a Jewish hermeneutic. For a challenge to Girard's claim to the Gospels' uniqueness, see Goodhart, 33–55.

6. For the application of Girard's theories to other religious traditions, see Girard, *Sacrifice* and Palaver and Schenk.

Works Cited

Alison, James. "Some Thoughts on the Atonement." James Alson. *Theology*, August 2004, www.jamesalison.co.uk/pdf/eng11.pdf. Accessed April 15, 2018.

"Atonement." *The Oxford Dictionary of the Christian Church*. Edited by F.L. Cross, Oxford UP, 2005, pp. 124-125.

"Atonement." *The Westminster Dictionary of Christian Theology*. Edited by Alan Richardson and John Bowden, Westminster Press, 1983, pp. 50–53.

Burke, Kenneth. *A Grammar of Motives*, University of California Press, 1969.

—. *A Rhetoric of Motives*. U of California Press, 1950.

—. *Attitudes Toward History*, University of California P, 1984.

—. *Permanence and Change: An Anatomy of Purpose*. University of California Press, 1984.

—. "The Rhetoric of Hitler's 'Battle.'" *The Philosophy of Literary Form: Studies in Symbolic Action*. University of California P, 1973, pp. 191–220.

—. *The Rhetoric of Religion*. Beacon Press, 1961.

—. "Toward Hellhaven." *On Human Nature: A Gathering While Everything Flows, 1967-1984*. University of California Press, 2004, pp. 54–65.

Carter, C. Allen, *Kenneth Burke and the Scapegoat Process*. University of Oklahoma Press, 1996.

Catholic Study Bible. Edited by Donald Senior, Oxford UP, 1990.

Condit, Celeste Michelle. "Post-Burke: Transcending the Sub-stance of Dramatism." *Quarterly Journal of Speech*, vol. 78, no. 3, 1992, pp. 349-55.

Crusius, Timothy. "A Case for Kenneth Burke's Rhetoric and Dialectic." *Philosophy and Rhetoric*, vol. 19, no. 1, 1986, pp. 23–37.

Desilet, Gregory. *Cult of the Kill: Traditional Metaphysics of Rhetoric, Truth, and Violence in a Postmodern World.* Xlibris, 2002.

Girard, René. *A Theater of Envy: William Shakespeare.* Oxford UP, 1991.

—. *I See Satan Fall Like Lightning.* Translated by James G. Williams, Orbis, 2001.

—. *Sacrifice.* Translated by Matthew Pattillo and David Dawson, Michigan State UP, 2011.

—. *The Scapegoat.* Translated by Yvonne Freccero, Johns Hopkins UP, 1989.

—. *Things Hidden Since the Foundation of the World.* Translated by Stephen Bann and Michael Metteer, Stanford UP, 1987.

—. *Violence and the Sacred.* Translated by Patrick Gregory. Johns Hopkins UP, 1979.

Goodhart, Sandor. *The Prophetic Law: Essays in Judaism, Girardianism, Literary Studies, and the Ethical.* Michigan State UP, 2014.

Harrison, Robert Pogue. "The Prophet of Envy." *The New York Review of Books.* 20 Dec. 2018, www.nybooks.com/articles/2018/12/20/rene-girard-prophet-envy/. Accessed January 1, 2018.

Haven, Cynthia. *Evolution of Desire: A Life of René Girard.* Michigan State UP, 2018.

Jasinski, James L. "Scapegoating." *Sourcebook on Rhetoric.* Sage Publications, 2001, pp. 503–08.

Johnson, Elizabeth. *Creation and the Cross: The Mercy of God for a Planet in Peril.* Orbis, 2018.

Kirwan, Michael. *Discovering Girard.* Cowley Publications, 2005.

Palaver, Wolfgang, and Richard Schenk, editors. *Mimetic Theory and World Religions.* Michigan State UP, 2018.

Pernot, Laurent. "The Rhetoric of Religion." *Rhetorica*, vol. 24, no. 3, 2006, pp. 235–54.

Smith, Jonathan, et al. *Violent Origins: Walter Burkert, René Girard, and Jonathan Smith on Ritual Killing and Cultural Formation*, Stanford UP, 1987.

Worsham, Lynn. "Moving Beyond the Logic of Sacrifice: Animal Studies, Trauma Studies, and the Path to Posthumanism." *Writing Posthumanism: Posthuman Writing.* Parlor, 2015. 19–55.

Inspiration as Invention: Continuing Reflections on the Relationship between Religion and Rhetoric

Joonna Smitherman Trapp

> *That rhetoric and religion are somehow related has been obvious to everyone who has thought about it.*
>
> —Wayne C. Booth

The very beginnings of the Rhetoric Society of America (RSA) were grounded in a belief that interdisciplinary communication among people interested in rhetoric, "language, and in the nature of language in use" was possible and sustainable. In the first newsletter in 1968, the Society imagines itself as rhetoricians, "linguists, literary theorists, literary critics, psychologists, sociologists, teachers of English composition, and English editors from textbook publishing houses" (1). By 1969, the newsletter references computer science and anthropology as disciplines of connection (3), and in 1972, Ross Winterowd adds philosophy to the list. Even though religion is omitted in these lists, interest and research into the linkages between religion and rhetoric have always been part of RSA's interdisciplinary goals. As early as 1972, the fourth edition (vol. 3 actually, since the first two volumes both carried "vol. 1" designations) of the newsletter contains a review of Murphy's influential *Three Medieval Rhetorical Arts*, which includes a section on the art of preaching. Efforts were reported in 1972 ("Bibliography") to begin a bibliography with varied subjects including philosophy and rhetoric as well as medieval rhetoric, which would likely have included topics related to religion and rhetoric. And in the first partial bibliography published the next year, seven works are listed which, at varying degrees, deal with rhetoric and religion ("Selective"). Over the 50-year history of RSA, books, articles, and conference presentations have continued the vibrant interest in religious thought and practice and rhetoric. In 1973 in the communication side of the discipline, the Religious Communication Association was founded and continues today. In addition to regular conferences, a newsletter, a listserv, awards, and a website of information, the group publishes the *Journal of Communication and Religion*, which celebrates diverse religious viewpoints and welcomes a variety of disciplinary perspectives. According to a history of the organization, various groups for the study of religious rhetoric had existed prior to this as part of the larger communication organization (Gehrke and Keith).

Recently a new group has arisen (many of us RSA members). Rhetoric and Religious Traditions originally began as a group focused on Christian tradition and rhetoric. It has morphed over time to include other faith traditions, and it has standing group status with the Conference on College Communication and Composition (CCCC). The first conference for the group occurred at De Paul University in 2005, which grew out of a study group with several key scholars sharing interest in rhetoric and religion—Anne Ruggles Gere, Beth Daniell, Elizabeth Vander Lei, Tom Amorose, David Jolliffe. Thirteen years later a second conference was held at the University of Tennessee in 2018 with a subtitle of "Publics, Partnerships, and Possibilities," echoing the interdisciplinary goals of RSA. According to the organizers of the conference, attendance was about 135 in number, demonstrating a significant interest in the subject (Ringer).

Those of us in rhetorical studies interested in these connections normally have other disciplinary specialties, but we continue to find ways to bring our research interests into perspective with religious history, religious literature, religious speech acts, and examination of sacred texts. This essay draws upon work already accomplished in the connections between rhetoric and religion, and it continues the investigations fostered by our professional organization by also considering a subject needing further attention—inspiration as a method of rhetorical invention. Here Harriet Beecher Stowe serves the subject, as well as a touchstone example of inquiry.

Inspiration—A Form of Rhetorical Invention

Harriet Beecher's Stowe's 1852 novel, *Uncle Tom's Cabin*, contains a passage that has stayed with me from my first reading of the novel to this very day.

> For the soul awakes, a trembling stranger, between two dim eternities,—the eternal past, the eternal future. The light shines only on a small space around her; therefore, she needs must yearn towards the unknown; and the voices and shadowy movings which come to

> her from out the cloudy pillar of inspiration have each echoes and answers in her own expecting nature. Its mystic imageries are so many talismans and gems inscribed with unknown hieroglyphics; she folds them in her bosom, and expects to read them when she passes beyond the veil. (380)

This quotation is, in my opinion, one of the most compelling expressions in nineteenth-century American literature of the uncertainty individuals face as they attempt to examine their past and make decisions regarding their future. For Stowe, both past and future were inexorably intertwined with notions of the Divine. She would later claim to have been divinely inspired to write the journey of Uncle Tom, the central idea of the novel coming to her in a vision (Wilson 256). Like other reformers of her day, she also understood the destiny of America in those same religious terms. Since the late 1700s when Benjamin Rush began to actively promote social reform in order to create the perfect moral nation in preparation for a millennial age, antebellum reformers increasingly used both religious language and the political vocabulary of the Republic in their attempts to build a divinely based civic virtue (Abzug 3-8).

This fusion of vocabularies was most frequently encountered in speeches from the pulpit and the podium during the 1800s, and Stowe grew up absorbing the strong oratorical traditions of the socially active and religious culture that surrounded her. The spiraling world of sermons, discussions, and religious disputations, in the center of which sat the young, attentive, and bright Harriet Beecher, affected the way she thought, spoke, and wrote. Like many young preachers preparing for the ministry, she committed to memory "a wonderful assortment of hymns, poems, and scriptural passages, which enabled her . . . to use and quote these valuable adjuncts of her writings during her mature life" (Fields 23). The major difference perhaps between her preparation and the young ministers' was her age—Stowe was only five-years old when she began exercising her memory. As a consequence, she was successful in "reproducing the continuous scriptural allusion that flowed through such speech in the days when people still went to meeting twice every Sabbath day" (Westbrook 23). Using this rich source of religious language, Stowe responds to the call of social reform and the strong, moral urging within her. She appropriates a form of discourse accessible to women in the nineteenth-century, the novel, and adapts the primarily aural rhetorical nature of the sermon into her own highly rhetorical work—*Uncle Tom's Cabin*—in an effort to move an entire nation to change its practices and save itself from destruction.

We should not be surprised to find that, given the cultural climate and values of that time and place, writers such as Stowe used religious terms and imagery when describing rhetorical practices. In Stowe's statement from *Uncle Tom's Cabin* quoted above, we see a writer describing the rhetorical process of invention. We learn from the ancients that invention affords writers and speakers ways to discover proofs, creating arguments fit for the situation at hand, or in Aristotle's words, "to see the best available means for persuasion" (I.2.1, Kennedy 37).

The inspiration Stowe describes is quite different from the inspiration so often pictured in literature of nineteenth-century America in such scenes as Reverend Dimsdale's election speech in Hawthorne's *Scarlet Letter*, in which the crowed witnessed a near miracle.

> According to their united testimony, never had man spoken in so wise, so high, and so holy a spirit, as he that spake this day; nor had inspiration ever breathed through mortal lips more evidently than it did through his. Its influence could be seen, as it were, descending upon him, and possessing him, and continually lifting him out of the written discourse that lay before him, and filling him with ideas that must have been as marvellous to himself as to his audience. (Chapter 23)

In this passage, Hawthorne depicts a scene in which the speaker is divinely filled with words not his own. In Hawthorne's version of inspiration, God controls the discourse, making the discourse of non-human origin and imbuing it with heavenly eloquence. Stowe's notion of inspiration is quite different. The past and the future are dark, unknown. The "soul" receives "movings" which have "echoes and answers" in the human experiencing inspiration. Here, the human, moving toward the future, draws on past knowledge and experiences, and uses the self's own nature to invent the actions, thoughts, and speeches that propel toward the future. Human will is not co-opted; rather, inspiration connects to the human will causing rhetorical agency, recognition of imperfection, and exigence to communicate to an audience.

Ralph Waldo Emerson helps us understand this sort of inspirational working in his essay entitled "Inspiration."

> Inspiration is like yeast. 'T is no matter in which of half a dozen ways you procure the infection; you can apply one or the other equally well to your purpose, and get your loaf of bread. Everything which we hear for the first time was expected by the mind; the newest discovery was expected. In the mind we call this enlarged power

> Inspiration. I believe that nothing great and lasting can be done except by inspiration, by leaning on the secret augury.

In a similar manner to Stowe's notion of light and its association with understanding and knowing, Emerson also focuses on light, comparing this sort of insight to "a flash of light, then a long darkness, then a flash again." The "insight" or "thought" may not be connected or consecutive; however, the moment of inspiration is powerful, more powerful, he claims, than "magic" or "religious tradition." These powerful moments of thought "let us into realities" or something "expected." Again, this is not a loss of will, but rather an igniting of something creative, something generative that exists in the human, that exists in realities that humans needed to enter.

Roger Thompson, in his book on *Emerson and the History of Rhetoric*, notes that Emerson asks the preacher to submit the "private soul" to the "great and public and divine Soul from which we live" (67). In so doing, Thompson argues, Emerson encouraged preachers "to embrace new visions of the self in deploying their particular forms of rhetoric" (67). This seems radically different from Dimsdale's leaving the written page, speaking as a pure conduit of the Divine. Rather, this inspiration provides "illumination" of what it means to step forward, to make progress (66).

Not taking time to rehearse the long and complicated history of the understanding of invention's place in rhetorical theory and practice, I'll employ the expedient notion, taken from Robert Young, that the function of inventional heuristics are "to prompt memory, observation, and inference in the conduct of inquiry" (351). Using this as a guide and viewing invention as a social act, we can understand what Stowe describes and what Emerson envisions—"inspiration" as taking on the role of prophet in a community.

Railton writes that Stowe, like Melville, "gave the novelist a prophetic office. Fiction was a means, not an end; ultimately, it was a way to tell the truth" (144). Traditionally, prophets pinpoint gross errors in their nations and communities, and they deal directly and openly with the problems and try to change the course of the perceived corruptions. According to Brueggemann,

> [Prophets] were concerned with most elemental changes in human society and they . . . understood a great deal about how change is effected. The prophets understood the possibility of change as linked to emotional extremities of life. They understood the strange incongruence between public conviction and personal yearning. Most of all, they understood the distinctive power of language, the capacity to speak in ways that evoke newness "fresh from the word." (9)

Prophets are firmly rooted in human existence, remain connected to the human world, and are users of human language. Their connection to a divine mission or inspiration allows them to invent speech and issue calls to action in difficult and even impenetrable situations.

In her book, *The Gendered Pulpit*, Roxanne Mountford also takes up the idea of the rhetor/preacher as prophet. Female ministers found that the role of prophet allowed them to resist "the culture's ideals," to lead the community in moral thinking and action, and "preach reform to the people" (116-7). One of Mountford's subjects of study used "her narrative vision" for her church to "win over her people" (117).

A key feature of prophetic utterances in both preaching and literature is narrative. The vision Stowe had was part of the narrative that became her novel. Mountford draws upon the writing of Fred B. Craddock to explore the importance of narrative in preaching. Craddock, as Mountford explains, suggests that beginning a sermon with a narrative allows "distance from the Scripture and, paradoxically, participating in it." He advocates turning the sermon into a narrative that the congregation "overhears." The narrative, then, will "draw the audience inductively into their own conclusions" (Mountford 61). Prophets invite audiences to enter into narratives, not just "overhearing" them as Craddock suggests, but actually living them in the retelling. Through the narrative of Uncle Tom, Stowe invents the sermonic force of the book. By way of example, we see Stowe turning from the inspirational narrative to the sermonic purpose of the novel while describing the scene of Tom's grief when he hears he has been sold by Mr. Selby:

> . . . [H]e turned to the rough trundle bed full of little woolly heads, and broke fairly down. He leaned over the back of the chair, and covered his face with his large hands. Sobs, heavy, hoarse and loud, shook the chair, and great tears fell through his fingers on the floor. . . . For, sir, he was a man. . . . (43)

"For, sir, he was a man"—an understated argument spun so artfully throughout the novel has its invention in the inspirational moment.

In her book *Invention in Rhetoric and Composition*, Janice Lauer traces the relationship between inspiration and invention—their mergings and their conflicts in the nineteenth century. "In the nineteenth century, epistemic rhetorical invention still took a back seat to logic, inspiration, and observation," and from there, she argues it continued diminishing due to the rise of romanticism and its emphasis on "intuition and inspiration as the sources of ideas and motivations for writing" (41). While certainly Laurer is correct about this, perhaps it is possible in the light of how Stowe and Emerson understand inspiration to see it less as competition with rhetorical invention and rather as another developing stage in how various cultures and peoples "prompt memory, observation, and inference in the conduct of inquiry." Lauer has certainly demonstrated in her book on invention that it is not static and is, instead, rather dynamic, useful to different times and people in differing ways.

In 1985 as part of an important bibliographic essay on invention in the technical and scientific fields, Carolyn Miller posits that invention includes "all the means by which writers come to their matter, whether consciously and systematically or intuitively and routinely." Her list of possible tools of invention include "presupposition, premises, value, inspiration, work activities—anything that leads to or is taken as 'good reason'" (123-24), further connecting invention to inspiration.

The Past and the Future—"Yearning Towards the Unknown"

Thinking of these terms, invention and inspiration, calls to mind Wayne C. Booth's 1991 essay "Rhetoric and Religion: Are they Essentially Wedded?" in which he endeavors to take this bonding one step further by claiming that the study of either discipline must inevitably lead to the other. In this particular case, adjusting our thinking about what inspiration is and how it functions in the practice of rhetoric in the United States helps us to value the force for change in this country that texts of inspirational origin, both oral and written, indeed have been. We can also think in solid civic and cultural terms about how inspiration as a function of invention allowed writers and speakers a heightened authority and position as people-to-whom-we-should-listen.

I hope this essay will spur more work on the relationship between inspiration and rhetorical invention, especially in American literature and rhetoric where the connections, given our national and regional histories, seem so very important and crucial. It is striking that in our history, religious rhetoric is both a place, as Mountford says, that has restricted the female body (67); yet the female voice, either in print or orally, has managed to gain an audience using religious rhetoric. The moral claim of inspiration and the authority it imbues to a rhetor seems key in understanding the intimate relationship between religion and rhetoric.

Works Cited

Abzug, Robert H. *Passionate Liberator: Theodore Dwight Weld and the Dilemma of Reform*. Oxford UP, 1980.

Aristotle. *On Rhetoric: A Theory of Civic Discourse*. Translated with Introduction, Notes, and Appendices by George A. Kennedy, 2nd ed., Oxford UP, 2007.

"Bibliography Plans." *Newsletter: Rhetoric Society of America*, vol. 3, no. 1, 1972, p. 1. *JSTOR*, www.jstor.org/stable/3885126.

Booth, Wayne C. "Rhetoric and Religion: Are They Essentially Wedded?" *Radical Pluralism and Truth*, edited by Werner G. Jeanrond and Jennifer L. Rike, Crossroad, 1991, pp. 62-80.

Brueggemann, Walter. *The Prophetic Imagination*. Fortress P, 1978.

Emerson, Ralph Waldo. "Inspiration." *The Complete Works of Ralph Waldo Emerson*. Biographical Introduction and Notes by Edward Waldo Emerson. Vol. VIII. *Letters and Social Aims*. Houghton Mifflin, 1904. www.bartleby.com/90/.

Fields, Annie, editor. *The Life and Letters of Harriet Beecher Stowe*. Houghton Mifflin, 1897.

Gehrke, Pat J., and William M. Keith. "Introduction: A Brief History of the National Communication Association." *A Century of Communication Studies: The Unfinished Conversation*, edited by Pat J. Gehrke and William M. Keith, Routledge, 2015, pp. 1-25.

Hawthorne, Nathaniel. *The Scarlet Letter, A Romance*. Ticknor, Reed & Fields. 1850.

Journal of Communication and Religion, http://www.relcomm.org/journal-of-communication-and-religion.html.

Lauer, Janice M. *Invention in Rhetoric and Composition*. Parlor P, 2004.

Miller, Carolyn. "Invention in Scientific Research in Technical Communication." *Research in Technical Communication: A Bibliographic Sourcebook*, edited by Michael G. Moran and Debra Journet. Greenwood P, 1985, pp. 117-62.

Mountford, Roxanne. *The Gendered Pulpit: Preaching in American Protestant Spaces*. Southern Illinois UP, 2003.

Murphy, James J., editor. *Three Medieval Rhetorical Arts*, [*Principles of Letter Writing*; *New Poetics*; *Form of Preaching*]. U California P, 1971.

Newsletter: Rhetoric Society of America, vol. 1, no. 1, 1968. *JSTOR*, www.jstor.org/stable/3885049.

Newsletter: Rhetoric Society of America, vol. 1, no. 1, 1969. *JSTOR*, www.jstor.org/stable/3885077.

Railton, Stephen. "Mothers, Husbands, and Uncle Tom." *Georgia Review*, vol. 38, no. 1, 1984, pp. 129-144.

Ringer, Jeffrey. Personal email. 4 Feb. 2019.

"Selective Bibliography on Rhetoric and Books and Articles Relevant to Rhetoric." *Newsletter: Rhetoric Society of America*, vol. 3, no. 3, 1973, pp. 13–20. *JSTOR*, www.jstor.org/stable/3885092.

Smith, Robert W. "Reviewed Work(s): *Three Medieval Rhetorical Arts*, [*Principles of Letter Writing*; *New Poetics*; *Form of Preaching*] by James J. Murphy." *Newsletter: Rhetoric Society of America*, vol. 3, no. 1, 1972, pp. 7-8. *JSTOR*, https://www.jstor.org/stable/3885132.

Stowe, Harriet Beecher. *Uncle Tom's Cabin or, Life among the Lowly*, edited with an introduction by Ann Douglas, reprint of first-edition text established by Kenneth S. Lynn (Harvard, 1962), Penguin Classics, 1986.

Thompson, Roger. *Emerson and the History of Rhetoric*. Southern Illinois P, 2017.

Westbrook, Percy D. *Acres of Flint: Writers of Rural New England, 1870-1900.* Scarecrow P, 1981.

Wilson, Forrest. *Crusader in Crinoline: The Life of Harriet Beecher Stowe.* Greenwood, 1941.

Winterowd, W. Ross. "The Prospect (And the Future) of Rhetoric." *Newsletter: Rhetoric Society of America*, vol. 2, no. 1, 1972, pp. 4-5. Taylor & Francis, www.jstor.org/stable/3885098.

Young, Richard E. "Invention." *Encyclopedia of Rhetoric and Composition: Communication from Ancient Times to the Information Age*, edited by Theresa Enos, Garland P, 1996, pp. 349-355.

Enlivening the Rhetorical Imagination: Rorty, Vico, and the Poetics of Rhetorical Invention

Scott Welsh and Laura Leavitt

In the concluding section of Morris Dickstein's seminal collection, *The Revival of Pragmatism,* Richard Poirier asks, "Why Do Pragmatist Want to Be Like Poets?" (1998). While this essay makes no attempt to answer for pragmatists in general, it does take the side of those who have argued that the value of the pragmatism to the rhetorical tradition, and Richard Rorty's value to the rhetorical tradition, in particular, is in its attention to things like art and irony as much as its attention to science and deliberation (Horne, 1993). Rorty is especially interesting, in the present political climate, because he did not speak about public discourse in a way that assumed cooperative argumentation in which interlocutors engage in a give-and-take of reasoned arguments in efforts to convince each other. In contrast, Rorty insisted that our beliefs, or what he called "final vocabularies" frequently shift without our conscious awareness or intent and hardly ever in response to what we tend to think of as argument or reasoning (75). This has led rhetoricians to sometimes accuse Rorty, and even pragmatism in general, of being insufficiently attentive to the rhetorical enactment of public deliberation (Danisch 162). The eighteenth century professor of eloquence, Giambattista Vico, however, might wholeheartedly embrace locating poetic reframing, alone, at the core of rhetorical engagement. Like Rorty, Vico does not imagine that people change their minds because they are argumentatively convinced to do so (Schaeffer 67).

Instead, Vico similarly makes the case, with Rorty, that persuasion is a function of poetic re-conception, or that we change our minds only when we are imaginatively inspired to do so. Although separated by three centuries and following distinct disciplinary paths, Rorty and Vico converge in their interest in describing the experience of persuasion from the point of view of audience members in a surprisingly contemporary fashion, which is to say from the point of view of those who may resist, out of fear or frustration, engaging those who are not already known to be political allies. What each independently concludes is that the experience of persuasion, rather than an act of being convinced in argumentative exchange, is instead a matter of unforeseen poetic delight. More specifically, the delight each describes is an experience of creative, ironic juxtaposition in which new connections are made that confound the rigid binaries and conceptual boundaries that often impede or undermine public deliberation. In other words, each imagines a mode of rhetorical invention especially well-suited to deliberation in which trust is in short supply and tensions run high. What they offer is a language of invention that challenges speakers to attempt not to win consent in the moment, but instead invites speakers to pursue the raw experience of conceptual delight. Speakers address themselves to the immediate pleasure of the audience by deliberately side-stepping or eliding pressure, tension, and risk through novel, poetic ways of thinking.

Rorty's account of what he terms "persuasion," primarily in *Contingency, Irony, and Solidarity,* introduces a mode of rhetorical invention that directly avoids what we think of as direct disputation or argumentative engagement (78). His view of persuasion is rooted in the assumption that people do not often change their minds in argumentative contests of refutation and assertion (7). Instead, Rorty argues that persuasion is the consequence of a gradual adoption of alternative vocabularies, not through accepting another's lobbying on their behalf, but by their ability to allow hearers to think about issues in new ways. Such vocabularies, by Rorty's account, do so by offering alternative, creative metaphors that cast subjects in a new light or otherwise disorient the rhetorical imagination (20).

Rorty's well-documented resistance to engaging rhetorical theory, however, has often led rhetoric scholars to underestimate his value to rhetorical theory's purposes (Danish 157). More often than not, they regard Rorty's work as philosophically compatible with parts of the rhetorical tradition but as failing, ultimately, to comprise a coherent or compelling rhetorical theory on its own. In contrast, we argue that Rorty's account of how change occurs within "public rhetoric" of a culture, primarily through the resources of irony, builds upon Giambattista Vico's account of rhetorical invention (Rorty 87). More specifically, Rorty's vision of ironic re-description advances Vico's argument that ingenium is the result of the recombination of images and terms within the *sensus communis*.

Rhetorical theorists have been prone to reducing Rorty's figure of the "liberal ironist" to people devoted to the cosmopolitan upending of parochial ideologies (Danisch 171). Our view is that Rorty's liberal ironists, insofar as they are public figures, are best understood not as poetic iconoclasts but as everyday poets creatively redeploying terms within the *sensus communis*, composed of what he calls the "final vocabularies" of fellow citizens. This approach to persuasion, Rorty argues, is not only more effective, as Vico suggests, but is also democratically essential. It is essential because citizens need to be able to trust others to avoid asking them to give up cherished ways of speaking, whenever possible, if they are going to be willing to put their trust in democratic politics.

I

Perhaps better than anyone else, Robert Danisch has detailed all the instances in which Richard Rorty sidled up to rhetoric before ultimately backing away. He notes how Rorty agrees with the Sophists that "truth is made rather than found" and that while "the world is out there," "descriptions of the world are not" (Danisch 165; Rorty 5). This places Rorty fully within a rhetorical epistemology, building on Protagoras's insight that "man is the measure of all things" (Danisch 161-62). By Rorty's lights, personal and social change occurs through a process of learning to speak differently about the world. Over time, people half creatively, half absentmindedly invent (or stumble upon) new vocabularies that either resolve problems or make them seem hardly worth noticing any longer (Rorty 16). Those who are especially well-suited to inventing new ways of speaking Rorty calls "ironists," or those who are able to creatively juxtapose elements from within the vast reaches of human culture in order to see the world and its problems in new ways (73).

Danisch's problem with Rorty is that he didn't follow the Sophists far enough. The Sophists' location of truth in the faculty of human imagination "led to the development of a robust pedagogy" in which students were offered "training in the strategic art of public speaking so as to equip people with the capacity to shape perceptions" (162). In contrast, Danisch argues, the only advice Rorty offers students who wish to pursue social change is to "redescribe lots and lots of things in new ways, until you have created a pattern of linguistic behavior which will tempt the rising generation to adopt it" (166). Yet Rorty makes little attempt, Danisch notes, to understand how one might go about tempting "the rising generation" (166). Instead, Rorty merely explains that as new words come into use, old words slowly die off, leading to the evolution of vocabularies employed within a culture. "He has nothing to say," Danisch explains, about why one vocabulary would be taken up and another would not (175). The art of persuasion, he argues is reduced to something like creative genius, which isn't of much help to someone struggling to figure out how to effectively engage others in public deliberation.

"To say that persuasion is a matter of imagination," Danisch concludes, "is not to offer a very substantive account of persuasion" (176). What those who seek to persuade truly need, instead, he argues, is instruction in "practices capable of guiding and improving public deliberation" (180). Although, Rorty may well be right that "imagination creates the games that reason proceeds to play," we nevertheless need accounts of, and instruction in, such reasoning if citizens hope to be effective in "transforming public policy" and improving "sociopolitical conditions (175, 158). This is because such transformation and improvement, according to Danisch, primarily comes through citizens, within particular language games, engaging in some sort of "face-to-face dialogue" in which they arrive at "intersubjective agreement" (173, 176). Danisch, like other critics of Rorty, is not so quick to divorce, as Rorty does, "the talent for 'speaking differently'" from the "talent for 'arguing well'" (166). "It's as if," Danisch writes, "the process of argumentation [for Rorty] does not require imagination and the imagination does not require argument" (166).

II

What is particularly interesting about Vico in light of Danisch's careful and sustained critique of Rorty is that Vico sounds an awful lot like Rorty. In *On the Most Ancient Wisdom of the Italians*, Vico directly takes up the relationship between argument and imagination and concludes that they are essentially one, and all but excludes "argument" as a helpful concept. In other words, he doesn't describe an interaction between the two as if each has a role or its own distinct function. Like Rorty, effective speech is, indeed, reduced to a species of ingenuity. In fact, Vico's account of the history of the word argument connects it to Latin words for acuity, sharpness, and clarity—which he reduces to the product of "sharp men" who "are able to find a likeness or ratio between things very different and far removed from one and other." He calls this "mother wit" or "acumen." He concludes, "Hence, wit is essential to invention because, in general, to find new things requires both the work and the activity of wit alone" (102).

John Schaeffer's brilliant 1990 study of Vico on rhetoric explains how Vico arrived at the conclusion that rhetorical invention is fundamentally a matter of poetic ingenuity. In his chapter, "Orality and *Sensus Communis* in Vico's Early Writings on Rhetoric," Schaeffer recounts how Vico attempted, in essence, to reverse engineer the process of persuasion by beginning with the feeling one has when one changes one's mind. That feeling for Vico, Schaeffer painstakingly shows, is the feeling of delight. Delight occurs, by Vico's account, in those moments when a speaker invites an audience to collaboratively discover a connection between two things that were previously considered to be entirely separate. In Vico's handbook on rhetoric, he writes, "The orator, in presenting an acute saying, makes beauty which is left for the hearer to discover; for it is present by virtue of the rational connection (*ligamen*) which, when the hearer discovers it, unites the extremes to allow for the contemplation of similarity and thus reveals the beauty which the orator brought to pass" (Schaeffer 66). This connection between two separate things Vico calls the "conceit," and "conceits," he says, "are the arguments" (Schaeffer 67). Schaefer further explains that "there is no question of a 'clear' argument with the mere addition of a decorative figure." Rather, for Vico, "the metaphor is the argument" (67).

Orators who are able to effectively do this require a particular sort of training according to Vico and, remarkably, that training is often indistinguishable from Rorty's suggestion that the ironist needs a wide engagement with the ways of speaking of lots of different people. Vico refers to this as a deep engagement with the *sensus communis*, the collection of shared knowledge, history, art, literature, and religion that makes up the vocabulary of one's hearers (Schaeffer 76). It is only through deep engagement with the *sensus communis* that one can produce unlikely or unheard-of connections between disparate things that an audience will nevertheless understand and recognize as having an ironic yet seemingly undeniable connection when viewed through the vocabulary of the orator.

Such connections, however, do not simply exist, but must be forged by the orator in a deliberate pursuit of what Vico calls "poetic logic" (*New Science* 127). As Lewis Hyde similarly argues, this practice is often as much a result of the cultivation of randomness and chance encounters as much as anything else (150). A primary question, as Danisch rightly insists, is then how to operationalize something like poetic logic or poetic invention. The new metaphors Rorty asks us to pursue do not automatically suggest themselves.

In the classroom, we attempt to operationalize the pursuit of delight through the discovery of meaning in random juxtaposition. Recently, one of us (Welsh) asked a class tasked with giving persuasive speeches on controversial issues to suggest a controversial subject as an example for the class to consider. A student proposed the always popular subject of marijuana legalization. As anyone who encounters this subject with students knows, it has become increasingly difficult for students to imagine new ways of speaking about the issue. Ahead of time, Welsh decided to ask students with pictures on their shirts to stand, and that the class would attempt to connect the issue to one of the pictures. The only shirt with a picture on it that day showed a rocket launching into space. When invited to comment on what was happening in the picture, a student said it was a rocket "escaping earth's atmosphere." With that, the metaphor was set and Welsh asked, "In what sense might marijuana be related to 'escape'"? Predictably, students said, marijuana can be used as an escape from pain or as an escape from the pressure and anxiety of everyday life. These initial responses seemed to largely invite students to repeat lines of arguments that were already familiar to them. So, Welsh invited students to return to the picture and ask what else was happening in it. In that moment, someone volunteered that "the earth is being left behind." The key question then emerged: "Other than pain or anxiety, who or what is left behind when one uses mind-altering drugs?" Hesitantly, a student volunteered that children often feel abandoned when their parents drink. Another student followed with the suggestion that whenever people use drugs or alcohol to escape, there are often other people who are left behind to deal with the consequences. A sort of sad beauty settled over the class as a new connection was formed: someone is always left behind when someone else tries to escape—and marijuana use is no different. Marijuana and alcohol are connected to children, in other words, less as the potential users or abusers, but as those indirectly harmed by these substances' very ability to produce mental and emotional escape among adults upon whom children depend. And how did we get there? It was the cultivation of random connection and looking for a *ligamen*. Or, as Schaeffer says, "The image makes sense in spite of appearing to be non-sense" (64).

What we especially like about this example is that, by explicitly affirming the value of the drug, it side-steps "argument" in which we enter established language games in order to win an argument on pre-existing terms. In other words, it does not engage the audience in debate. Instead, it solely and entirely affirms elements of the *sensus communis*, marijuana, pain, relief, relaxation, adults, and children, and in a way that does not drive immediately toward a conclusion or policy. It is perhaps an example of what is often called "reframing," but it may be more subtle than that. It suggests a trajectory, but does not complete the thought. It leaves it to the audience to decide what value the conceit has and how it should be permitted to affect their pre-existing commitments or beliefs. It is, as Rorty says, merely an addition to our vocabulary for thinking about drug legalization. It doesn't attempt to prove anyone wrong or attempt to win any particular argument. Rather, it begins and ends in a moment of unsettling, although not joyous, delight in seeing something in a slightly different way.

This may be part of what Rorty means when he talks about making "utterances" "without a fixed place in a language game" (18). As Janet Horne observed not long after, Rorty essentially identified what she calls "fictions," or connections produced in imagination, as the source of new vocabularies and hence new arguments (175). It is, indeed, more "poetic invention" than "strategy," as Danisch puts it, because it attempts to resist being fixed to a particular pre-existing side in a particular pre-existing debate. This troubles Danisch because it isn't immediately wedded to a particular program of institutional or political change, which is the ultimate concern he attributes to the rhetorical tradition. Rorty and Vico, in contrast, both take a much longer view of life in society, one which is sustained by addressing oneself to others' capacity for discovery and delight, and not merely through addressing others as objects to be moved or affected in pursuit of a clearly defined political or ideological goal.

Unfortunately, Rorty and Vico may be even more right now than ever, when so much of political discourse is conducted as attack and defense, and "owning" one's opponent, or what Rorty would have called "humiliation" seems to be the name of the game (92). Of course, it may be that in times of relative cultural uniformity, in which final vocabularies overlap considerably or the *sensus communis* lacks diversity, rhetoric can proceed as argument rendered as tactics, strategy, and debate. At the same time, amid extensive ideological and cultural diversity, perhaps speech that seeks insight and delight rather than proof and victory might give audiences the space they need to genuinely listen without the fear of being asked to give up too many of the commitments that give their lives meaning.

Works Cited

Danisch, Robert. "The Absence of Rhetorical Theory in Richard Rorty's Linguistic Pragmatism." *Philosophy and Rhetoric*, vol. 46, no. 2, 2013, pp. 156-181.

John Dewey. *The Public and Its Problems.* Swallow, 1957.

Horne, Janet. "Rorty's Circumvention of Argument: Redescribing Rhetoric." *Southern Communication Journal*, vol. 15, no.3, 1993, pp. 169-181.

Hyde, Lewis. *Trickster Makes This World: Mischief, Myth, and Art.* North Point, 1998.

Poirier, Richard. "Why Do Pragmatists Want to Be Like Poets?" *The Revival of Pragmatism: New Essays on Social Thought, Law, and Culture*, edited by Morris Dickstein, Duke UP, 1998, pp. 347-361.

Rorty, Richard. *Contingency, Irony, and Solidarity.* Cambridge UP, 1989.

Schaeffer, John D. *Sensus Communis: Vico, Rhetoric, and the Limits of Relativism.* Duke UP, 1990.

Vico, Giambattista. *The New Science of Giambattista Vico.* Revised and unabridged ed. Translated by Thomas Goddard Bergin and Max Harold Fisch, Cornell UP, 2010.

Vico, Giambattista. *On the Most Ancient Wisdom of the Italians.* Translated by L. M. Palmer, Cornell UP, 2010.

Inventing in Our Own House: Theorizing Democracy from the Standpoint of Rhetoric

Michelle Iten

Our conference theme of invention comes at a time when it's crucial to remember that democracy as a way of living together is something we must invent with all available resources. As we sustain the critical work of strengthening the "mutually interdependent and complex relationship" between rhetoric and democracy (Todd McDorman and David Timmerman xii-xiii), we are at a particularly rich intersection of memory and invention. To recall that democracy is not a guarantee is to recognize that it requires deliberate, ongoing, and wide-ranging invention. Building democracy for the future requires our discipline to sharpen its vision, ready to see and grasp all the available rhetorical means of inventing democracy. This includes our creative expansion of such invention as well as our scrutiny of lost, rejected, and overlooked means: practices that we may not typically count as having democratic potential. One practice that invites a longer look is the building of theory. Of the many means of crafting and caring for democracy, theorizing "democracy" itself from the standpoint of rhetoric is a vital means of invention.

Of course, though we import it freely, is crafting political theory really our business? Not necessarily. But rhetorical theory is, and democracy conceived as a particular method of human relations is a rhetorical phenomenon, the invention of which can benefit from theory that employs our discipline's ways of seeing associated life, human motives, and symbol use. Moreover, at a time when understandings of democracy seem increasingly reductive, our discipline should aim for copia, proliferating a number of rhetorical theories of democracy and keeping them green in disciplinary crosstalk. We are fortunate right now to have a broad and powerful core of democracy studies in rhetoric, populated by such scholars as Robert Asen, Nathan Crick, Robert Danisch, Jeremy Engels, Gerard Hauser, Patricia Roberts-Miller, Candace Rai, and Karen Tracy, to name just a few. In addition, our discipline's scholarship on publics and counterpublics, on deliberation, and on rhetorical citizenship—though not precisely the same things as democracy—intersects with and informs our understanding of it. But at a time when democracy can be hard to see, we can benefit from even more theory-lenses to help us to discern new and unnoticed rhetors, genres, and practices that "count" as democratic rhetoric.

Primarily, the rhetorical practice of theorizing democracy means to think about it at the level of concept. What does the word mean? What is the nature of democracy? At what point does democracy become something else? Prior to these questions, though, is thinking about theory itself, its affordances and its consequences. This includes the range of different purposes theory can take on: description, explanation, systemization, prescription, speculation, or—in an obsolete definition that's worth recovering—theory as contemplation, an act of mental beholding. Also prior to the act of building theory is thinking about discipline-specific methodology: the approaches, methods, and types of questions for theorizing that fit a rhetorician's hand. In this paper, I share a few methodological moves we in rhetoric can use to reveal the implicit theories of democracy that underlie our work and to stimulate the invention of new, explicit theories. I put these in the form of questions we as individual scholars and teachers might ask ourselves in order to unearth our assumptions about democracy; deepen our understandings of it; and most important, clarify our hopes for ourselves and our students.

The first question is, how can we benefit from bringing the theorization of democracy more firmly into rhetoric's tent? In my own case, the need to theorize democracy from a rhetorical standpoint begins in, and circles back to, the classroom. I've taught some form of discourse for democracy every semester for several years. Each time I ask, "For these students and in this time, out of the many capacities and practices I could teach as democratic, which should be priority? Which are most democratic? Which are most needed now?" At the same time, resilience is also priority: which rhetorical skills should I select to help students embody democratic relations over the long haul, through upheavals in governance, technologies, and conditions? And, I'm concerned for equality: of any rhetorical practice that I designate and teach as integral to enacting democracy, who has more access to that practice, and who has less? These curricular questions always drive me right back to theoretical ones: what is democracy, and what lets us call a rhetorical practice "democratic"?

At times it's been hard to find theories that fit my particular hand as a rhetorician and whose consequences I can live with. I'm uneasy, for example, with theories that describe democracy solely as a constitutional form, in which discourse and human motives—a rhetorician's bread and butter—are epiphenomenal. I'm uneasy with normative theories that posit equality as inherent, something that we need only let emerge, as opposed to actively cultivating it through rhetorical action. Similarly, I've also found it hard to draw sustenance from theories that posit democracy as an empty signifier; a horizon event (e.g., Derrida's "democracy to come," as explained by Paul Fritsch); or otherwise un-seeable. Somewhere along the line I realized, "I teach rhetoric, and I need rhetorical theory about democracy." Such theory will not disdain ideas from political science and political philosophy, but in true rhetorical fashion will synthesize and chasten these received notions of democracy with knowledge about the everyday use of human symbol systems.

Another reason we might need more explicitly rhetorical theories about democracy itself is that we sometimes tend to leave the word unexplained. In rhetoric, we use "democracy" to do heavy lifting—to justify the value of our research and pedagogy in our institutions and beyond; to provide grounds for judgments of ethics in our rhetorical criticism; to signal our commitments to the humane, the just, and the larger good. But the word itself may appear early in our materials, and then give way without much explanation to subsequent words. The implication of this is that the term democracy, while vital as a justification, is self-evident, having a stable meaning and signaling a particular hierarchy of political virtues that all readers can supply.

Yet, for rhetoricians especially, words used as pieties should automatically trigger deep examination. Part of that examination includes articulating what *kind* of democracy we mean: constitutional, Athenian, creative, radical, liberal, rhetorical, pragmatic, deliberative, aggregative, algorithmic, actually lived, and so on, to name a few. Each is underpinned by somewhat or very different views of what counts as discursive action, of what is possible in associated life, and of which hierarchy of political virtues is most democratic. This means, in turn, different assumptions, often unexpressed, of what counts as democratic rhetoric and who can be a democratic rhetor—questions whose answers have significant consequences for what we research and teach as "the" rhetorical practices of democracy. Again, our aim needn't be the dominance of one model, but rather sustained and explicit exchanges about the many ways we conceive of democracy in our discipline, and our reasons for those ways. Such multiplicity is vital defense against becoming complicit in democracy's dilution or neglect. Our multiple definitions will keep the word prominent and cared for. In this way, we can avoid leaving the word and concept vulnerable to erasure and co-option by neoliberal, technocratic, and other authoritarian agendas.

A second question to explore is, is it suitable to regard theory as a means of inventing democracy? And if so, what can rhetoric bring to the task; what disciplinary resources do we have that can make new knowledge about democracy this way? At first glance, the enterprise of theory, with its search for definitions and abstract principles, might chafe, and even seem somewhat irresponsible, when the times so compel us to analyze and cultivate on-the-ground rhetorical action for democracy in the here and now. But such analysis and cultivation are already involving us in thinking about democracy at the level of theory. If we use the word democracy and assume a meaning for it, there's some theory there, below the surface. If we make certain selections about what artifacts to criticize or what skills to teach as democratic discourse, then some larger principle is directing our vision and providing criteria for our selections. In any case, the study of women's rhetorics has shown us that it's difficult and maybe even misleading to definitively separate rhetorical theory and rhetorical practice, along with similar dyads of theory–pedagogy, theory–criticism, and theory–experience. We can better think of rhetoric's ways of making knowledge as a dynamic Mobius strip, with one surface and one edge.

This understanding, in fact, is a primary resource that the discipline of rhetoric can bring to the theorization of democracy. It can help us grant equal validity to the different purposes of doing theory. At a time when democracy needs all the friends it can get, it seems wasteful to posit a bright line between purposes in order to assert superiority—arguing, for example, that theories of democracy must stem from the description of actually existing democracy or that theories of democracy must prescribe ideals and aims. As rhetoricians, we don't need to have this fight because we already understand the ways in which description can function as prescription—the way "is" turns into "should"—and the reverse—that an allegiance to a "should" shapes our perception of "what is." We know that whether case-based or speculative, theories are always arguments and as such mature one another.

Another disciplinary resource that rhetoric can bring to the theorization of democracy is the ability to shift among a wide range of apertures and scales. Thus we have rhetoric scholarship that examines democracy through the lens of a specific site or artifact, but we also have scholarship that examines democracy as it intertwines with other concepts, such as pragmatism (Danisch), Deweyan aesthetics (Crick), performative deliberation (Arabella Lyons), and so on. This sort of epistemological breadth is one of rhetoric's greatest strengths. Somewhere between a purely philosophical or scientific theorization of democracy and a purely descriptive one lie rhetorical notions of democracy, aimed at both deep knowledge and contextualized action. Finally, rhetoricians bring to the practice of theory a familiarity with reading negative space (Jacqueline Jones Royster and and Gesa E. Kirsch 72). As students of influence and the directing of attention, we know how to notice the unnoticed. Rhetorical theories of democracy will help invent more democracy, period, by creating the conceptual frameworks to help us look and listen for missing democratic agents, muted and inaudible voices, overlooked sites and practices of democracy, non-obvious language for conceiving democracy, and neglected sources of democratic power. A second method, then, to spur our invention of democracy at the level of rhetorical theory is to take stock of the disciplinary methods and resources we bring to such an endeavor.

A third question that opens us up to making rhetorical theory about democracy is to ask ourselves, what does the word democracy mean? As a method, definition and its techniques can help us plumb our assumptions about democracy. Again, rhetoricians bring a unique resource to this task: a tolerance and even a preference for multiplying such things as definitions, a sort of exuberance in excess that is itself deeply democratic (Daniel Bensaïd 43; Chantal Mouffe 74), standing in contrast to the desire to subdue all alternatives to one authoritative definition in the search for epistemic certainty. Formulating a definition of democracy engages us in, for example, delineating its characteristic features; naming its parts; examining its intersections with cognate terms; and choosing which political virtues take precedence as most characteristic of democracy as opposed to other ways of associated life. In addition, pondering different translations of the Greek word *demokratia* can help us with our definitions. Not because we think such etymology will provide definitive proof of what "democracy" *is*, but because our individual choices among possible versions of *demokratia's* historical origin are likely to reflect what we find most valuable in the concepts of group life and human nature (Cynthia Farrar 171).

For example, we can choose to translate *demos* as "the" people or "all" people, each of which carries different implications (Mouffe 45); the simultaneous ruler-and-ruled; dwellers in a particular deme; the common people; the non-aristocratic, working class (Farrar 175; Ellen Meiksins Wood 61-62); the multitude or majority; legal citizens; or equal sharers. Similarly, there are options for translating *kratos*: as force enacted on others, with the potential for violence (Christopher Hobson 647); as the economic and materially productive power of the *demos* (Josiah Ober 94-95); or as stemming from the verb for "grasp" or "grip" (Paul Cartledge 162). As a brief example of the utility of pondering different translations and their consequences, in my teaching, I choose this latter meaning of *kratos* as "grip" because it highlights citizens' direct handling of power. This translation helps me emphasize the deliberate intentionality of exercising democratic power: to place our hands around something and curl our fingers to hang on to it requires ongoing attention and conscious intention. While definitions are part of theory-making in general, I argue that rhetoricians have particular facility in understanding that how we choose or construct a term's definition is functional, setting up clear trajectories for what we will be able to use the term to do for us, whether we use it as a frame of perception, a justification for our work, or both.

A final question that invites us into the rhetorical theorization of democracy is a subset of definition: what kind of thing is democracy? Here, too, our answers set up lenses through which we will perceive rhetorical action for democracy. For example, theorizing democracy as a form of governance sets up the theorist to look for and validate democracy as it inheres in certain boundaried structures (Sheldon S. Wolin, "Norm" 34), the shapes of which serve as proof of democracy's presence in a particular time and place. Theorizing democracy as a form directs critical and pedagogical attention to the invention of democracy through constitutions, laws, structures of representation, and codified processes and procedures, such as elections, meeting structures, and discussion protocols. On the one hand, conceiving democracy as form poses challenges: the risk of valorizing containment and fixity (Wolin, *Politics of Vision* 601-602); issues of exclusion, including what to do about all the leftovers and spillovers that don't fit the form; and the tendency to center democratic life on the State. At the same time, pursuing democracy as it inheres in forms provides necessary correctives to views that would consign democracy to ephemerality or indefinition (what Hauser describes as the meaning of democracy being "up for grabs" ["Rethinking" 225]), and offers the opportunity to invent genres and procedures of rhetorical action that help people manifest democratic values and relations.

Another way to answer the question, what kind of thing is democracy? is to conceptualize democracy as an energy. This directs the theorist's attention to tracking the rhetorical invention of democracy as it happens through movement and through methods of conducting, channeling, and using democracy. Through this theoretical lens, we can, for example, explore proliferation: by what rhetorical practices does democracy-as-energy multiply and spread, and by which does it dwindle? And mobility: how does democracy travel through rhetorical actions? Which practices fuel or halt it? We can also think about democracy's varieties of energy, such as tension, propulsion, and expansion. For example, theorizing democracy as an energy of expansion can lead us to count as democratic the ingenious, subterranean, or anachronistic rhetorical actions that resist the encroachment of modes of discourse whose ubiquity tends to get conflated with their necessity. On one hand, challenges to theorizing democracy as energy include the temptation to look for the source of democratic energy rather than looking for how it is invented, as well as the risk of theorizing democracy as something inherent, metaphysical, or otherwise existing outside our invention of it. On the other hand, conceiving democracy as an energy can help us, quite simply, ask new questions about democracy and rhetoric. In addition, thinking of democracy as an energy—a thing that flows through and around forms, that exists in effects rather than containers—can also help us perceive opportunities for the rhetorical invention of democracy in times and places where a paucity of traditional forms of democracy would seem to make democratic relations impossible. Together with exploring benefits and resources, questions of democracy's definition and nature hint at the breadth of possibilities for inventing democracy by theorizing it from the standpoint of rhetoric.

In conclusion, democracy is something we must continually invent, using all available resources. If the rhetorical actions involved in governance and legislating democratic conditions make up the front of the tapestry, the back is made up of the rhetorical practices we use to relate to others in ways that make democracy a lived and visible experience, what Greg Clark describes as the play of influence in interpersonal experiences that help build a common life and democratic culture (114). It's a propitious moment to craft some theoretical lenses for seeing the back of the tapestry, using rhetoric's epistemological resources to sharpen our vision of democracy itself.

Works Cited

Asen, Robert. *Democracy, Deliberation, and Education*, Pennsylvania State UP, 2015.
Bensaïd, Daniel. "Permanent Scandal." *Democracy: In What State?* edited by Giorgio Agamben, translated by William McCuaig, Columbia UP, 2009, pp. 16-43.
Cartledge, Paul. "Democracy, Origins of: Contribution to a Debate." *Origins of Democracy in Ancient Greece*, edited by Kurt A Raaflaub, Josiah Ober, and Robert W. Wallace, U of California P, 2007, pp. 155-69.
Clark, Gregory. "Rhetorical Experience and the National Jazz Museum in Harlem." *Places of Public Memory: The Rhetoric of Museums and Memorials*, edited by Greg Dickinson, Carole Blair, and Brian L. Ott, U of Alabama P, 2010, pp. 113-35.
Crick, Nathan. *Democracy and Rhetoric: John Dewey on the Arts of Becoming*, U of South Carolina P, 2010.
Danisch, Robert. *Pragmatism, Democracy, and the Necessity of Rhetoric*, U of South Carolina P, 2007.
Engels, Jeremy David. *The Art of Gratitude*, SUNY Press, 2018.
—. *Enemyship: Democracy and Counter-Revolution in the Early Republic*, Michigan State UP, 2010.
—. *The Politics of Resentment*, Penn State UP, 2015.

Farrar, Cynthia. "Power to the People." *Origins of Democracy in Ancient Greece*, edited by Kurt A Raaflaub, Josiah Ober, and Robert W. Wallace, U of California P, 2007, pp. 170-95.

Fritsch, Matthias. "Derrida's Democracy to Come." *Constellations: An International Journal of Critical & Democratic Theory*, vol. 9. no. 4, 2002, pp. 574-97.

Hauser, Gerard. "Rethinking Deliberative Democracy: Rhetoric, Power, and Civil Society." *Rhetoric and Democracy: Pedagogical and Political Practices*, edited by Todd F. McDorman and David M. Timmerman, Michigan State UP, 2008, pp. 225-64.

—. "Rhetorical Democracy and Civic Engagement." *Rhetorical Practices: Discursive Practices of Civic Engagement: Selected Papers from the 2002 Conference of the Rhetoric Society of America*, edited by Gerard Hauser and Amy Grim, Erlbaum, 2004, pp. 1-14.

Hobson, Christopher. "Beyond the End of History: The Need for a 'Radical Historicisation" of Democracy in International Relations." *Millenium—Journal of International Studies*, vol. 37, 2009, pp. 631-57.

Lyon, Arabella. *Deliberative Acts: Democracy, Rhetoric, and Rights*, Pennsylvania State UP, 2013.

McDorman, Todd F. and David M. Timmerman, editors. Introduction. *Rhetoric and Democracy: Pedagogical and Political Practices*, Michigan State UP, 2008, pp. xi-xlii.

Mouffe, Chantal. *The Democratic Paradox*, Verso, 2005.

Ober, Josiah. "'I Besieged That Man': Democracy's Revolutionary Start." *Origins of Democracy in Ancient Greece*, edited by Kurt A. Raaflaub, Josiah Ober, and Robert W. Wallace, U of California P, 2007, pp. 83-104.

Rai, Candace. "Power, Publics, and the Rhetorical Uses of Democracy." *The Public Work of Rhetoric: Citizen-Scholars and Civic Engagement*, edited by John M. Ackerman and David J. Coogan, U of South Carolina P, 2010, pp. 39-55.

Roberts-Miller, Patricia. *Deliberate Conflict: Argument, Political Theory, and Composition Classes*, Southern Illinois UP, 2004.

—. *Demagoguery and Democracy*, The Experiment, 2017.

Royster, Jacqueline Jones and Gesa E. Kirsch. *Feminist Rhetorical Practices: New Horizons for Rhetoric, Composition, and Literacy Studies*, Southern Illinois UP, 2012.

Tracy, Karen. *Challenges of Ordinary Democracy: A Case Study in Deliberation and Dissent*, The Pennsylvania State UP, 2010.

Wolin, Sheldon S. "Norm and Form: The Constitutionalizing of Democracy." *Athenian Political Thought and the Reconstruction of American Democracy*, edited by J. Peter Euben, John R. Wallach, and Josiah Ober, Cornell UP, 1994, pp. 29-58.

—. *Politics and Vision: Continuity and Innovation in Western Political Thought*. Revised ed, Princeton UP, 2004.

Wood, Ellen Meiksins. "Democracy: An idea of Ambiguous Ancestry." *Athenian Political Thought and the Reconstruction of American Democracy*, edited by J. Peter Euben, John R. Wallach, and Josiah Ober, Cornell UP, 1994, pp. 59-80.

The Mt. Oread Manifesto and the Realities of 2018

Joseph Good

"The Mt. Oread Manifesto on Rhetorical Education" was published in *Rhetoric Society Quarterly* five years before the 2018 RSA conference. But its message may be even more important today. Taking full consideration of the political realities and social issues of 2018 and 2019, I distill three general tenets from the Manifesto that deserve more careful consideration. First: Listening. As in honestly listening to those who we might disagree with. Second: Ethical Consideration. As in fairly and fully presenting any alternate or opposing viewpoints. Third: The Public Good. As in the workable compromises needed to function and thrive as a community, as a society, or as a democratic state. To explore these tenets, I will begin with an introduction to the Manifesto. Then I will consider the Academic Writing Program at the University of Maryland. Finally, I will try to enact these ideas with a brief consideration of "citizenship."

In 2003, a group of rhetoric scholars convened at the Alliance of Rhetoric Societies in Evanston, Illinois. At that conference, Jeffrey Walker sought to unify rhetorical study through its teaching tradition. He stated that "The main line of the rhetorical tradition has been…a 'teaching tradition' in an 'educational theater,' devoted to certain ideals that might be summed up as 'civic'" (quoted in Hauser 39). Gerard Hauser echoes this ideal and also summarizes the findings of the ARS conference in his *RSQ* article, "Teaching Rhetoric: Or Why Rhetoric Isn't Just Another Kind of Philosophy or Literary Criticism." Therein, Hauser seeks to "advance a collective assertion of what we study and teach, what binds our several traditions together as a disciplinary practice… and why this mode of education is valuable for a free society" (40). This "mode of education" is urgent and lacking; Hauser asserts that "without rhetorical competence, citizens are disabled in the public arenas... and democracy turns into a ruse disguising the reality of oligarchic power" (52). In order to unify the traditions of civics and rhetoric, Hauser invokes the classical example of Isocrates:

> Isocrates was not just a scholar of his culture but an *activist*. His activism took the form of his own compositions *and* his pedagogy. He taught pupils the agonist and seductive arts of speech, but also to aspire beyond the pugnacity of the *agon* and the dazzle of seduction, to seek *arête* through rhetorical practices aligned with the narratives of their intellectual and moral traditions. He taught them to be *public* speakers, which means his pedagogy taught them to be externally oriented as interventionists for change. (42-43)

From there, Hauser declares that "We—scholar-teachers of rhetoric—require a manifesto reclaiming this tradition as rhetoric's role in civic education" (43).

"The Mt. Oread Manifesto on Rhetorical Education" came roughly 10 years after the ARS conference, but maintains the same zeal for rhetorical education. The Manifesto is authored by William Keith and Roxanne Mountford and, like Hauser's article, speaks on behalf of a group of rhetoric scholars.[1] Recalling the historical (and largely extinct) division between Speech and English, the Manifesto seeks to bridge the contemporary divide between communication departments and the English departments (1-2). The authors see this bridge as already begun, noting that "writing teachers assign formal presentations, and speaking teachers require writing" (2). Yet the authors believe that rhetoric has not been given its due: "Though their history within separate disciplines obscures it, rhetoricians have a common interest... that is disguised by the current separation of writing and speaking instruction" (2). From there, the authors lay down the tenets of the Manifesto itself (which will be observed more closely in the sections to follow). The Manifesto seeks to unify the work of rhetoricians in First-Year Writing and basic Communication courses – both usually taken in a student's first year at a university. This practical strategy anticipates a "transdisciplinary field" under the rule of Rhetoric, where "rhetoricians...implement an integrated curriculum" (3). The new integrated curriculum would "develop citizen participants, not simply future employees or more literate students" (3). Furthermore, the authors state this consolidation is a step towards "a world in which

---

1. In their first footnote, Keith and Mountford list the "conceptual contributions from the participants in the "Rhetoric in/between the Disciplines" Seminar at the 2013 Rhetoric Society of America Institute in Lawrence, Kansas."

... average citizens can perform rhetorical analyses of discourse around them and ask productive questions" (3).

In reaction, some scholars note the distance between the ideals of the Manifesto and the realities of university administration. Cristina Hanganu-Bresch considers the possibility of an integrated curriculum in her article, "Quo Vadis, Independent Writing Programs? Writing about Writing and Rhetorical Education." Therein, Hanganu-Bresch observes that "where old alliances with English/literature programs crumbled, new ones started to be forged with Rhetoric and Communication programs" (199). This burgeoning alignment included "university-wide academic initiatives that transcended old curricular allegiances (such as writing across the curriculum, writing in the disciplines, or the writing center)" (199). Hanganu-Bresch sees the Manifesto as part of this trend of initiatives and calls Roxanne Mountford a pioneer in the "Communication across the curriculum" movement (213). Hanganu-Bresch further acknowledges that "since Rhetoric is the disciplinary home and the foundation of all our writing pedagogies... the Mt. Oread Manifesto call makes sense" (213). However, she also admits that her university's attempts to begin the discussions on an integrated curriculum have "fallen flat," and that "not all academic institutions are well equipped to tolerate that degree of overlap" (213). Thereafter, Hanganu-Bresch sides with a different model of integrated curriculum (writing about writing) and asserts that "the conversations surrounding [rhetorical education] are by comparison less robust and the implementation of its vision ... still fluid" (214).[2] Seemingly aware of these practical difficulties, William Keith's 2016 article concedes that "systems are entrenched enough that it may be difficult to get people to understand why one would change" ("Understanding" 122). Keith remarks that "external commentators laud the potential for university education to produce better citizens," but then reluctantly concludes that real change would take a series of shifts from books to instructors to entire departments (122).

Despite these practical difficulties, the University of Maryland's Academic Writing Program honors the goal of developing citizen participants. It was built and modernized by highly qualified and celebrated rhetorical scholars such as Jeanne Fahnestock, Jane Donawerth, Shirley Logan, and Jessica Enoch. That said, there are some noteworthy difficulties in developing and running a civics-friendly First-Year Writing curriculum. Especially at a large public university, the education level of incoming freshmen is disparate. Ex-

---

2. "Writing about Writing" is a practice where the fields of Rhetoric and Writing Studies are the main subjects (i.e., content) of a writing course (Hanganu-Bresch 203).

perience can vary from students of private schools with several years of A.P. classes, to other students who were mostly coached for standardized tests at a large public school. Of course, all college students must learn how to properly research, to cite, to build a term paper, etc. The University of Maryland understands, respects, and deals with those practical issues. But, the program also intends to instill certain scholarly principles, like *dissoi logoi*, *stasis*, inquiry, responsible use of data, and ethical representation of opposing views. One of the major goals of Maryland's program (and I quote the standard syllabus) is "to be able to enter intellectual conversations inside and outside the academy."

Before getting deeper into the program at Maryland, please consider a few points directly from the Manifesto:

> *We seek a world in which*
> - Students are exposed to authentic projects and audiences that connect them to the public sphere, rather than artificial, textbook-driven, assignments . . .
> - Instruction in writing and speaking serve primarily to offer rhetorical education, even though this education may also prepare students for the job market . . .(3)
> - Business and political professionals [. . .] understand why compromise is vital to a republic and how collaboration grounded in a strong ethical understanding serves the public good." (4)

These tenets reaffirm the commitment to honest listening, ethical consideration, and the public good. Aimed at an audience of university students, these tenets more specifically call for public interaction, a rhetorical education, and ethical compromise.

Honoring similar goals, the University of Maryland's Academic Writing Program is built on principles of rhetoric. One of the main ambitions is to teach *stasis*. Instructors aim to show students how *stasis* is a valuable tool for resolving differences as well as the invention of writing content. Students typically approach the unfamiliar *stasis* with hesitation and frustration. But the program considers it a necessary, if painful, first step towards developing citizen participants. Later in the semester, students must produce an Inquiry paper. In that Inquiry, students must ask genuine, open, and scholarly questions around their chosen issue. Students must genuinely consider opposing views. They must envision the entire scope of an issue. They must question their own entrenched ideas. Accordingly, many students struggle with the Inquiry assignment. Students have grown accustomed to certain patterns of thought and written discourse. Instructors work with students to help them understand the value in a difficult inquiry process. Students are encouraged to ask difficult questions. As with stasis, many students do not consider this an easy process. Many instructors frequently ask for "re-writes" on the Inquiry assignment. But by the end of the semester, most students come to see the value in questioning and considering multiple perspectives.

Building on the Inquiry, students move to a "Digital Forum." Students must produce a simple website that shows three different "stakeholders" in an issue. This further encourages students to consider alternate and opposing viewpoints. Each stakeholder must be represented fairly and equally. This encourages students to reconsider their own viewpoints. Students may also develop a healthy respect for other opinions and arguments within their chosen issue. The core of the semester is the Position Paper—a ten-page piece of formal academic writing. For this assignment, instructors teach a rhetorically-based structure that includes a "consideration" section. Students see how a rhetorical consideration of opposing arguments can make their argument stronger. After the process of the Inquiry assignment and the Digital Forum, most students can ethically consider alternate and opposing views. Advanced students can even work towards something like a proper refutation.

Because students can choose their topics, many students naturally choose public issues. And after the progression of writing assignments, many students produce position papers that can actually contribute to the public good. Instructors at the University of Maryland would testify to such development. Other programs at other universities are making similar strides. The writing programs at Penn State and Oklahoma, with populations similar to the University of Maryland, have developed writing programs with comparable goals. Based on feedback from panels at the RSA 2018 conference, there are many other programs with interest in developing citizen-participants in their First-Year Writing programs. Hoping to lead by example, the University of Maryland shows that some key goals of the Manifesto can be realized within a First-Year Writing program.

The Manifesto's message is not only limited to First Year Writing students. Modern composition professors can use similar tenets to better inform themselves in social discussions with their students. For instance, citizenship is a key issue in modern social and political discussions. Many rhetorical scholars are researching and addressing citizenship issues. Among them is Amy J. Wan, who released *Producing Good Citizens: Literacy Training in Anxious Times* in 2014. Wan asserts that "anxieties about citizenship persist in the United States" (146). This is especially true over the past few years, with issues like DACA, NAFTA, and visas becoming ever-more contentious. She also asserts that a teacher's calls for citizenship or civics are not "neutral" (147). National programs such as the DREAM Act "interact with the intellectual work [of] universities ... as they prepare students to be 'citizens'" (150). Some forms of legislation represent a kind of citizenship that is based on "the exercise of exclusion and control, particularly among those students with the most tenuous citizenship status" (150).

Teachers may believe they provide a genuinely good and politically neutral service of civic education. Wan helps us realize that producing "good citizens" is not a politically neutral act. Indeed, making a value statement about citizenship means having a workable idea of what a good citizen looks like. Wan therefore believes "we must seek to answer what specific kind of citizenship we hope to produce through literacy, or risk situating citizenship as simply another assessable learning goal in our curriculum" (176). In order to teach a responsible and equitable form of citizenship, "literacy teachers and other educators need to consider their place in the process of the achievement of full citizenship... that allows an individual full access to society's resources" (175). There are sets of circumstances that put limits on what a citizen can aim to be, and on how a university can teach students how to be good citizens (Wan 175). Only when all those limits are recognized "can the influence of the writing classroom on the production of good citizens be evaluated fully" (175). Wan does not claim to have the final answer, but she is confident that teachers must regard the process of citizenship training as collaborative:

> Students arrive with their own ideas about goals and expectations for both class and citizenship, but so do teachers. The role of the teacher-citizen is not one in which the teacher awards or judges the citizenship of students, but rather a more delicate one in which the teacher recognizes his or her role, both implicit and explicit, in a larger process of citizenship production. (176)

Because of this, an education that is based on citizenship must consider what effects are already being produced by teachers, as well as evaluate the (privileged) status of teachers as the defenders of citizenship.

The Mt. Oread Manifesto embraces the ideals of ethical citizenship—based largely on democratic participation. But, as Wan reveals, any education must consider the privileged status of teachers. In some ways, teachers are the "defenders of citizenship." This is especially important today, when citizenship is such a contentious and potentially violent issue.

Indeed, recent political and social issues re-emphasize the need for a comprehensive civic and rhetorical education. At places like the University of Maryland, we are trying to begin such an education. And we are having some success. Yet, as teachers and defenders of citizenship, we should also remember the principles that we preach. Any education program should consider the reality of social and political circumstances across the nation. We should listen, ethically consider our opposition, and then work towards a public good for the *whole* public. Fortunately, it is not too late to re-examine, improve, and work towards the goals of the Mt. Oread Manifesto. First-Year Writing is a popular domain of rhetoric scholars, and those programs should seriously consider the Manifesto's tenets.

Works Cited

Hanganu-Bresch, Cristina. "Quo Vadis, Independent Writing Programs? Writing about Writing and Rhetorical Education." *A Minefield of Dreams: Triumphs and Travails of Independent Writing Programs*, edited by Justin Everett and Cristina Hanganu-Bresch, University Press of Colorado, 2016, pp. 199-219.

Hauser, Gerard A. "Teaching Rhetoric: Or Why Rhetoric Isn't Just Another Kind of Philosophy or Literary Criticism." *Rhetoric Society Quarterly* vol 34, no. 3, 2004, pp. 39-53.

Good, Joseph and Woody, Cassandra, panelists. "Engaging the Mt. Oread Manifesto on Rhetorical Education." Rhetoric Society of America Conference 2018: Reinventing Rhetoric, 1 Jun 2018, Downtown Minneapolis Hilton, Marquette 9, 2nd Floor, Minneapolis, MN.

Keith, William. "Understanding the Ecology of the Public Speaking Course." *Review of Communication*, vol. 16, no. 2-3, 2016, pp. 114-124.

Keith, William and Roxanne Mountford. "The Mt. Oread Manifesto on Rhetorical Education 2013" *Rhetoric Society Quarterly*, vol 44, no. 1, 2014, pp. 1-5.

The University of Maryland Academic Writing Program. Standard Syllabus for English 101: Introduction to Academic Writing. College Park, MD, Fall 2018.

Wan, Amy J. *Producing Good Citizens: Literacy Training in Anxious Times*. University of Pittsburgh Press, 2014.

Some Reflections on the Wideness of the Atlantic

Kristian Bjørkdahl

As *exordium*, two age-old insights. The first: When in Rome, do as the Romans do. The next: At the start of an oration, always strive to establish rapport with the audience.

These imperatives compel me to declare at the outset that I regard the Rhetoric Society of America—of which RSA50[1] will here be *pars pro toto*—as the undisputed avantgarde of rhetorical studies. Thus, that merry band of Europeans who traversed the Atlantic to attend the Society's 50th anniversary had travelled from the periphery to the center, from the provinces to the imperial capital of rhetoric. These Europeans had sought out the hub of their own field of research, and had now arrived—as you Americans say—to *where the action is*.

For European scholars of rhetoric, the proverb about the Romans is quite superfluous; most of the time, we already strive to do what you Americans do. There are certain—Francophone—exceptions to this rule, but overall, the rhetoric community in Europe has had a pronounced tendency to look across the Atlantic for inspiration, guidance, insight, and, well, most everything else. This is fact, not flattery. The United States is far ahead of the old world with regards to the institutionalization and professionalization of rhetoric studies. American rhetoricians might find that statement either depressing or hard to believe, considering the discipline's many institutional entanglements in the United States. It is nevertheless true. Certain European pioneers aside, the resurgence and professionalization of rhetoric in the twentieth century was largely an *American* accomplishment.

---

1. The 18th Biennial RSA Conference, in Minneapolis in 2018, marking the Society's 50th anniversary.

But let's move beyond encomium. After all, any doxa is tied to a particular time and place, and those who travel will therefore at some point have to confront difference. Like the provincials who travelled to the *urbs aeterna* in Antiquity, many of us Europeans who came to Minneapolis for RSA50 felt not only gratitude and awe and kinship and a deep connection, but also a certain strangeness. I am not referring to the absurdly low indoor temperatures or the ridiculous amount of meat in your sandwiches, but to the contemporary configurations of American rhetoric, as they were on display at RSA50. In some quite specific ways—though certainly not in every way—these configurations seemed to many of us quite *strange*.

Before I elaborate on this feeling of estrangement and speculate about some of its causes—which is my modest aim here—I should perhaps explain why I feel so curiously entitled to speak on behalf of Europeans, using pronouns like "us" and "we." The explanation is quite banal, and will have to stand in as my exposition of method.

AN *IMPROMPTU* FIELDWORK EXPANDED

Having had an experience, *in situ* Minneapolis, of feeling somewhat estranged from certain aspects of the scholarship on display there, I began wondering whether my reaction was unique. I approached a few of my European colleagues in attendance: What did they think about that particular panel, the one on X? Did they hear the key note last night, and what did they make of it? What was their take on the ubiquity of panels on the subject of Y? Had they tried one of those ridiculously meat-filled sandwiches? And so forth. On the whole, this micro-ethnography led me to believe that I was in fact *not* alone in feeling somewhat estranged: many of my European colleagues thought that American rhetoricians were strange on just the same counts that I found them to be so.

Having returned home, I expanded this micro-ethnography into something a tad more systematic, by approaching all the Europeans listed in the RSA50 program, requesting short interviews.[2] The interviews were in principle open-ended and semi-structured, but in practice most of them ended up

---

2. The interviews were done by telephone, chat or e-mail. In total, I did 13 interviews. I made requests for interviews only to scholars from Europe. I excluded from the sample all Europeans currently working in the United States, as well as Americans working in Europe. This left 17 relevant scholars, of whom one turned out never to have made the trip. Three scholars never responded to my request. I promised those interviewed that their responses would be anonymized, and consequently, I have removed certain details concerning geography as well as some references to the respondents' own scholarship. I have also randomly changed certain other pieces of

having a fairly similar structure: they all began with a question about the Europeans' general impressions of RSA50; next, I would typically prompt them to compare what they had experienced at RSA50 with what they were used to from Europe; finally, most interviews ended with a question that touched on the main cause of my own estrangement—namely activism, partisanship, and conceptions of the political.

I will not pretend that this little reception study of the RSA50 gives us the European rhetoric community's "official" view of its American counterpart. The number of interviews is much too small for any such pretense, and the selection is skewed; for one thing, I've only talked to those Europeans who actually traveled to RSA50, that is, those who expected the event to be interesting enough to cross the Atlantic. In addition, the very notion of a "European rhetoric community" is troubled, as there are some notable differences among the rhetorical traditions in various parts of Europe.

But if the scope is limited and the selection skewed, these interviews do convey a sense of the "backstage" conversation among Europeans about our American friends, and in this sense, they are no more than an extension of the *impromptu* "interviews" that I did with my colleagues while still in Minneapolis. During these conversations, neither interviewer nor interviewee have been terribly concerned with matters of fact—that is, whether or not the views expressed are in fact correct. Rather, what surfaced in the interviews were impressions and (more or less well-argued) opinions. The reader will therefore have to forgive our gross simplifications and misunderstandings, and take what follows as a first step towards learning more about the differences and relation between these two academic communities.

As the Romans Do

With only a very few exceptions, my European colleagues expressed unforced and enthusiastic appreciation of RSA50, of RSA, and of American rhetoric in general. The basic tone among the Europeans was that, "the US, and RSA, is where you find the research front" (E1). More concretely, many of the Europeans expressed appreciation—one might even say awe—of the *diversity* and *audacity* of American rhetoric. One scholar said that rhetoric at RSA50 "was much wider in scale and more diverse in content than I had experienced at similar events in Europe," and added that, "the scale of rhetoric seemed vast." This contrasted with what he had experienced in his own country, where he was "used to struggling to make a case for drawing attention to rhetoric" (E3).

---

information, to disable identification of the respondents. The interviewees quoted are identified as *E1* and so on.

Many of the Europeans were struck simply by the size of the conference, and talked about the "enormous variety of topics in the panels and sessions" (E6) or the "width of topics covered" (E9). One confused European found himself constantly wondering "whether I had actually picked the right one to go to" (E11). Another scholar complimented the "breadth and energy represented by all [the] young and coming rhetorical scholars," as well as "the depth of discussions, particularly in so far as conceptual and theoretical perspectives of rhetoric are concerned" (E8). Another scholar remarked, as did several, that the "general quality of the papers is high," adding that, "the organization does an increasingly good job in inviting and organizing different panel and presentation formats" (E4).

Finally, a few remarked on the exceptionally collegial tone of the conference. One said that, "as a foreign participant, I felt welcome" (E4), while another said that she in the course of the conference began noticing "how polite everyone was," complimenting the Americans on their "friendliness and notable willingness to congratulate, thank and positively listen to all papers regardless of the theme or the claims being made," as well as on their "patience and attentiveness" (E3).

Admittedly, some of my European colleagues were more critical of what they encountered at RSA50. One was particularly disgruntled with the experience. He did not see "RSA50 as an 'event' in the true meaning of the word," he said, but rather as an expression of "an ever more hard-pressed scholarly industry struggling for financing and educational and societal acceptance." The "sheer volume of the event makes it overwhelming," he argued, and added that the conference was rather more like a showground for "the latest intellectual trend" and for "isolated, short-lived fads." He felt that the RSA50 was more accurately seen as an "epideictic gesture," as "more like a carnival or pop concert than an actual conference" (E7).

Rhetorical Sprawl

While this particular scholar was alone in making an assessment this harsh, his response hinted at issues that surfaced in several of the other interviews. These objections had to do partly with the size and format of RSA50, but also partly with certain more substantial trends within American rhetoric. Much of the scholarship at RSA50 "seemed to have very little, if any, relation to what traditionally has been understood by rhetoric," argued the same scholar. He added that this "lack of focus and structure left the impression that rhetoric is an all-encompassing theory, which I think in the long run could harm the very core of rhetorical studies," specifically by robbing it of its "power to critically analyze the pressing questions of today's society" (E7).

As a witness to the academic sprawl at RSA50, this scholar felt that American rhetoric lacks a *core*—a word he did in fact use, which he apparently connected to rhetorical *tradition*—another word he used. And he suggested that without these things, rhetoric would forfeit its chance of addressing the pressing questions of the day. Another scholar remarked similarly that, "The sheer breadth of the rhetorical field is generous in its inclusivity but diminished a sense of feeling urgent or in some way dangerous" (E3).

It seems strange that Europeans' estrangement should come from the perceived political impotence of American rhetoric studies, considering how the American tradition seems, in many ways, thoroughly infused by politics. As a case in point, Andrea Lunsford proposed, in her key note speech, that "narrative justice" should become the goal towards which the discipline should strive. What makes the European reaction even more perplexing is that remarks such as those above were balanced by explicit statements of *disapproval* of the political nature of the research on display at RSA50. One said: "From the vantage point of the European tradition, one could accuse some American rhetoric scholars with a penchant for intervention and activist scholarship of substituting scientific inquiry and knowledge production with political advocacy" (E5). Another noted that "the activism rolled into much of the research presented at RSA is too much, and there were panels I opted out of because I expected them to be more about displaying 'solidarity' than about inquiry into the matter at hand" (E4).

The Political Impotence of the Partisan

This conundrum, how Europeans could fault the Americans for being politically impotent and too political at the same time, needs some unpacking. One explanation could be that while certain Europeans adhered to the former view, others subscribed to latter. That is not exactly what emerges from my interviews, however, and I suspect that a somewhat more complex explanation is needed. The conundrum has something to do, I think, with how the Atlantic forms a divide between two different conceptions of "politics." It is not that European rhetoric scholars strive to be apolitical. To the contrary: one often finds among European rhetoricians a deep-seated desire to give back to society, and European rhetoric often justifies itself by the service it can provide to politics. For a European, however, to offer "service to politics" means, roughly, to contribute insight that might somehow help improve our public lives together, where "our" refers to more or less everyone. The common attitude in Europe is that if and to the extent rhetoric is to serve politics, it cannot—it *must* not—assume a partisan conception of politics.

I believe this is where many European rhetoricians have a somewhat more "traditional" conception of the utility and purpose of their own discipline than do the Americans, since for us Europeans, "politics" by definition refers to matters of collective, socially universal concern. An understanding along these lines was elaborated by one of the European scholars:

> Especially in Germany, rhetoric is seen as a people's art. Rhetoricians at Scandinavian universities are also preoccupied with the idea that rhetoric is to be of use to the common person, to everybody. There is normativity in Europe too, but in a different way. In Scandinavia and many other European countries, the universities are all public, and because of that, there is this basic notion that the tax payer is paying for the work I do as a rhetorician. In addition, there is here a pedagogical idea that the function of rhetoric is to teach people to express themselves, as well as to demask those who express themselves deceptively, a broad understanding that includes everyone. (E1)

It might look as if European rhetoricians have a tendency to conceive of politics as a harmonious, consensus-driven utopia, but this does not follow strictly from the basic assumption. The *universalism* embedded in the European view does not presuppose *unity*. It does entail, however, that the contribution rhetoric offers to politics, and the way in which rhetoric can give back to society, is seen as something more general and indirect than what many American scholars apparently assume.

On Not Identifying with Identity Politics

For several of the European scholars, the Atlantic marked a distinction, most basically, between different views of the salience and role of *groups* in society. American rhetoric scholarship, noted several of the European scholars, is far more distinctly branded by identity politics than is its European equivalent. The Americans are "more preoccupied by identity politics and by the condition of particular groups in society," noted one, and added that there is hence "more of a focus in the American tradition on rhetorical activism" (E1). Another implicitly framed the issue in terms of an opposition between the particular and the general:

> To put it very bluntly, and certainly overstating it, I at times felt that panels were more oriented toward professing *particular political views* and confirming each other in their correctness, and this *at the expense of more general points* educating me about rhetorical

phenomena in the world or how they are theoretically interesting. (E4, emphasis added)

The same scholar said that he had no illusions that his own work was objective or neutral, noting that "I think almost every aspect of it is value laden in one way or another." His complaint with some of the American scholarship, then, was that "it sometimes is downright political in ways that make it irrelevant to colleagues with different political views" (E4). Again, for the Europeans, rhetoric can be placed in the service of politics, as long as it, in the process, does not become irrelevant to those with different political views.

Another scholar elaborated the issue of groups nicely when she said that, "I think European and American rhetoric parts ways in their respective ideas of *whom* rhetoric is there *for*."

> In Europe there is no idea that rhetoric is supposed to serve *particular groups*. In the US, this is different. It might have to do with the role of slavery in American culture, this thinking along group lines, that over time, concern is supposed to encompass a steadily larger number of "groups"; rhetoric is seen to do work that aids the cause of, say, black people, and then another group, and then another one, all the way until you get to dolphins. (E1, emphasis added)

In the United States, she continued, many rhetoricians appear to think that it is the job of rhetoric "to fight for disenfranchised groups, whereas here, in Europe, we tend to think that they must fight their own causes. And rhetoric is then seen as a more *overarching* art, which is there to teach *everyone* how to demask manipulation and so on" (E1, emphasis added).

This goes some way towards explaining the conundrum above, since if you assume that rhetoric can serve politics only if "politics" refers to a set of socially universal concerns, then activism on behalf of a particular group— i.e. partisanship, advocacy—will be a dead end. On the one hand, it will be poor scholarship, since it, as one scholar noted, substitutes "scientific inquiry and knowledge production with political advocacy," and on the other it will be poor politics, since it diminishes, as another noted, "a sense of feeling urgent or in some way dangerous." The assumption underlying this view is that, while it is easy to be a partisan, to be a *citizen* is hard work.

THE RETURN

As *peroratio*, reparations. The Europeans who travelled to RSA50 came not because they had nothing better to do. They came because they desired to be part of the global research front of rhetoric, which they agreed was in the

United States. These same Europeans left Minneapolis feeling enlightened, emboldened, and inspired on behalf of their own discipline. At the same time, some of them also felt the estrangement that almost invariably ensues when one moves from one doxa to another.

It is of course a gross simplification to talk of "American rhetoric" as my informants (and I) have done here. The American rhetoric community, no less than the European, is divided. So when I leaked some of the Europeans' impressions to an American colleague of mine, he said simply that, "I am not as sanguine as some people about [what] you saw on display." Instead of identity politics-based scholars who tended to "see their power almost purely in resistance," he referred me to resources in the American tradition that could conceive of rhetoric's service to politics in a more comprehensive and optimistic way, namely the Deweyan one. And it is indeed a paradox that, while the great American philosopher John Dewey is "not such a big deal in Europe," as my American colleague also noted, there is a great deal of overlap between his ideas and what I have described as a European view of politics.

What, then, is to be done? The question is misplaced, since the purpose here has been more epideictic than deliberative. Just as Europeans' ideas of optimal indoor temperatures and appropriate meat-to-bread ratios will continue to differ from that of their American counterparts, the same is probably true of their respective conceptions of rhetoric. We may nevertheless hope to develop more effective means of transport across the intellectual Atlantic that separates European from American rhetoricians, so that exchanges can be made in a spirit of appreciation, and not resentment. A first step towards that aim will be to study each other's ways.

Why Do We Study Rhetoric? How Should We Do It? Who Should We Do It For? Greetings from a Rhetorical Cousin Living at the Edge of Europe

Jens E. Kjeldsen

What can rhetoricians from the United States learn from their Scandinavian cousins? Not much, perhaps. On the other hand, though, it does seem that Scandinavian rhetoric scholars may offer a different perspective on the role and function of rhetorical scholarship. Hopefully, this may contribute to a joint effort of Europe and the US in building the future of rhetoric.

In Scandinavia, where I am from, the study of rhetoric has mostly followed American trends in research. When I studied rhetoric at the University of Copenhagen in the early 1990s, the United States stood out as a magical place, from where all relevant and significant rhetorical theory flowed. I can still remember the utter excitement when I as a young student went to the university library to pick up a research article by the American Professor David Zarefsky. I had waited for weeks. The text had been sent by mail all the way from the United States. Yes, this was before Internet and email. Leaving the library, I felt I was holding a gem of knowledge in my hand – and of course, I was. Now, as a professor of rhetoric and visual communication I have attended the RSA conferences many times. I have lived in the cradle of modern rhetorical theory and criticism as a visiting scholar at the University of California, Berkeley, and at Northwestern University. I have even had coffee with David Zarefsky.

So, the US has come to Europe, and Europe has come to the US. Even though the two once-separate worlds have now been bridged, Scandinavian scholars appear to have developed a distinctive approach that differs somewhat from the American. As I have mentioned elsewhere ("The Rhetoric of Sound"), there seems to be an epistemological and stylistic divide between rhetoric and communication studies in the US and Europe. European, and especially Scandinavian, studies in rhetoric are predominantly occupied with exploring the objects of rhetoric in their own right: What is rhetoric? How do people use rhetoric? How is rhetoric performed in different genres and changed by new media? Many American rhetoric and communication studies appear to be predominantly occupied with political engagement on behalf of groups that are considered disenfranchised or oppressed. From a Scandinavian point-of-view, the approach to rhetoric in some US communication departments seems strangely foreign. In many ways, these US studies in rhetoric appear to do what we have been taught not to do, and now teach our own students to refrain from: Taking political sides. So, we are puzzled by the amount of US publications that are openly activist, politicized, and acting on behalf of groups.

We are also slightly puzzled by the style of writing. The Scandinavian tradition of rhetorical studies aims at writing and communicating research as accessible and clearly as possible – even in research journals. It is seen not only as a scholarly ethos, but also as a public duty. From this Nordic point of view, much rhetorical work from the US carries an excessive amount of theorizing and conceptualization. To some of us, it sometimes seems that the more zealously we theorize, the more we transform our objects of study into concepts used to create other concepts, the more we end up moving away from the very object that we seek to understand, and into a self-sustaining exegesis of concepts. In contrast to this trend, I carry a feeling of obligation that research must be relevant, understandable and of value to the general public, and I believe that many of my Scandinavian colleagues feel the same way. You are expected to share your insights with people outside academia, and you are expected to do it in a way that may enlighten or help them in their everyday lives. This sense of public obligation affects both the topics chosen for research and the way research is written. Plain understandable prose is the preferred writing style. I can still remember one of the central tenets of my teacher at the University of Copenhagen, Professor Jørgen Fafner (1925-2005), who was the founding father of the study of rhetoric in Denmark – and in Scandinavia in general. He often told us: you have only understood something properly, if you are able to explain it to others, so that they may also understand it (cf. Fafner).

This is what most Scandinavian rhetoricians try to do: Examine issues that are relevant to the public, write research papers as accessible as possible, and participate in the public debate by communicating the scholarly insight in an enlightening and educational way to the population. Such communication is done by writing articles for newspapers, being interviewed in broadcast media, participating in debates, and giving talks to the general public – from pupils to pensioners. There is even a specific Scandinavian word for this kind of communication: "formidling." Germans would say "Vermittlung," but the word does not really exist in English. Normally, it is translated to dissemination, mediation or simply communication. However, none of these words captures the sense of translation from research to everyday prose, or the informing and educational character of this kind of public communication. Actually, such communication, "formidling," is one of three duties established by law for Scandinavian scholars: research, teach, and communicate ("formidle").

Of course, not all rhetoric research and scholars in Scandinavia fit the picture I have described.[1] Similarly, not all American scholars fit the contrasting picture. Still, it is a picture that does help distinguish the study of rhetoric in Denmark, Norway, and Sweden from the study of rhetoric in the United States. In general, Scandinavian research is less abstractly theoretical than research in the US Mostly, studies are about political rhetoric examined through rhetorical criticism. This is the case for Denmark, where the main approaches in the study of political rhetoric are either rhetorical criticism of selected specimens, representing genres or themes, *or* theoretically informed approaches, leaning on political theory and practical philosophy, but still based on qualitative studies of examples (Kock). In both approaches, an evaluative orientation is often central in the sense that the scholar seeks a normative assessment of the studied discourse. Scholars apply concepts and criteria for democratic communication that they seek to develop in a combination of analysis and theory.

Sweden has focused on historical and pedagogical studies as well as studies of climate rhetoric, which is dominant at Södertörn University. Literary studies was the field that rhetorical research first began in the 1970s and 1980s at the Universities of Uppsala and Stockholm. Today, these institutions continue this approach, but also do historical and political work, as well as philosophically oriented work inspired by Chaïm Perelman (Rosengren) and Cornelius Castoriadis. The University of Lund, on the other hand, has specialized in didactics and pedagogy; Örebro has a tradition of feminist rhetoric and studies on non-verbal rhetoric.

---

1. For an account of the study of rhetoric in Scandinavia see Kjeldsen, Jens E. and Jan Grue. *Scandinavian Studies in Rhetoric. Rhetorica Scandinavica 1997–2010*. Retorikförlaget, 2011. The introductory chapter, "The Study of Rhetoric in Scandinavia" (7-38), provides a historical overview from the 1970s to 2010.

In Norway, research and teaching in rhetoric is primarily done at the University of Oslo and the University of Bergen. In Oslo, the main interests are texts norms and text cultures, conversations analysis, and the study of non-fiction prose. In Norwegian, this field is termed "saklitteratur," which does not have an English equivalent, but in German would translate into "Sachliteratur." These studies look at a wide range of everyday prose texts ranging from children's drawings, to documents from public authorities, or speeches by politicians (cf. Berge). In Bergen the study of rhetoric has been focused on political speechmaking and speechwriting (Johansen and Kjeldsen; Kjeldsen et al.) and political rhetoric in general. Political debates in broadcasting, for instance, is a growing field of interest. A large project on the Scandinavian immigration debate, called *Scanpub,* has several researchers examining rhetorical aspects of the debate, such as argumentation and the rhetorical constitution of actors in the debate.[2] Another theme in Bergen has been visual rhetoric and multimodal rhetoric (Kjeldsen, "Visual Rhetorical Argumentation"). A recent move in the study of rhetoric initiated and lead from the rhetoric group at the University of Bergen is the project *Rhetorical audience studies.* This project involved scholars from Denmark and Norway as well as the UK and US. It is worth mentioning, because it illustrates the Scandinavian inclination towards the practical and the empirical, and the orientation towards the public and the rhetorical life of the everyday. At the same time, it breaks with parts of the dominant tradition of rhetorical studies in both Scandinavia and, I believe, the US. It does so by introducing the field of *rhetorical reception studies* and insisting that rhetoricians should more often study rhetorical audiences empirically. This is done in the book from the project (Kjeldsen, *Rhetorical Audiences*).

The move towards empirical audience studies was attempted in the US already in 1998 by Jennifer Stromer-Galley and Edward Schiappa, when they published the paper "The Argumentative Burdens of Audience Conjectures: Audience Research in Popular Culture Criticism." Here, they argued that rhetoricians should do more empirical reception and audience analysis through the use of focus groups. This methodological move met resistance and twenty years later, in 2018, they admitted that the effect of the paper had been modest in their "initial target audience." They admit that: "Among rhetorical scholars in the United States, at least, our position did not gain widespread acceptance" (Stromer-Galley and Schiappa).

Like Stromer-Galley and Schiappa, my colleagues and I in Bergen found it peculiar that so few rhetoricians carry out audience and reception studies. After all, without audiences, there simply is no rhetoric. If we do not un-

---

2. See: https://scanpub.w.uib.no/

derstand how empirical audiences react to rhetoric, then we simply do not understand rhetoric. So, why do rhetoricians not examine these audiences empirically more often? There are, of course, many reasons for this. One may be the redefinition of rhetoric as the study of meaning and symbol use beginning in the late 1960s (Blair 41). Another may be the fact that doing empirical audience studies is cumbersome and time consuming. However, a reason for the neglect of reception studies, which is more closely connected to the theme of the present paper, is the ideological aspects of academic identity and scholarly self-understanding. The rhetorician sees herself as an intellectual who interprets the world and its rhetorical complexities through her special intellectual capacities and her academic ability to analyze and provide judgement. This puts the scholar in a privileged position. The scholar becomes the "expert reader", the brilliant, discerning mind (Middleton et al. 10f.). From this point of view, doing reception studies and listening to audiences entails a loss of position and power. Instead of explaining the world to people, you listen to people in order to understand the world. In a more modest version of this self-image, rhetorical critics see themselves as surrogates for audiences. However, critics cannot function as surrogates for audiences, simply because they are very different from those audiences.

There are good reasons for rhetoricians to do empirical audience studies through interviews, focus groups, and ethnographic methods. First, audience studies provide an opportunity to examine the rhetorical, interpretative labor done by audiences. Rhetorical utterances have neither one unequivocal and definite meaning nor a universal deterministic effect on audiences. That is why rhetoric has been termed the study of misunderstanding and its remedies (Richards). We also know this from a broad spectrum of theories, which teach us that audiences are always active participants in any communicative exchange. Reception theory describes how a reader must cognitively fill out the gaps and open places in any text (Holub). Semiotics demonstrates how communication in general is polysemic and open (Barthes; Eco). Pragmatics and relevance theory shows how language works through implicature, requiring conversational partners to constantly make inferences (Clark; Wilson and Sperber). This is particularly relevant for rhetorical argumentation, because it is enthymematic and leaves it to the audience to fill in the gaps and missing premises (Bitzer). If we want to find out how the communicative work done by audiences is carried out, and establish what it means—which are essential rhetorical tasks — then the best way to find out is do audience studies.

Not only are rhetorical texts polysemic, it can be difficult to determine exactly what and where the rhetorical text is. Traditional rhetorical criticism analyzed discrete and clearly demarcated texts. However, in in our contemporary and fragmented media environment it can be challenging to determine which text an audience has actually experienced. This is especially pertinent online where communication is constantly produced, copied, shared and changed. Online communication is interactive, intertextual and transitory. It is increasingly segmented and personalized by the use of algorithms creating different texts for different groups—even for individuals. In this situation, the best way of finding out which texts—or rather flow of communication—people have experienced is to talk to them or observe them. Audience studies not only help us see that texts are polysemic and audiences are active, but also that audience interpretation and decoding are not completely free and incidental (Condit).

Audience studies, then, are not only a way of understanding the power of the audience; it is also a way of understanding the power of rhetoric—in situ and in general. Audience and reception studies also offer a way to understand "the other." If we truly wish to understand the persuasiveness of appeals we find surprising or even worrisome, we will not find good answers by speculating about the values or (lack of) intelligence of the audience.

If we seek answers only by putting ourselves in the place of "the other," playing the role of people different than ourselves, we will neither understand them nor the rhetoric they find appealing. It is obvious, for instance, that the rhetoric of Donald J. Trump in the US election campaign of 2016 was received very differently by supporters and opponents. To many, the appeal and success of Mr. Trump's rhetoric was surprising, almost inexplicable. The answers could have been found by paying more attention to the audiences that found his rhetoric convincing, for instance, through studies of the reception of his speeches and tweets, or through ethnographic conversations with supporters of the tea party movement and Trump (as done by Hochschild).

Audience and reception-oriented approaches offer a way for rhetorical research to acknowledge the impact and effect of rhetoric without relying on a simple transmission model of communication. Rhetorical reception studies acknowledge that rhetoric has the power to do something to audiences they encounter. The main aim of rhetorical audience studies is to understand the interaction between the rhetorical situation, the characteristics of the utterances, and the audience uptake and its negotiation of the rhetoric. Instead of moving conjecturally from textual traits to assumed effect, reception studies allow the researcher to also move from response to text, in order to establish the rhetorical traits that may have contributed to the response.

The modern study of rhetoric began in America, and the US is still the leading nation. However, other nations and regions have followed, and different perspectives and methods have evolved. One of these regions, as I have described, is Scandinavia. In order to make sure that rhetorical research continues to be relevant in our time, it is imperative that we pay attention to the audience and to the different scholarly perspectives and research methods around the world. This is how we may evolve together. This is how we simultaneously celebrate the past and build the future.

Works Cited

Barthes, Roland. *Image, Music, Text.* edited by Stephen Heath, Hill and Wang, 1977.
Berge, Kjell Lars. "Rhetoric and the Study of Texts, Text Norms and Text Cultures." *Scandinavian Studies in Rhetoric. Rhetorica Scandinavica 1997-2010*, edited by Jens E. Kjeldsen and Jan Grue, vol. 2010, Retorikförlaget, 1997, pp. 88-105.
Bitzer, Lloyd F. "Aristotle's Enthymeme Revisited." *Quarterly Journal of Speech*, vol. 45, no. 4, 1959, pp. 399-408, doi:10.1080/00335635909382374.
Blair, Carole. ""We Are All Just Prisoners Here of of Our Own Device" Rhetoric in Speech Communication after Wingspread." *The Effects of Rhetoric and the Rhetoric of Effects*, edited by Amos Kiewe and Davis W. Houck, University of South Carolina, 2015, pp. 31-58.
Clark, Billy. *Relevance Theory*. Cambridge University Press, 2013.
Condit, Celeste Michelle. "The Rhetorical Limits of Polysemy." *The Routledge Reader in Rhetorical Criticism*, edited by Brian L. Ott and Greg Dickinson, Routledge, 2013.
Eco, Umberto. *The Role of the Reader. Explorations in the Semiotics of Texts*. Indiana University Press, 1979.
Fafner, Jørgen. "The Focal Point of Rhetoric." *Scandinavian Studies in Rhetoric. Rhetorica Scandinavica 1997-2010*, edited by Jens E. Kjeldsen and Jan Grue, Retorikförlaget 2011, pp. 56-75.
Hochschild, Arlie Russell. *Strangers in Their Own Land. Anger and Mourning on the American Right*. The New Press, 2016.
Holub, Robert C. *Reception Theory. A Critical Introduction*. Routledge, 2003.
Johansen, Anders, and Jens Kjeldsen. *Virksomme Ord: Politiske Taler 1814-2005*. Universitetsforlaget, 2005.
Kjeldsen, Jens E. "The Rhetoric of Sound, the Sound of Arguments. Three Propositions, Three Questions, and an Afterthought for the Study of Sonic and Multimodal Argumentation." *Argumentation and Advocacy*, vol. 54, no. 4, 2018, pp. 364-371.
—, editor. *Rhetorical Audiences and the Reception of Rhetoric. Exploring Audiences Empirically*. Palgrave Macmillan, 2018.
—. "Visual Rhetorical Argumentation." *Semiotica: Journal of the International Association for Semiotic Studies*, vol. 2018, no. 220, 2018, pp. 69-94.
Kjeldsen, Jens E., and Jan Grue. *Scandinavian Studies in Rhetoric. Rhetorica Scandinavica 1997-2010*. Retorikförlaget, 2011.
Kjeldsen, Jens E. et al. *Speechwriting in Theory and Practice*. Palgrave, 2019.
Kock, Christian. "The Identity of Rhetoric as a Scholarly Discipline and a University Program." *Scandinavian Studies in Rhetoric. Rhetorica Scandinavica 1997-2010*, edited by Jens E. Kjeldsen, Retorikförlaget, 2011, pp. 40-55.

Middleton, Michael et al. *Participatory Critical Rhetoric: Theoretical and Methodological Foundations for Studying Rhetoric in Situ.* Lexington Books, 2015.

Richards, I. A. *The Philosophy of Rhetoric.* Oxford University Press, 1936.

Rosengren, Mats. "On Doxa." *Scandinavian Studies in Rhetoric. Rhetorica Scandinavica 1997-2010*, edited by Jens E. Kjeldsen and Jan Grue, Retorikförlaget, 2011, pp. 156-167.

Stromer-Galley, Jennifer, and Edward Schiappa. "The Argumentative Burdens of Audience Conjectures: Adience Research in Popular Culture Criticism." *Rhetorical Audience Studies and Reception of Rhetoric. Exploring Audiences Empirically*, edited by Jens E. Kjeldsen, Palgrave Macmillan, 2018, pp. 43-83.

Wilson, Deirdre, and Dan Sperber. *Meaning and Relevance.* Cambridge University Press, 2012.

RHETORICAL INTERVENTIONS

Do I Look Fat in this Essay?

Abby Knoblauch

In their 2015 *Peitho* article "Embodiment: Embodying Feminist Rhetorics," Maureen Johnson, Daisy Levy, Katie Manthey, and Maria Novotny argue that "to think about rhetoric, we must think about bodies" (39). Those working in embodied rhetoric would certainly agree; within the last few decades, scholars have turned more pointed attention toward embodied writing and embodied rhetoric: an explicit referencing of the body within scholarly texts as a way to make clearer the role of the physical body in the making (and interpretation) of knowledge, and as a way to challenge the presumption of a white masculinist cis-het rhetorical agent as the sole or primary theory-producer.

Those practicing embodied rhetorics work to reinscribe—or sometimes to simply recognize—the body within the text itself to make clearer that the body one lives in impacts the way one makes sense of the world, as well as the sense the world makes of them. In short, the way we move in the world is in and through our bodies, and the knowledge we make can therefore never be totally separated from our physical form. All knowledge is embodied knowledge. In this way, embodied rhetorics shares much with fields such as disability studies, critical race theory, feminist theory, and queer and trans* theory. Often left out of these conversations, however, are issues of body mass, body size. Jackie Wykes tells us that "fatness was largely elided in scholarship on the body prior to the emergence of fat studies. Even in work that explicitly engaged with 'embodied difference' or 'subversive' bodies, fatness was rarely mentioned, and the question of fat subjectivity and identity was almost never addressed" (3). Despite a cultural obsession with fatness (and nearly ubiquitous and desperate attempts to avoid it[1]), and despite work on thin privilege

---

1. While different cultural groups within the U.S. (and certainly worldwide) have varying relationships to fat and fatness, the hegemony of thinness is difficult

in feminist studies, legal studies, health and socio-medical studies, and the body positivity and fat activist and acceptance movements that Wykes references, I would argue that there is still a dearth of such scholarship in composition and rhetoric, a gap in our field concerning the intersections of fat studies and embodied rhetoric.

Given that the fat body has historically been tagged as hyper-corporeal, as really the most body-ish of bodies, the lack of discussion of the fat body within embodied rhetorics is striking. So I ask, is there no room for fat bodies in embodied rhetorics? Maybe such bodies, fat bodies, are really "out of bounds," as Jana Evans Braziel and Kathleen LeBesco have dubbed them in their fantastic collection of the same name. Maybe it's because it's not polite to talk about fat bodies in public[2]. It's something we're told we should be ashamed of, should be trying to hide. It's the horizontal stripes, the arm jiggle, the VBO—visible belly outline—of embodied rhetoric. Maybe rhetoric is meant to be the new black—slimming on everyone.

Or perhaps it's more that many of us can imagine linguistic, textual markers of race, ethnicity, sexual orientation, or gender identity, but we can't imagine textual or linguistic markers of fatness. And yet, that wasn't always the case. In 2003, William P. Banks wondered if, like his *physical* performance of queerness, there aren't textual performances in his writing that "out" him as queer. Ultimately, he concludes that there must be (30). Sixteen years later, many of us are now familiar with queer rhetorics and queer time; something that, to many, didn't seem textually visible now seems obvious, or at least often accepted, by the field. So, if a text can not only gesture to or reference the physical queer body, but if a text itself can be queer or queered, might the same be true of the fat body? The fat text? In other words, might there be linguistic markers or textual performances of fatness? I don't mean do fat people represent themselves in texts—of course they do and they always have; instead, if we can imagine queer rhetorics, trans*-rhetorics, African-American rhetorics, Chicanx rhetorics, rhetorics of disability, can we also imagine fat rhetorics? If so, what might that be? What would it mean to embody fatness in writing? And what do we risk by continuing to *ignore* fat bodies when we talk about embodied rhetorics?

To put it simply—probably too simply, to fail to reposition or recognize the fat body within the text further reinscribes a very limiting body privilege,

---

to ignore.

2. Oh, you're not fat. Don't call yourself fat. You're pleasantly plump. It upsets me when you call yourself fat. I don't think of you as fat. (When you call yourself fat, I don't know how to respond. It makes me uncomfortable.) You're not fat; you're beautiful.

reinforces thin-presumption, and reminds those with bodies that cross the boundaries of socially acceptable size that they should be neither seen nor heard, that their bodies should not be acknowledged as producers of knowledge, that their bodies are flawed and therefore not to be trusted, that their bodies are best kept secret, that their bodies are best hidden or erased, that their bodies are kept corseted and/or closeted. And since I'm a fat chick[3] who rarely stays quiet, I say screw that.

But embodied rhetoric is more than simply saying that you're one of the fat folk. Simply "outing" one's self as fat on the page, in the text, in your next article does little epistemological work[4]. Embodied rhetoric asks that we mark the ways that our bodies participate in knowledge-making. And my fat body impacts how I make meaning[5]. It impacts how meaning is made of me. Merleau-Ponty is helpful here, arguing that bodies aren't simply objects in the world, but are instead "our point of view in the world" (5). Elizabeth Grosz reframes this in particularly useful ways when she says that "The body is my being-to-the-world and as such is the instrument by which all information and knowledge is received and meaning is generated. It is through the body that the world of objects appears to me; it is in virtue of having/being a body that there are objects for me" (87). As theories of embodiment and embodied rhetoric illustrate, my body both shapes and is shaped by its experiences. It is through my body that I encounter the world. The self, whatever that is, isn't the body, that's true, but the two are intertwined; they make and are made by each other.

Before I try to flesh out what a fat rhetoric might look like (see what I did there), let me pause to note that I understand the potential problems with treating the body as a static object, as a fixed or discrete or stable entity, as a bounded thing. The body might be a symbiosis, a conglomeration of cells and bacteria. It might be a cyborg. It might be an assemblage. It might be a post-modern post-human myth. It might be, it might be, it might be. I'm

---

3. Oh, you're not fat. Don't call yourself fat. You're pleasantly plump. It upsets me when you call yourself fat. I don't think of you as fat. (When you call yourself fat, I don't know how to respond. It makes me uncomfortable.) You're not fat; you're beautiful.

4. Or outing yourself as thin, for that matter, although the cultural weight of thinness is, of course, quite different than the cultural weight of weightiness. The power dynamics are decidedly different.

5. Oh, you're not fat. Don't call yourself fat. You're pleasantly plump. It upsets me when you call yourself fat. I don't think of you as fat. (When you call yourself fat, I don't know how to respond. It makes me uncomfortable.) You're not fat; you're beautiful.

down with a lot of that. But when I walk into a room, when my body walks into the room, carrying that colony of bacteria in my gut with me, what people see aren't the bacteria. What people judge isn't the space between my cells, or the indeterminacy that is always already in process and progress when the body is in motion, all the possible motions and choices held in that potential, as Brian Massumi might say. They see a *body*—bounded if not fixed—and that body is visibly, inarguably FAT[6].

So, while the socio-medical definition of who "counts" as fat, as well as the assumptions and meanings that accompany this label, change over time and space and culture and place, right now, today, I sit here and am fat[7]. Sure, this might be a temporary state of being; certainly weight is always in flux, as are bodies. As Rosemarie Garland and Jasbir Puar both remind us, all bodies are in a state of decay, are in only temporary stages of ability. We might also consider that all bodies are only in temporary and varying states of mass: we will all gain weight, lose weight, and as all of the research shows, those of us who lose large amounts of weight are almost certain to gain it back again within a few years (can you see my hand raised? Is your hand raised, too?). The body is always in process[8], but most of us live in what Gayle Salamon (and others) explains as a state of proprioception, the sense that makes it possible to feel our bodies as whole, contiguous entities rather than as separate parts (2-4). Similarly, most of us live our day-to-day lives as if we were at least somewhat stable: we experience that felt sense not only in that our limbs and torso are a coherent whole (for many of us, at least), but also the sense that there is an "I" here, that when I reference myself there's some sense of self that holds it all together, despite the problems with that assumption. And that when I reference my body, there's an "it" that I'm referring to. I recently had

---

6. Oh, you're not fat. Don't call yourself fat. You're pleasantly plump. It upsets me when you call yourself fat. I don't think of you as fat. (When you call yourself fat, I don't know how to respond. It makes me uncomfortable.) You're not fat; you're beautiful.

7. Oh, you're not fat. Don't call yourself fat. You're pleasantly plump. It upsets me when you call yourself fat. I don't think of you as fat. (When you call yourself fat, I don't know how to respond. It makes me uncomfortable.) You're not fat; you're beautiful.

8. And here I resist the cultural assumption that fat bodies are works in *progress*— that those fat folk who are attempting to lose weight are working toward a "better" version of themselves. The progress narrative of diet and change is flawed from the jump, presuming that the body you live in, if not thin (and if not white, if not "abled," if not particularly pleasing in particularly pleasing—often patriarchal— ways) is not, itself, enough. Is not, itself, complete.

one of my big toenails removed and "aggressively cauterized" and I can tell you that in that moment I was *very* rooted in my body.

So, that caveat notwithstanding, it might be this very nature of flux and plurality—the fact that a person's weight varies not only over a lifetime, of course, but over the course of a day—that can point us toward some possible characteristics of a fat rhetoric. Not simply the description of fatness, nor the revelation of fatness, nor analyses and discussions and unpackings of how fat folk are represented in fiction, television, movies, magazines; nor the facile "admission" in an article that I am, in fact, a fat chick[9]. What I'm interested in in this particular project is not so much how fat folk represent themselves or are represented in media—there's some fantastic work already being done in those areas, but instead, to carve out a space for fat embodied rhetorics. To imagine what a fat rhetoric might look like within that theoretical framework. In order to do so, we need to look at how the fat body, and perhaps especially the fat female body, has been, *scare-quotes,* "understood."

For example, Sarah Shieff (citing Mary Russo who draws on Bakhtin), has explained that the perception of the ideal body has historically been marked as male; more specifically, as the "static, self-contained male body" (217). In opposition, the female body, and particularly what is considered the fat and therefore often grotesque female body, has been imagined, in Russo's words, as an "open, protruding, extended, secreting body. It is the body of becoming, process and change" (qtd. in Shieff 217). The ideal body, then, is contained, tidy, ordered (and male), in part because such physiques were believed to embody the ideal of rationality, also coded male. The rational MIND was ordered and logical, so the ideal BODY, too, reflected the desire for rationality, mastery, and control. Jana Evans Braziel, however, illustrates ways in which the body itself has historically been associated with mutability and fluctuation, contrasting that with the "metaphysical ideas of immutability, stasis, and solid resistance to transformation" (242). In other words, the changeable body is of this world; to find big "T" truth one must transcend the body, to move beyond the messy corporeality of bodily function. To marshal the body, to deprive it of base and worldly desires, was a step in the right direction.

Within this framework, the ideal body reflects the rational mind, but the body AS BODY is believed to drive one toward irrationality, emotion, corporeal excess. We can attempt to control the body, and, according to such bina-

---

9. Oh, you're not fat. Don't call yourself fat. You're pleasantly plump. It upsets me when you call yourself fat. I don't think of you as fat. (When you call yourself fat, I don't know how to respond. It makes me uncomfortable.) You're not fat; you're beautiful.

ries, SHOULD attempt such control, should attempt to force the body to not only respond to the ordered drive of a rational mind, to be contained within a tight package, but also to correspond to the organizational schemas of rationality itself. But the fat body is very much body, is literally *lots* of body, is SO body, and as such is generally read, both historically and contemporarily, as a sort of failure of rationality written in flesh, a reflection of desire over reason, of emotion over logical thought.

And the fat body has long been associated with excess—excess adipose tissue, excess flesh, excess skin, but also excessive eating and drinking, and, at times, excessive bodily gasses and fluids. The fat body, especially the fat female body, has been imagined as liquid, uncontainable, intent on escaping its boundaries, spilling over the attempts to bind it, leaking and seeping actual bodily fluids (Braziel). Even more pointedly (and complicatedly) Braziel argues that by hyper-embodying the very nature of flux, a concept of mutability that posed complications for the perceived intransience of metaphysical binaries, "fat female bodies undermine the stability of Western metaphysical and dualistic thought: they topple philosophical binarisms," binarisms in which thought and reason are divorced from the body itself (232).

Of course, such characterizations of the fat body and of fat folk are deeply problematic, but they persist. Oh do they persist. Fat folk are believed to be less intelligent, less driven, less capable than thinner folk. They're seen as slovenly, lazy, messy, animalistic; they suffer from too much body, too little control, too little restraint, too little *mind*. This is not only hurtful and prejudiced, it's also just crap. But fat activists are working to reclaim the fat body and perceptions of it, so I want to set that aside for now, important as it is. Instead, I want us to consider what would happen if we think about fat bodies as those that *refuse* to be controlled (as many fat activists have been encouraging us to do)[10]. What happens if we see fat bodies as taking up space in a way that challenges the allotments of space that apparently, somewhere along the line, we were "allocated." And then what happens if we replace the word "bodies" in those sentences with the word "rhetorics?"

Let me start to pull this all together. If fat bodies make hyper-visible the constantly fluctuating body-ness of the body itself (and keeping in mind, of course, that the mind is also body), then might fat *rhetoric* challenge not only the mind-body split, but also the valorization of *disembodied* academic prose that focuses on mind over matter and continually attempts to erase the impact and influence of the body? This is embodied rhetoric writ large, pun

---

10. Andrea Shaw, for example, argues that the fat black female body "resists both imperatives of whiteness and slenderness as an ideal state of embodiment" (9). This notion of resistance implies a sense of agency that is often denied fat folks' bodies.

intended. Given what we've been told about fat bodies, might fat rhetoric, then, be writing that intentionally resists overly-rational control, resists the constructed boundaries of genre or propriety? Could it be writing that spills over the edges, escapes its container, opens up space in parentheticals, footnotes, asides, ellipses, dashes, lists, insisting on making visible a-bit-of-that-some-of-that-much-of-that-all-of that that we're often told to hide? Could it challenge that masculinist fetish (you heard me) for neat and tidy prose? Could it refuse to excise the excess the excess the excess the excess the excess the excess? Could it redefine excess itself? Could it literally flow over, push at the margins, push past the boundaries, make itself and mark itself as large? As containing multitudes?

And I know what some of you are thinking. I'm asking those questions and you're thinking, "No. No it can't do that. That's sloppy writing." Ah, such a loaded term, sloppy, so often associated with food and with fatness and with fat folk eating fat-folk-food. But don't worry, this isn't to say that anything goes—this is *rhetoric*, after all, and our symbol usage must be purposeful. But might fat rhetoric, like fat folk in fat bodies, attempt to resist the too-often damaging, dehumanizing, debilitating, destructive restrictions and, instead, celebrate that which is made to be cut out, FORCED to be cut out, that which is deemed shameful and removed? Might it, like the fat chick rocking the bikini, might it just say oh screw you, I'm not hiding myself, not removing from sight those things that YOU deem unsightly? Might it be organized in ways that are not necessarily rational, and yet are functioning just fine thank you? Might it luxuriate for a moment in the joys of language, the sound of words in the ear, the feel of words in the mouth? The lick of those Ls and the pucker of those Ps? Might it remind us that there are other ways of being, other ways of expression, other ways of rhetoric-ing? And might it remind us that other doesn't have to be Other?

Le'a Kent tells us that valuing images of the fat body "requires undermining the process of abjection that makes fat women's bodies synonymous with the offensive, horrible, or deadly aspects of embodiment. It requires finding a way of representing the self that is not body-neutral or disembodied (and therefore presumptively thin), but intimately connecting with the body in a new vision of embodiment that no longer disdains the flesh" (131). Let's hear that again: "Intimately connecting with the body in a new vision of embodiment that no longer disdains the flesh" (131). Making room for fat rhetorics might do the same: recognize an attempt to connect with the fleshy body in the text in a way that challenges normative assumptions about both bodies and texts. Because "when bodies take up spaces that they were not intended to inhabit, something other than the reproduction of the facts of the matter happen" (Ahmed 62). Fat rhetorics, then, might claim aspects of embodiment and textuality that have often been abject, and, therefore, unimaginable, unspeakable, certainly unpublishable, meant only for the private sphere. They might find a new way to take up textual and intellectual public space, refusing to stay hidden and quiet, pushing beyond reproduction and toward creation. "You might be fat," the discourse community whispers, "but do you have to be so public about it?[11]" I think it might be time that I answer, unashamed, yes.

Works Cited

Ahmed, Sara. *Queer Phenomenology: Orientations, Objects, Others*. Duke UP, 2006.
Banks, William P. "Written Through the Body: Disruptions and 'Personal' Writing." *College English*, vol. 66, no. 1, 2003, pp. 21-40.
Braziel, Jana Evans. "Sex and Fat Chics: Deterritorializing the Fat Female Body." Braziel and LeBesco, pp. 231-254.
Braziel, Jana Evans and Kathleen LeBesco, editors. *Bodies Out of Bounds: Fatness and Transgression*. University of California Press, 2001.
Garland Thomson, Rosemarie. *Extraordinary Bodies: Figuring Physical Disability in American Culture and Literature*. Columbia UP, 1997.
Grosz, Elizabeth. *Volatile Bodies: Toward a Corporeal Feminism*. Indiana UP, 1994.
Johnson, Maureen, Daisy Levy, Katie Manthey, and Maria Novotny. "Embodiment: Embodying Feminist Rhetorics." *Peitho Journal*, vol. 18, no. 1, 2015, pp. 39-44.
Kent, L'ea. "Fighting Abjection: Representing Fat Women." Braziel and LeBesco, pp. 130-150.
Massumi, Brian. *The Politics of Affect*. Polity, 2015.
Merleau-Ponty, Maurice. *The Primacy of Perception*. Translated by James M. Edie, Northwestern UP, 1964.
Puar, Jasbir K. *Terrorist Assemblages: Homonationalism is Queer Times*. Duke UP, 2007.
Salamon, Gayle. *Assuming a Body: Transgender and Rhetorics of Materiality*. Columbia UP, 2010.
Shaw, Andrea Elizabeth. *The Embodiment of Disobedience: Fat Black Women's Unruly Political Bodies*. Lexington Books, 2006.
Shieff, Sarah. "Devouring Women: Corporeality and Autonomy in Fiction by Women Since the 1960s." Braziel and LeBesco, pp. 214-230.
Wykes, Jackie. "Introduction: Why Queering Fat Embodiment?" *Queering Fat Embodiment*, edited by Cat Pausé, Jackie Wykes, and Samantha Murray, Ashgate, 2015, pp. 1-12.

---

11. Oh, you're not fat. Don't call yourself fat. You're pleasantly plump. It upsets me when you call yourself fat. I don't think of you as fat. (When you call yourself fat, I don't know how to respond. It makes me uncomfortable.) You're not fat; you're beautiful.

What Happened to Hubert Humphrey?

David Zarefsky

Seventy years ago, Hubert Humphrey was a hero among liberals because of his courageous stand for human rights over states' rights at the 1948 Democratic National Convention in a speech that was instrumental in passing the minority platform plank on civil rights. But twenty years later – fifty years ago, in the year of RSA's birth – he was a pariah among the sons and daughters of those same liberals, who shouted him down with chants of "Dump the Hump," while his strongest supporters were the Southern party bosses whose ancestors would have found him an anathema twenty years before.

The eighteen-year-old vote not yet having been passed, I cast my first ballot for Hubert Humphrey in 1968, but I did so with a distinct lack of enthusiasm. My attitude was fairly common among liberals. Humphrey had been transformed from a liberal hero into what columnist Stewart Alsop called a "national whipping boy" (Cohen, 291) in the space of two decades.

How to explain this change? Conventional wisdom focuses on Vietnam. Unsupportive of escalation, and having expressed his doubts to President Lyndon Johnson, Humphrey was barred from participation in Vietnam decision-making until he learned his lesson and became a sycophant, thereby alienating his erstwhile supporters. This account is true as far as it goes. After the Pleiku attack of February 1965, Humphrey wrote a long memo to Johnson urging him not to start a campaign of bombing North Vietnam and warning that he would lose public support if he did (Humphrey, 318-19). Johnson pointedly kept Humphrey off the invitation list for National Security Council meetings for a year (Prados, 114), then tested him to make sure that he would not be an obstacle.

But Humphrey's predicament was not limited to Vietnam, and it started quite early in his vice presidency. He had been forewarned. When considering vice presidential possibilities in 1964, Johnson said he wanted someone who would "kiss my ass in Macy's window and say it smells like a rose" (Dallek, 160). Presumably, Humphrey had accepted this condition, although there is no record of it. In early 1965, just a few weeks into the term, Harvard-mathematician-cum-nightclub-satirist Tom Lehrer sang, "Second fiddle's a hard part, I know, / When they don't even give you a bow," and "Does Lyndon, recalling when he was VP, / Say, I'll do unto you as they did unto me?" (Lehrer, 1965).

But it wasn't all President Johnson's fault, either. Humphrey made some unwise rhetorical choices. To explore this claim, I'd like to re-examine a rather quotidian speech he delivered in July of 1966 to the convention of the National Association for the Advancement of Colored People (NAACP). Just a few weeks earlier, the March Against Fear, going from Memphis to Jackson, Mississippi, had been interrupted by the shooting in the leg of the march leader, James Meredith. The sponsoring organizations, the Student Nonviolent Coordinating Committee (SNCC), the Southern Christian Leadership Conference (SCLC), and the Congress on Racial Equality (CORE), took over where Meredith left off. As the march went on, leaders of the three organizations got into an ideological (or, perhaps, ideographic) conflict between the slogans "Freedom Now" and "Black Power." The former slogan was associated with Martin Luther King and the SCLC; the latter, with younger radicals who were taking over SNCC. Having been released from jail several hours after he had been arrested for trespassing, Stokely Carmichael addressed a rally in Greenwood, Mississippi, and proclaimed, "We been sayin' freedom for six years and we ain't got nothin'. What we got to start saying now is Black Power! We want Black Power!" (Branch, 486).

Like most ideographs, "Black Power" was not defined with precision, but it was understood as a challenge by the younger generations to the leadership of the NAACP. Roy Wilkins, the organization's president, was the first major civil rights leader to denounce the slogan (Carson, 219). He had taken a clear stand against Black Power the day before Humphrey spoke to the NACCP. And President Johnson had told a press conference, "We are not interested in black power, we are not interested in white power, but we are interested in American democratic power, with a small 'd'" (Scott and Brockriede, *Rhetoric*, 75). This context created an exigence that probably made it impossible for Humphrey just to ignore the matter.

Anyone tempted to see this as an arcane dispute might think of a more current analogy: the difference between "Black Lives Matter" and "All Lives Matter." In part, this dispute turns on whether "Black Lives Matter" means something like "*Only* Black Lives Matter" or something like "Black Lives Matter *Too*" although it also involves a contested history of law enforcement and is not just a quibble over meanings. Similarly, in 1966 the question was whether power was necessarily redistributive or possibly additive, although it also raised the question of whether civil rights advocates must remain committed to nonviolence. Did gaining Black Power necessarily mean diminishing white power? Or could gaining Black Power be understood as filling a power vacuum, taking control of a community (for example) and providing leadership and influence when none seemed to exist?

Undefined but charged terms are invitations to rhetorical action. Advocates compete for possession of the term by giving it meaning, which they do more often by indirect means (such as stipulation, stigmatization, exemplification, or repetition) than by overt claims and reasons that a term ought to be understood as meaning thus-and-so. The process of rhetorical definition involves choices that can be made either strategically or otherwise.

Humphrey had some choice of how to understand "Black Power." Although an overt attempt by whites to control the term's meaning would have aroused resistance, the summer of 1966 was a moment when meaning remained fluid, and as Carson wrote, "Carmichael's purposeful ambiguity allowed his followers and his opponents to attribute their own meanings to the black power phrase" (Carson, 218-19). Humphrey instead acted as if the understanding of the term were fixed and his choice was how to evaluate it. His view required him to take sides between Carmichael and Wilkins (or, to lesser degree, between Carmichael and King). Not only that, but he took the side that, while popular with his immediate audience at the NAACP, would put him in more conservative company in a very short time, exalting procedural rights over material gains and concerned heavily with the avoidance of white backlash. This does not seem like the visionary who reset the hierarchy between states' rights and human rights.

Humphrey's speech is reprinted and analyzed in Scott and Brockriede's anthology *The Rhetoric of Black Power*. It has not received much attention since. My comments will bear out the acuity of Scott and Brockriede as contemporaneous critics. They claim that Humphrey regarded Black Power unfavorably when he could have regarded it favorably. I back up a step and suggest that he acted as though the term had a known meaning when he could have participated in the effort to bestow meaning upon it, at least suggesting a meaning that was less confrontational. He passed up the opportunity to transcend the dispute between Carmichael and Wilkins.

Humphrey began the speech by celebrating the fact that "America is marching on the road to freedom." The metaphorical use of "march" was common in the discourse of the civil rights movement and probably is not a specific reference to the recent March Against Fear that took place in Mississippi. Humphrey completes the introduction to the speech by stating, "We have learned that there is no single road to follow . . . no one program . . . no one slogan that will bring us to the end of our march" (ellipses in original). The reference to "no one slogan" was an opportunity to set up a discussion linking slogans to actions, which could have led into an attempt to interpret the "Black Power" slogan expansively and favorably. But Humphrey did not make this move. Instead he associates the movement's achievements with the claim that the NAACP has been in the lead. Under ordinary circumstances this might seem merely like paying tribute to one's host, but in the immediate context it seems like taking sides in an imagined conflict between the NAACP and SNCC. (While the controversy between "black power" and "freedom now" pitted SNCC against SCLC, the strongest opposition to "black power" came from the NAACP, whose leaders interpreted the slogan as a call for black separatism. King, by contrast, declined to sign a statement repudiating black power [Carson, 223]).

Humphrey then says that "we turn now to confront the work which remains" but he implies that it can be confronted with the tools of the past. Instead of saying something like "new work requires new tools," Humphrey dissociates the old "freedom now" slogan of the SCLC to make it accommodate the new tasks. Dissociation is a term used by Perelman and Olbrechts-Tyteca (411-459) to refer to the process of breaking a concept or term into two, in order to identify one's cause with the (new) preferred dimension, which then is claimed to be the "real" meaning of the older term. What Humphrey says is, "It is one thing to cry 'freedom now' on a picket line. But it is another to achieve true freedom in the squalid work of the ghetto . . ." This is not an appealing image, especially when he goes on to explain that this "squalid work" is to face problems "which no man can overcome in a day, week, or year." As a counterfactual, suppose instead that the vice president had talked about the slow but steady achievement of power over the forces of exploitation that he says have produced the problems of the ghetto. This could have been an opportunity for Humphrey to interpret the "Black Power" slogan as power over impersonal but real economic forces rather than power of Stokely Carmichael over Roy Wilkins, which Humphrey disparaged.

There follow two more antitheses ("It is one thing . . ."/ "It is another . . .") that are not linked to the "Freedom Now" slogan or to the "Black Power" slogan. They relate to the difference between making demands and expressing commitments, and the difference between overcoming flagrant prejudice and eliminating more subtle and sophisticated forms of racism. Both of these, however, could have been reformulated as differences between the trappings of power and the exercise of real power. These were opportunities, in other words, for Humphrey to pick up the "Black Power" term but to influence its definition.

Humphrey then moves into the longest section of the speech: his policy agenda of "certain problems demanding priority attention as we strive to translate legal promises of equality and freedom into reality" – another dissociation of the old term "freedom" with the additional drawback that it seems to regard "legal promises" as somehow not "real." His agenda was divided into tasks for the federal government, for state and local governments, and the private sector. Between the second and third of these agenda lists, Humphrey praises the NAACP for long ago making "the decision to stay in your communities and do the work that has to be done." This sounds like Booker T. Washington's "Cast down your buckets where you are," but also like an endorsement of SNCC's long-term commitment to community organizing. It is another missed opportunity to extend an olive branch to "Black Power" supporters, because these local activities could have been described as the achievement and exercise of power where it really matters.

Humphrey also expands the third agenda list to talk about enlarging employment opportunities. Interestingly, he calls for "vigorous affirmative action." But he used that term in its original sense, equating it with compensatory measures to help those unprepared for the start of life's race. The phrase he used in the speech was ". . . vigorous affirmative action through skillfully designed training programs to help compensate persons who have been denied all opportunity to prepare themselves for today's job market." This formulation ultimately locates the problems preventing employment in the individual workers, even though it acknowledges explicitly that it is not their fault. It might have been getting ahead of the game for 1966, but maybe there was an opportunity to describe affirmative action as two-pronged: making individual workers more competitive, but also overcoming systemic or structural forces that denied employment opportunities. If so, such an approach could have been described using the language of power.

Now nearing the end of the speech, Humphrey moves, at least obliquely, to address the developing rift within the civil rights movement. After urging the NAACP to continue to seek cooperation with all sorts of other groups, he says, "This appeal cuts to the core of those questions of philosophy and of strategy which currently engage the civil rights movement." In one sense his language is gentle–he never mentions the phrase "Black Power"–but there is no mistaking the object of his remarks. He appears to regard Black Power as a call for separatism, a rejection of integration as a goal, and an assertion of racial superiority for blacks. He says that "we cannot embrace the dogma of the oppressors–the notion that somehow a person's skin color determines his worthiness or unworthiness." In this formulation, he regards radical young black militants as analogous to diehard segregationists, both animated by the same prejudice. And his very next statement is "racism is racism–and there is no room in America for racism of any color." He urges that "we must reject calls for racism, whether they come from a throat that is white or one that is black." His fairly clear implication—and the title sometimes given to the speech—is that "black power is black racism."

To make that equation, however, is to presuppose a certain understanding of what Black Power is—an attempt by blacks to seize power from whites, to substitute black supremacy for white supremacy and to replace segregation ordained by whites with segregation ordained by blacks. That is indeed a prospect that whites would find threatening and would want to resist before it develops. But that was not the only sense of Black Power that was available to the vice president to discuss. It was not the sense that was being openly espoused by most of the young militants, although it was often attributed to them by whites. It foreclosed opportunities for Humphrey, long a friend of civil rights and still probably enjoying high *ethos* among blacks, despite his efforts to achieve compromise in the conflict over seating the Mississippi Freedom Democratic Party at the 1964 national convention. He had a chance to influence the understanding of a new term whose meaning was still fluid. He could have tried to co-opt its use so that it would be more aligned with his and the administration's interests. That was what President Johnson had done so skillfully with the Howard University speech (Public Papers, 635-640) the previous year. Without any indication that Humphrey had reflected on his rhetorical options, he chose instead to regard the term in its most unfavorable light, and then object to that way of regarding it.

To be sure, Humphrey's condemnation was brief and somewhat indirect. He quickly distinguished his disfavored sense of Black Power from "legitimate pride in the achievements of one's forebears." He urged greater attention by all Americans to the study of black history. But, he said, pride in black history should be the basis to build "a new climate of mutual respect among all elements of society—not false doctrines of racial superiority." (There is that unfortunate dichotomy again.) And he reminded his audience, "always remember, we seek *advancement* . . . not *apartheid*" (italics in original). He delivered a short encomium to President Johnson and to integration, which he regarded as the means to the ends of freedom, justice, and equal opportunity. He closed with words from James Weldon Johnson's "Lift Every Voice."

It was not a bad speech. It was attuned to the needs of the immediate exigence and met the expectation that a keynote speaker at the NAACP convention would offer praise to the NAACP. And it was probably not a speech of sufficient policy significance to have called for an extensive or laborious process of preparation. My argument is that the fluidity of the particular moment offered Humphrey opportunities to participate in shaping the meaning of a largely undefined term and to use it in a way far more congenial to his and the president's purposes. And Humphrey systematically missed those opportunities. In doing so, he instead identified himself with one side of an emerging struggle rather than working to transcend the struggle.

These are not altogether original insights. Scott and Brockriede included in their anthology not only Humphrey's speech but an essay they wrote at the time and published in *Speaker and Gavel* (Scott and Brockriede, "Hubert"). There they suggest that Humphrey had no choice but to address the topic of Black Power, but that he could have regarded it favorably rather than unfavorably. I agree with this assessment and have tried to show, with the benefit of hindsight, how he might have done it.

I have examined only one speech. Perhaps it was an aberration, but I doubt it. The same pattern can be found in Humphrey's treatment of Vietnam. After his aborted dissent in 1965, he was careful not to depart from Johnson's position in any particular, and this decision discredited him as being just a Johnson sycophant. Even as late as the 1968 Democratic convention, Humphrey abandoned a "middle of the road" Vietnam platform plank that he had crafted as a compromise, demanding that the convention adopt a hard-line endorsement of Johnson's policies, which a divided convention did by a narrow margin. He did so after experiencing a browbeating by Johnson, who all but told him that to do otherwise would be unpatriotic in wartime and might jeopardize Johnson's son-in-law, future Senator Chuck Robb, who was then serving in Vietnam.

In his study of the 1968 election, Michael Cohen (not Donald Trump's former lawyer) describes Humphrey's retreat on the Vietnam "peace" plank as "a microcosm of his entire political career. Two decades of concessions to political reality . . . had made expedience Humphrey's overriding political impulse" (Cohen, 265). He argues that Humphrey persistently was willing to yield a principle if doing so would help him to achieve his short-term goals legislative goals while he was in the Senate, now the opportunity to be elected president. What we saw in the NAACP speech is not so much a sacrifice of principle as foregoing a rhetorical option, but the underlying dynamic was the same.

Humphrey asserted his independence from Johnson only once during the 1968 campaign, at the end of September. Frustrated with his lagging poll ratings, tired of having his speeches interrupted by heckling and chants of "Dump the Hump," he threw in his remaining resources to buy television time for a speech to be delivered in Salt Lake City (Schumacher, 431-434). There Humphrey spelled out a position only marginally different from Johnson's. Humphrey would stop all bombing of North Vietnam "as an acceptable risk for peace," the very step that Johnson took on October 31. But symbolically, the speech was perceived as a big break for Humphrey. He had become his own man at last, perhaps for the first time since he had championed human rights over states' rights twenty years before. The Salt Lake City speech began Humphrey's political recovery in the fall of 1968. It was almost enough to carry him to victory.

Works Cited

Branch, Taylor. *At Canaan's Edge: America in the King Years, 1965-1968*. New York: Simon and Schuster, 2006.
Carson, Clayborne. I*n Struggle: SNCC and the Black Awakening of the 1960s*. Cambridge, MA: Harvard University Press, 1981.
Cohen, Michael A. *American Maelstrom: The 1968 Election and the Politics of Division*. New York: Oxford University Press, 2016.
Dallek, Robert. *Flawed Giant: Lyndon Johnson and His Times, 1961-1973*. New York: Oxford University Press, 1998.
Humphrey, Hubert H. *The Education of a Public Man*. Garden City, N.Y.: Doubleday, 1976.
Lehrer, Tom. *That Was the Year That Was*. Reprise Records, 1965. Phonograph record.
Perelman, Chaim, and L. Olbrechts-Tyteca. *The New Rhetoric: A Treatise on Argumentation*, trans. John Wilkinson and Purcell Weaver. Notre Dame, Ind.: University of Notre Dame Press. 1958/1969.
Prados, John. *Vietnam: The History of an Unwinnable War, 1945-1975*. Lawrence: University Press of Kansas, 2009.
Public Papers of the Presidents: Lyndon B. Johnson, 1965. Washington: U.S. Government Printing Office, 1966. Vol. II.
Scott, Robert L., and Wayne Brockriede. "Hubert Humphrey Faces the Black Power Issue," *Speaker and Gavel,* 4 (November 1966), 11-17.
Scott, Robert L., and Wayne Brockriede. *The Rhetoric of Black Power*. New York: Harper and Row, 1969.
Schumacher, Michael. *The Contest: The 1968 Election and the War for America's Soul*. Minneapolis: University of Minnesota Press, 2018.

What Institutional Logics Can Teach Us About Institutional Rhetorics (And Why We Should Care)

Ryan Skinnell

Kenneth Burke ends *Permanence and Change* with one of his most memorably poetic images—that of men [sic], building their cultures by "huddling together, nervously loquacious, at the edge of an abyss" (272). That line, understandably, gets a lot of attention from rhetoricians who appreciate Burke's evocative imagery, but there's another line just above it in the same paragraph that is compelling for different reasons. In setting up his nervously loquacious dénouement, Burke refers off-handedly to "man-made institutions" as "tiny concentration points of rhetoric and traffic." Burke's theoretical engagements with institutions are rarely favorable—in fact, just a few paragraphs earlier he notes that a "philosophy of being" may necessitate open conflict with people who defend institutions that serve an anti-social function (272). It is not totally clear what institutions he means, but he may well be referring to every institution, responsible as they are for bureaucratizing imagination. Nevertheless, Burke's figuration of institutions at "concentration points of rhetoric and traffic" suggests both an important distinction between rhetoric and institutions and also an intimate relationship between them.

This tangle is worth attempting to unravel. It is hardly controversial to suggest that institutions play a crucial role in the maintenance, distribution, and intensification of rhetoric. Rhetorical scholars often acknowledge that institutions have an outsized influence on public discourse (see, e.g., Atwill; LaFrance and Nicolas; Lamos; Leon; Lynch; Porter, et al.; Skinnell). But there nevertheless remains significant opportunity for rhetoricians to develop additional theories of institutional rhetorics that help explain how institutions get the right to speak, how they exercise that right, how they convey the right to speak to other institutions and individuals, and how institutions shape discourse in powerful and distinct ways. I'm certainly not the first person to suggest that institutional rhetorics constitute an important area of research (see, e.g., Goodnight, "Rhetoric"; Keremidchieva; Thompson; Zarefsky), but in this chapter, I suggest that the *institutional logics perspective*, which I discuss in more detail below, offers rhetoricians a valuable avenue for pursuing this work.

Before I introduce the institutional logics perspective, I want to start with an example to illustrate a concern that I believe new theories of institutional rhetoric can help explain. In January 2010, the United States Supreme Court issued a landmark decision in the now-infamous Citizens United vs. Federal Election Commission case (United States). In brief, the US Supreme Court held that the First Amendment to the Constitution protects the free speech rights of corporations, unions, and other associations to make political expenditures. The principle formalized by Citizens United is often referred to by the catchy moniker "corporate personhood," which essentially grants corporations some of the same First Amendment rights as individuals. Citizens United is somewhat more complicated than this summary allows, but even in brief, it introduces two crucial concerns for studying institutional rhetorics. The first is to do with the so-called "corporate persons," which may be a loosely affiliated group of people with similar political leanings, but which in practice are more commonly large groups and associations—including multinational corporations—that are organized around not-explicitly-political goals. A labor union, for example, which is organized around the protection of labor rights, may "speak" on behalf of the membership and apply the membership's resources to partisan political ends that are tangential to, and even in contravention of, some members' class allegiances. In this example, as in many others, "corporate persons" are often significantly better organized and resourced than the average group of concerned citizens.

A second concern for studying institutional rhetorics is the function of institutional decision-making. That is, the Citizens United decision was not unanimous. It was a 5-4 decision in favor of the plaintiff, and while the minority got to file a (scathing) dissent, the decision is, ultimately, representative of the entire Court. That is, the institution of the Supreme Court votes in favor of the plaintiff, even if the individuals that make up the Court do not.

For rhetoricians, it is not hard to identify some issues worthy of our disciplinary expertise in Citizens United: the irony of equating a single person with a massive corporation, for instance, or the reification entailed in allowing a collective to speak as one (corporate) person *and* to speak as a group at the same time. But even as rhetoric specialists are well equipped to read the rhetoric of Citizens United, there are important institutional elements that are hard to understand within current models of rhetorical action—corporations as speaking beings that are not beholden to any individual speaker, the institutional inducement to identification (see Burke, *War* 224), persuasive exchange at the inter-institutional level, and many more. Our traditional models of rhetorical appeals are robust and important, but they have their limits where institutions are concerned.

My central concern in this chapter is just a single aspect of institutional rhetorics that I think is fundamental to what we stand to learn. Specifically, I am interested here in how institutions establish normative conventions, or how they become concentration points of rhetoric and traffic. According to G. Thomas Goodnight, "Institutions regulate behavior through providing norms that reward 'acceptable' conduct, sanction the 'inappropriate,' and order expectations of exchange" ("Strategic" 360). In other words, institutions regulate what counts as "normal" in a given culture. And what counts as "normal" obviously has profound effects on how people in a given culture act, speak, and believe—even for people who are explicitly pushing against those norms. In order to understand the conditions in which rhetoric exists in a given culture, then, it is useful to understand how institutions mediate norms and therefore establish and regulate rhetorical situations.

For that I turn to a growing body of research in sociology. Sociologists have been studying institutions for more than a century, led by Max Weber, Talcott Parsons, Thorstein Veblen, Emile Durkheim, and others. Classical theories of institutions predominated in the twentieth century, and they are generally characterized by macrostructural analyses. Within classical theories, one of the main objectives for much of the twentieth century was to try to identify how institutions impose continuity, conformity, and constraint. Weber and Parsons provided the baseline for institutional theories for decades. But in the 1980s and 1990s, scholars in sociology and other fields developed New Institutional Theory (also called neoinstitutional theory) to try and account for a developing awareness of things like individual agency within institutions, the reality of institutional contingency (particularly in the wake of Reaganite deregulation), the effects of cultural change, and more (e.g., Powell and DiMaggio).

More recently still, institutional theorists have begun to elaborate what Patricia H. Thornton, William Ocasio, and Michael Lounsbury call the "Institutional Logics Perspective." The institutional logics perspective seems especially promising for rhetoricians. It is defined by Thornton, Ocasio, and Lounsbury as "the socially constructed, historical patterns of cultural symbols and material practices, including assumptions, values, and beliefs, by which individuals and organizations provide meaning to their daily activity, organize time and space, and reproduce their lives and experiences" (2). In other words, the institutional logics perspective avails rhetoricians of a series of symbolic and material analytic frames for studying institutional rhetorics.

Theories of institutional logics are as appropriately complex as you might expect, and I don't intend to unpack the entire theoretical apparatus here. What I do want to do, however, is briefly introduce some key concepts in institutional logics and suggest how they may have the potential to enlighten the rhetorical work of twenty-first century institutions.

For starters, proponents of the institutional logics perspective argue that institutions have both material and symbolic elements. According to Thornton, Ocasio, and Lounsbury, material elements are "structures and practices" and symbols are "ideation and meaning" (10). For rhetoricians, the links between their definitions of materials and symbols and rhetoricians' definitions of and theoretical engagements with same should be clear. In addition, however, it is worth pointing out the institutional logics perspective is explicitly intended to help explain causality of the sort that often eludes rhetoricians (c.f., Houck and Kiewe). Although we do make claims about causality in our work, rhetoricians are not always on the strongest ground in making causal connections because we do not always have good methods for connecting symbolism to materiality in specific ways. But by describing how symbolicity and materiality build in relation to one another, the institutional logics perspective offers us some options for doing so that are already aligned with our methodologies.

There are two other concepts I want to briefly introduce. The first is motivation—obviously a preoccupation of rhetoricians in the Burkean tradition. According to Thornton, Occasion, and Lounsbury, building on other institutional logics theorists, people's motivations for acting are often framed by institutional norms, values, and procedures. At the same time, however, people in institutions maintain forms of embedded agency, within which they can act and create institutional change (77). In other words, institutions frame but don't determine, which is a key point of entry for rhetoricians. Institutions also shape other institutions by way of institutional logics, though again, not without the openness to being changed themselves by virtue of agents. This argument, again, is highly compatible with long-standing arguments in rhetoric—from models of deliberative democracy to Burke's motion/action distinction (*Grammar*) to Sharon Crowley's ideologic (*Toward*) to a number of more recent arguments about cultural rhetorics (Bratta and Powell). The added value of the institutional logics perspective is the ways in which it allows us to examine institutions without losing sight of these fundamentally rhetorical principles. One of the challenges of studying institutions is that they often appear static in ways that seem to confound rhetoricians' interest in situational/kairotic speech. But the institutional logics perspective suggests that there is considerable contingency and flexibility in institutions that bears rhetoricians' attention. Ultimately, the institutional logics perspective offers rhetoricians one way of analyzing institutions by looking at the play of power at and across individual, organizational, field, and societal levels—sort of like an institutional pentad—in ways that lend themselves to both empirical and theoretical study.

The final concept from the institutional logics perspective I want to introduce is "schemas." Of course, schemas are not new to rhetorical studies, especially for those of us who have read Piaget, Vygotsky, and other education theorists, but institutional logics offers a useful twist on the concept. Again, according to Thornton, Ocasio, and Lounsbury, schemas are top-down knowledge structures that help institutions process information and guide decisions (88-92). Institutions, fundamentally, are information managers. They are designed and intended to process, filter, and manage information so that large groups of people across complex and distributed networks can nevertheless work toward a common goal. Schemas are how institutions formalize and distribute information—they involve shared vocabularies, shared rules and procedures, shared values, and in many cases, shared identities. Institutional logics theorists are interested in how schemas get built—through processes of narrative, for example. It is common for companies, for instance, to have elaborate origin stories that build on widely shared commonplaces, like "the family business makes good," "a magical epiphany," or "a socially-conscious business provides some sort of social good." In those stories, more often than not, a series of values and vocabularies is elaborated, which then permeates the company culture in all subsequent moments. Those values and vocabularies become touchpoints for the ways that new members are introduced to the institution and trained to act within it. In short order, the values and vocabularies of origin stories can begin to seem natural, and even unassailable, because they are incorporated structurally.

Interestingly enough, however, some origin stories can change relatively easily. To give one example, I used to work at the University of North Texas (UNT) in Denton, TX, and for research I was doing about writing instruction in the institution's early years, I read several versions of their origin story. According to UNT's current origin story, the university was founded in 1890 by an enterprising educator, Joshua Crittenden Chilton, who wanted to bring teacher training to North Texas. That origin story was produced in a number of early institutional documents, much as it is now. But, there were other origin stories at different times in the institution's existence. Beginning in the early 1900s, a different origin story was produced that omitted the first

12 years of the institution because it had been a private, for-profit institution plagued by controversies. When UNT became a state-funded institution, they rewrote the origin story and introduced new values and vocabularies. After a number of decades had passed, however, the old origin story was resuscitated. In both versions, of course, institutional authors were telling the truth, but the two different stories emphasize different values, procedures, and vocabularies. And both stories provided their own schemas by which to orient the institution and the people within it. In short, how the institution is narrated and what schemas it develops over time have direct, in many cases measurable, effects on institutional materiality. To translate it back into rhetorical terms, the concept of institutional schemas is more or less an explanation of how institutions become and function as concentration points of rhetoric.

In the end, my central claim here is pretty modest—I think rhetoricians can develop the study of institutional rhetorics to attend to questions about how institutions speak, how the shape rhetorical norms, and how they use rhetoric to shape cultural norms. The institutional logics perspective gives us one—though certainly not the only—set of methods for doing so. The real advantage to the institutional logics perspective is that it resonates well with the kinds of critical and rhetorical lenses that take advantage of what we already know and do. By developing additional theories of institutional rhetorics, we stand to learn a lot about what it means to act rhetorically in a fundamentally institutional world, and by extension, to act institutionally in a fundamentally rhetorical world.

WORKS CITED

Atwill, Janet M. "Rhetoric and Institutional Critique: Uncertainty in the Postmodern Academy." *JAC*, vol. 22, no. 3, 2002, pp. 640-5.

Bratta, Phil, and Malea Powell. "Introduction to the Special Issue: Entering the Cultural Rhetorics Conversations." *Enculturation*, vol. 21, 2016, http://enculturation.net/entering-the-cultural-rhetorics-conversations. Accessed 21 Feb. 2019.

Burke, Kenneth. *A Grammar of Motives.* U of California P, 1969.

—. *Permanence and Change: An Anatomy of Purpose.* 3rd ed., U of California P, 1984.

—. *The War of Words.* U of California P, 2018.

Crowley, Sharon. *Toward a Civil Discourse: Rhetoric and Fundamentalisms.* U of Pittsburgh P, 2006.

Goodnight, G. Thomas. "Rhetoric and Communication: Alternative Worlds of Inquiry." *Quarterly Journal of Speech*, vol. 101, no. 1, 2015, pp. 145-50.

—. "Strategic Maneuvering in Direct to Consumer Drug Advertising: A Study in Argumentation Theory and New Institutional Theory." *Argumentation*, vol. 22, no. 3, 2008, pp. 359-71.

Keremidchieva, Zornitsa. "The US Congressional Record as a Technology of Representation: Toward a Materialist Theory of Institutional Argumentation." *Journal of Argumentation in Context*, vol. 3, no. 1, 2014, pp. 57-82.

Kiewe, Amos, and Davis W. Houck, editors. *The Effects of Rhetoric and the Rhetoric of Effects: Past, Present, Future.* U of South Carolina P, 2015.

LaFrance, Michelle, and Melissa Nicolas. "Institutional Ethnography as Materialist Framework for Writing Program Research and the Faculty-Staff Work Standpoints Project." *College Composition and Communication*, vol. 64, no. 1, 2012, pp. 130-50.

Lamos, Steve. "Institutional Critique in Composition Studies: Methodological and Ethical Considerations for Researchers." *Writing Studies Research in Practice: Methods and Methodologies*, edited by Lee Nickoson and Mary P. Sheridan, Southern Illinois UP, 2012, pp. 158-70.

Leon, Kendall. "*La Hermandad* and Chicanas Organizing: The Community Rhetoric of the *Comisión Femenil Mexicana Nacional*." *Community Literacy Journal*, vol. 7, no. 2, 2013, pp. 1-20.

Lynch, John. "Institution and Imprimatur: Institutional Rhetoric and the Failure of the Catholic Church's Pastoral Letter on Homosexuality." *Rhetoric & Public Affairs*, vol. 8, no. 3, 2005, pp. 383-403.

Porter, James E., Patricia Sullivan, Stuart Blythe, Jeffrey T. Grabill, and Libby Miles. "Institutional Critique: A Rhetorical Methodology for Change." *College Composition and Communication*, vol. 51, no. 4, 2000, pp. 610–42.

Powell, Walter W., and Paul J. DiMaggio. *The New Institutionalism in Organizational Analysis.* U of Chicago P, 1991.

Skinnell, Ryan. *Conceding Composition: A Crooked History of Composition's Institutional Fortunes.* Utah State UP, 2016.

Thompson, Mark A. "Institutional Argumentation and Institutional Rules: Effects of Interactive Asymmetry on Argumentation in Institutional Contexts." *Argumentation*, vol. 31, no. 1, 2017, pp. 1-21.

Thornton, Patricia H., William Ocasio, and Michael Lounsbury. *The Institutional Logics Perspective: A New Approach to Culture, Structure, and Process.* Oxford UP, 2012.

United States, Supreme Court. Citizens United v. Federal Election Commission. *Hein Online: U.S. Supreme Court Library*, 2010, https://heinonline.org/HOL/P?h=hein.usreports/usrep558&i=472. Accessed 9 Jul. 2019.

Zarefsky, David. "Strategic Maneuvering in Political Argumentation." *Argumentation*, vol. 22, no. 3, 2008, pp. 317-30.

A Rhetoric of Food Justice Movements: An Exploration in Rhetorical Quilting

Shelley Sizemore and Ron Von Burg

Food is national security. Food is economy. It is employment, energy, history. Food is everything.

—José Andrés

The time has come to reclaim the stolen harvest and celebrate the growing and giving of good food as the highest gift and most revolutionary act.

—Vandana Shiva

Introduction

Food is a universal staple for human sustenance, but access to food presents a vexing and troubling reality. The universality of such a necessity creates a unique challenge to food justice movements that seek to ensure the availability of sufficient, nutritious food to underserved populations. Rhetorically distinguishing themselves from anti-hunger advocacy often grounded in charitable giving or global food production, food justice movements invariability draw upon diverse threads of race, class, gender, culture, religion, history, identity, international relations, zoning, science, environmentalism, just to name a few, in an effort to address the needs of underserved or threatened populations. The numerous strands that inform food justice efforts present a challenge to rhetorical scholars searching for generative metaphors for engaging the process of rhetorical invention in such diffuse social movements. To that end, we offer a new conceptual strategy and generative metaphor to navigate the tensions of stitching together disparate discourses into a cohesive argument. We present "rhetorical quilting" as a mode of reinventing extant approaches to discursive invention.

Quilting is a traditional fiber art form that recycles or repurposes discarded fabrics into a new whole, namely a blanket or quilt. These pieces of fabric, which are often parts of larger fabrics such as worn-out clothing, find renewed purpose as representing meaningful memories and histories associated with such materials. Quilting is an art form of pragmatic nostalgia, as the quilts themselves often become heirlooms, telling a story through the fabrics pieced together, that function to keep one warm and comfortable. Similarly, food justice movements do not exist as efforts to address individual exigences or situated responses to isolated social conditions, rather, they rely on various discursive reservoirs that are often both locally informed and globally connected. They are uniquely grounded in the tropes of adjacent movements, often using food as a metaphor for broader community sovereignty. Because food is a necessity for survival, access to food intersects with many other social justice efforts focused on economic disparity, discrimination, and environmentalism. Food justice movements borrow discourses from various movements to create a coherent whole on the importance of food access and increasingly, the importance of control over food production. Such movements stitch these discourses onto tropes associated with food: nutrition, health, and the cultural importance of culinary traditions.

Understanding food justice rhetoric requires stitching together discourses that address the ubiquitous appeal to food and social justice with the particular and distinct features of culture, tradition, and locality. This essay harvests the interpretative power of rhetorical quilting by first exploring the opportunities and limits of existing rhetorical approaches to food justice movements. Second, we present a vision of rhetorical quilting as a generative metaphor for discursive production that weaves together various lines of argument into a more cohesive rhetorical appeal. Finally, we apply rhetorical quilting to food justice movement rhetoric as a way of exploring how this metaphor broadens our view of the discursive field of movement rhetoric, amplifying themes across justice movements by sewing them together, mirroring the very interconnectedness of food systems with an interwoven rhetoric.

Spatial Metaphors of Rhetorical Invention

Rhetorical scholars exploring the process of discourse production have long relied on spatial metaphors to generate critical insight into rhetorical invention. The history of rhetorical theory is particularly rife with generative metaphors that reference space and location. Aristotle's *topoi* tied rhetorical invention to orators moving from topic to topic, drawing from places of knowledge best suited to the available means of persuasion. Likewise, the commonplaces of Cicero and Quintilian provide orators with a series of universal, inventional resources for argumentation production. More recently, philosopher Stephen Toulmin, in *The Uses of Argument*, presents argument fields as a metaphor for navigating the tensions between absolutism and relativism, suggesting that some arguments are 'field-dependent' while other arguments transcend fields. His model for practical argumentation, known as the Toulmin model, provides a heuristic for charting the constituent ingredients of an argument, largely based on the warrants that are common to particular epistemic fields.

Most salient to this project is Thomas Goodnight's conceptualization of argument spheres. Inspired by Toulmin's analysis of argument fields, Goodnight presents argument spheres as a tool for understanding how interlocutors draw from certain discourses in developing arguments. Goodnight introduces three types of arguments spheres--the personal, the public, and the technical--to explore how interlocutors generate arguments in deliberative spaces. Even though there are subjects and warrants that are germane to specific spheres, such as legal arguments in the technical sphere or matters of family finances in the personal sphere, Goodnight identifies the "colonization" of spheres in which arguments from one sphere will shape the judgment process on matters typically associated with another sphere. Specifically, Goodnight warns of the colonization of the personal and public spheres by the technical sphere, in which expertise and technical knowledge drive deliberations over putatively private or public matters. To be sure, these spheres often do amalgamate and there are many more than three argument spheres, creating new inventional possibilities when such blending occurs. The intersections of these argument spheres can change the norms of invention and the standards of judgment. To wit, Olson and Goodnight's exploration of a fur controversy demonstrates how protesters employed various argumentative techniques to shift supposedly personal matters, such as fashion choices, into an issue of public concern, thereby altering the norms of argumentation typically associated with certain spheres.

Food justice movement rhetoric often lies at the intersections of various argument spheres. Food is typically a private event; the relationship with food preparation and dining, and the rituals that attend meals, are often rooted in familial and cultural traditions. Yet, issues related to accessibility, food safety, and nutritional value are matters associated with public and technical policy arguments. As rhetors increasingly construct arguments that straddle Goodnight's argument spheres in discussions of hunger alleviation and/or environmental sustainability, we can observe how his model works in some food movement rhetoric, for example, as when appeals to technical arguments regarding food safety blend with personal and public appeals that champion the importance of food availability to maintaining familial bonds and educational performance. The intersections of such argument appeals, we suggest, exist within what Edbauer calls "rhetorical ecology," which broadens the situatedness of rhetoric to refigure the relationships between exigence, audience, and constraints. However, as food rhetoric continues to evolve into a push for food justice, it becomes tethered to contemporary and historical justice movements in a way that expands beyond existing spatial metaphors. In addition to the specific complexities of evolving food justice rhetoric, social fragmentation and diffusion of media limit the efficacy of many conventional metaphors for understanding rhetorical invention in the contemporary moment. As no single text or rhetor could be said to represent a movement's rhetorical fabric, we seek to understand the construction of individual and group identities relating to the food justice movement as assemblages, or what Jabir Puar calls a "collections of multiplicities" (211). Rhetorical quilting seeks to honor the ways these collections of multiplicities from across identities, across movements, and across times inform and are informed by each other. Objects, history, power, class divisions, resource distribution, for example, all exert forces that shape or constrain rhetorical agency. Food justice rhetoric relies on all of these material realities at the same time as it finds grounding in philosophical questions of equity, justice, and sovereignty.

Food Justice Themes

Much of the most visible food rhetoric comes out of the anti-hunger movement and is thus deeply steeped in the rhetoric of charity, altruism, and policy. As a basic human survival need, anti-hunger movement rhetoric appears almost completely material, often with primary connections to nutrition and economics. Similarly, food rhetoric grounded in sustainability or ecological considerations is largely technical, often framing food as a manifestation of broader climate or ecological problems. Both rhetorics position food as a means towards a broader end whether that end is improved educational outcomes in low-income children, the reversal of climate change, or reductions of hazardous chemicals. Food justice movements are distinct from other kinds of movements related to food in the ways that their arguments are framed through social justice. Defined by LeAnn Bell as "the full and equal participation of all groups in a society that is mutually shaped to meet their needs" (2), a framing grounded in social justice highlights the centrality of self-determination and interdependence, participation by all groups, the process and the goal. Food Justice movements draw upon various strands of political, social, economic, and scientific discourses, often all at the same time, and include themes that address race, gender and sexuality, economics and class, cultural pastimes and traditions, city planning and zoning, and nutrition and health policy, to name a few. Existing rhetorical approaches might encourage critics to isolate these themes from each other or to focus on the ways that arguments migrate from sphere to sphere. While there is great value in this specified approach, rhetorical quilting, inspired by Edbauer's rhetorical ecology, suggests rhetoric like that of food justice movements is more than the sum of its parts, a more that is only fully understood when we are able to expand our field of vision to better cover the intersections of these themes as well as the transcendence of their arguments across time and space. This shift has the potential to radically change what we think a rhetoric is doing simply by broadening how we understand the interconnectedness of its arguments.

For example, the 2010 film, *Lunchline* chronicles the growth of the National School Lunch Program. The film could be called a rhetorical artifact of the food justice movement as it frames audience understanding of the school lunch program as part of broader social safety net programs. The film touches on well-worn rhetorical arguments about the importance of school lunch for educational attainment while also launching a critique of popular understandings of the school lunch program by focusing on its role in perpetuating farm subsidies and big agriculture. However, even as the film aligns itself with the food justice movement in its critique of industrialized food (grounded in highly technical arguments about the production of said food), it misses an opportunity in its failure to acknowledge the interconnectedness of food and hunger with movements for racial and ethnic equality. As an anti-hunger program, the National School Lunch Program was framed as a response to poverty and food insecurity, which it was. *Lunchline* argues that, while public arguments in support of the program focused on relieving childhood hunger, policy arguments were more focused on maintaining farm subsidies through creating a market in schools for excess agricultural products (corn syrup etc.).

We argue that even this narrative is incomplete because it fails to recognize school lunch as an institutionalization of survival programs, notable examples of which were the Black Panther Party's free breakfast and re-education initiatives. Such a discursive expansion would mirror the evolution of food justice rhetoric from food security to food sovereignty, providing an opportunity for seeing the connection of food rhetorics to other social justice rhetorics, particularly those grounded in the experiences of indigenous peoples, people of color, and anti-globalization activists. Absences like these are representative of how the way we understand a rhetoric places constraints on the arguments and interconnections that we can see. As we unpack the anatomy of rhetorical quilting in the following section, we will do it through the trope of food sovereignty.

The Rhetorical Quilting of Food Justice Discourse

The concept of the quilt, and its power as a pastiche and vehicle for remembering, has not escaped the attention of rhetorical scholars. The most prominent references to quilts among rhetorical scholars reside with analysis of the NAMES AIDS Project Memorial Quilt. Notably, Blair and Michel explore the AIDS memorial quilt as a site for memory construction that refigures the relationship between invention and reception as well as troubles the boundaries between public and private memories. Likewise, Charles Morris's edited volume *Remembering the AIDS Quilt* brings together a notable collection of scholars to explore the rhetorical functions of the NAMES AIDS Quilt on its 25th anniversary. Scholars attend to how the AIDS quilt offers new rhetorical arrangements for capturing the complexity of the HIV/AIDS crisis. To wit, Ott, Aoki, and Dickinson suggest the concept of quilting as a mode of rhetorical criticism, noting that "[u]nlike more traditional rhetorical texts, the Quilt is decidedly protean, populist, mobile, material, multivocal, spatial, and fragmentary. It is, simply stated, a postmodern text(ile) whose rhetorical consequentiality is as colorful, compelling, and varied as its countless panels" (102). Our approach to rhetorical quilting as a mechanism for understanding the complexities of food justice movement discourse draws inspiration from this scholarly attention to the inventive potential of the quilt metaphor.

A quilt consists of three layers: the top (the recycled or repurposed fabrics), the batting (the insulating filling), and the backing (the bottom layer of a uniform piece of fabric). Quilting, however, is the actual stitching that binds the three layers together; such stitching is simultaneously artistic and pragmatic, demonstrating the artistry of one who binds the fabrics together to create a useful, comforting blanket. Rhetorical quilting provides a productive metaphor for the reinvention of rhetorical discourse, in that it relies on a process of discursive recycling, piecing together arguments and discourses steeped in their own history and meaning brought together through artistic and pragmatic stitchings that fuse together the layers at various points. This stitching together of disparate discourses requires other layers to generate cohesion, as the batting and backing do for the quilt. In other words, rhetorical quilting relies on interlocutors to stitch together these layers in artistic and pragmatic ways. To borrow the language McGee used to describe ideographic analysis, rhetorical quilting has both horizontal (the top layer of assembled fabrics) and vertical (the layers of the quilt and the process of quilting) dimensions. This study highlights how food justice rhetorically employs the horizontal and vertical dimensions of rhetorical quilting to reinvent new discursive structures.

The ways that the three components of the quilt interplay in food justice movement rhetoric is exemplified in the growing discourse of food sovereignty as a governing trope. Food sovereignty is the basic idea that individuals and communities have a right to accessible, affordable, culturally appropriate food. Increasingly, this argument includes a demand for control over the means of food production in addition to availability of food. Arguments for food sovereignty are best understood using rhetorical quilting largely because so much of this 'new' argument is a recycling or repurposing of past arguments. The top of the food sovereignty trope is a stitching together of rhetorics from the Black Panther Party's survival programs (exquisitely documented by Stanley Nelson's 2016 documentary *Vanguard of the Revolution*), American Indian Movement and contemporary indigenous activism about the sanctity of native land rights as they relate to traditional hunting and fishing practices, and even the hippie back to the land movement chronicled by Warren Belasco (2007). Globally, food sovereignty has been a central rallying cry from anti-globalization activists like Vandana Shiva whose anti-Monsanto crusade has been organizing rural women in India in opposition to industrial agriculture for nearly three decades. The batting or insulation, the part of this rhetorical quilt that gives it warmth and weight, is the discourse of social justice. Value-based claims of equity, equal opportunity, just access to and control over resources; these broader claims of social justice organizing provide the substance to food sovereignty claims. Finally, the bottom layer, the uniform piece of fabric that holds the full textile together, is the agreement that access to and control over material needs (like food but also water, housing, etc.) is itself a justice issue and not merely one of altruism. The quilt allows us to see how, in one key rhetorical part of the food justice movement, multiple discourses are not only stitched together, but are actually reliant upon each other for their meaning and structure.

Together, the process of rhetorical quilting focuses critical attention to the individual stories and effort fused together on a common struggle around a materially common need, in this case: food. Rhetorical quilting crafts a critical practice that highlights modes of invention that bring together diverse appeals around a shared theme, providing a richer account of complex appeals that form the tapestries of food justice rhetoric.

Works Cited

Aristotle. *The Art of Rhetoric*. Penguin Books, 1991.

Blair, Carole, and Neil Michel. "The AIDS Memorial Quilt and the Contemporary Culture of Public Commemoration." *Rhetoric and Public Affairs*, vol. 10, no. 4, 2007, pp. 595–626.

Cicero, Marcus Tullius. *De Oratore*. Edited by E. W. Sutton and H. Rackham, Harvard University Press, 1942.

Edbauer, Jenny. "Unframing Models of Public Distribution: From Rhetorical Situation to Rhetorical Ecologies." *Rhetoric Society Quarterly*, vol. 35, no. 4, 2005, pp. 5–24.

Goodnight, G. Thomas. "The Personal, Technical, and Public Spheres of Argument: A Speculative Inquiry into the Art of Public Deliberation." *The Journal of the American Forensic Association*, vol. 18, no. 4, Mar. 1982, pp. 214–27, doi:10.1080/00028533.1982.11951221.

McGee, Michael Calvin. "The 'Ideograph': A Link Between Rhetoric and Ideology." *Quarterly Journal of Speech*, vol. 66, no. 1, Feb. 1980, p. 1.

Morris, Charles E., editor. *Remembering the AIDS Quilt*. Michigan State University Press, 2011.

Olson, Kathryn M., and G. Thomas Goodnight. "Entanglements of Consumption, Cruelty, Privacy, and Fashion: The Social Controversy over Fur." *Quarterly Journal of Speech*, vol. 80, no. 3, Aug. 1994, p. 249.

Puar, Jabir. *Terrorist Assemblages: Homonationalism in Queer Times*. Duke University Press, 2007.

Quintilian. *The Orator's Education*. Edited by D. A. Russell, Harvard University Press, 2001.

Toulmin, Stephen. *The Uses of Argument*. Cambridge University Press, 2003.

Veterans Deployed to Standing Rock: The Rhetoric of Serving Country through Peaceful Protest

Heidi Hamilton

During the 2016 Indigenous peoples protest at Standing Rock against the Dakota Access pipeline (DAPL), thousands of U.S. military veterans "deployed" to Standing Rock to support efforts to block the pipeline. While the protests at Standing Rock are interesting and deserving of scholarly attention, in this essay, I focus on a small subset of rhetoric related to the mobilization of veterans. Looking primarily at two groups, Veterans for Peace and Veterans Stand (for Standing Rock), I contend that while these groups argued for the support of indigenous peoples at Standing Rock, they also were engaging in identity formation, fundamentally attempting to change the way others view veterans, but more importantly the way veterans view themselves and their military service.

A Brief Background

For the purposes of this essay, I will not go deeply into the history behind the actions at Standing Rock. For those unfamiliar with the 2016 actions there, briefly, protests started in spring 2016 by a small group opposed to the pipeline's potential to contaminate the tribe's water source and the destruction of sacred lands. The protest expanded as a site of solidarity for First Nations peoples as well as for climate and environmental activists (Iaconangelo). The Army Corp of Engineers was criticized for not consulting the Standing Rock Sioux, and for disregarding other federal agencies concerns about the project. As the protest expanded, members of more than 200 Native American tribes took part, as well as indigenous peoples from other nations (Linehan).

By late 2016, a large encampment was being maintained, and numerous demonstrations and other protest activities had been engaged in, while legal battles over the pipeline continued. It is in this context that veterans' groups entered the picture. Veterans for Peace (VFP) defines itself as "global organization of Military Veterans and allies whose collective efforts are to build a culture of peace by using our experiences and lifting our voices. We inform the public of the true causes of war and the enormous costs of wars, with an obligation to heal the wounds of wars" ("Who We Are"). The group issued a solidarity statement in September 2016, and group members and supporters began arriving at the encampment in the fall. By December, at least 70 VFP and IVAW (Iraq Veterans against the War) members were present ("A Significant Victory"). Veterans Stand for Standing Rock was formed by Wesley Clark, Jr., a former Army officer turned political commentator and activist, and Michael A. Wood, a Marine Corps veteran, former police officer, and advocate for police reform (Linehan). The group was formed with the explicit intention of mobilizing veterans to deploy to Standing Rock December 4-7, 2016, to "prevent progress on the Dakota Access Pipeline and draw national attention to the human rights warriors of the Sioux tribes" (Linehan). The group issued a letter announcing the problem, and provided the mission, the execution, and the logistics (Linehan). The accompanying GoFundMe site eventually raised over a million dollars for food, supplies, transportation, and legal costs (Wood).

This essay primarily looks at rhetoric from these two groups, as well as statements made by veterans identifying as members of one of the groups or acting under its auspices, and focuses on the period from September to December 2016, starting with the Veterans for Peace solidarity statement through the December "mobilization."[1]

Veterans and Social Movements

Veterans participating in social movement activism is not new. For example, in recent history, Vietnam Veterans Against the War participated in demonstrations and protests during that conflict. Iraq Veterans Against the War (IRAW) engaged in street performances in simulations designed to bring the conditions and actions in Iraq to citizens in US cities. Veterans for Peace, in fact, was founded in 1985, and has engaged in actions promoting peace both in the US and around the world ("History").

However, those actions by those groups were for causes directly related to their veteran status. They positioned themselves as stakeholders in the

---

1. Action has occurred since then, as legal battles have continued. These actions have largely been supported through supplies and continued statements.

anti-war cause because their military service provided them with a unique responsibility and authority. Standing Rock provides a more complicated case. Veterans are not a primary stakeholder; the tribe is, with the extension to other indigenous peoples, as the pipeline becomes a symbol of the violation of indigenous rights.[2] At Standing Rock, veterans' groups ceded authority to the tribes, explicitly pointing to the Sioux leadership ("A Significant Victory") and indicating that veterans were there to provide infrastructure and organization, as opposed to be the direct-action protesters (Iaconangelo). I argue then that the function of the groups' rhetoric, while in ways directed toward an outside audience, serves as a self-directed ego function, shaping the veterans' own identity.

Ego-Function and Coalitional Subjectivity

Theorizing on the ego-function of social movements, and the expansion of this to an understanding of coalitional subjectivity, helps explain how this identity shaping occurs. Richard Gregg first theorized the idea of the ego-function, suggesting that for the self-directed ego-function, one's rhetoric will not only be directed toward the self, but that rhetoric actually will constitute the self (74-75). Atkins-Sayre posited that "Social movements, if they are focused on identity work, must continually articulate particular identities in order to invite individuals—supporters and others—to view themselves in a particular way" (314). Stewart's theorizing on movements delineates between self-directed and other-directed movements. Self-directed movements see themselves as the oppressed group rather than other-directed movements which struggle on behalf of others who are oppressed. While this may seem an instance of an other-directed movement, the veterans acting on behalf of the tribes, I argue that the groups' rhetoric also positions them as a self-directed movement defining the veterans as a group needing this action. Particularly relevant here is Stewart's discussion that one function of self-directed movements is to increase self-worth, engaging in rhetoric that restores and enhances self-esteem and confidence.

Carillo-Rowe's theorizing on coalitional subjectivity further aids in understanding this case. In her discussion of feminist subjectivity, she argued for the need to understand power lines that connect. She stated, "I seek to advance the notion of a coalitional subject who is marked by a movement from the individual (a "politics of location") to the subject constituted through belonging (a "politics of relation")" ("Subject to Power" 26). In this way,

---

2. While some veterans were tribal members, that may have given additional incentive to them or may have been the primary incentive, but the rhetoric examined in this essay was aimed instead toward their veteran status.

the self-identity of veterans is not just rooted in their location as veterans, but in their relationship to the Standing Rock activists. Carillo-Rowe further argued

> Belonging is political—who we love is constitutive of our becoming. I mean "love" not necessarily in the narrow sense of lovers, or even friends, although I mean those relations too. "Love" may be considered in an expansive sense. Whose lives matter to us? Whose well-being is essential to our own? And, alternatively, whose survival must we overlook in order to connect to power in the ways we do? If questions of who we love are inseparable from the politics of subject formation, then belonging is political. The sites of our belonging constitute how we see the world, what we value, who we are becoming. ("Moving Relations" 3)

In this way, the formation of this identity becomes a political act. Chavez extends Carillo-Rowe's argument to social movements:

> For activists who engage in coalition building on behalf of multiple or broad social justice and human rights causes, rhetoric functions in two primary ways within enclaves. First, activists interpret external rhetorical messages that are created about them, the constituencies they represent, or both. In the case of coalition-building, these meaning-making processes serve as the rationale to build bridges with allies. Second, activists use enclaves as the sites to invent rhetorical strategies to publicly challenge oppressive rhetoric or to create new imaginaries for the groups and issues they represent and desire to bring into coalition. (3)

While Chavez's work on migrant and LGBT movements in Arizona focuses on the first function, I want to discuss the latter function here, using those coalitions, those enclaves, as points to invent rhetorical strategies to create the group itself.

Rhetorical Strategies

Turning then to the rhetorical strategies employed by these groups, this essay looks at three interrelated themes. First, the groups indicate their opposition to the violence being used by the energy company, its hired security forces, the police, and others. The Veterans for Peace position statement says, "We strongly condemn the violence being used against the resistance and believe it to be both a crime and a human rights abuse" ("Veterans for Peace Statement"). Stronger language is evidenced in its Thanksgiving statement:

"This Thanksgiving season, we are witnessing, yet again, brutal acts against Indigenous People and their lands. The Dakota Access Pipeline is yet another act of violence and genocide against Native people" ("Veterans for Peace Calls"). The Veterans Stand statement defines the violence more explicitly:

> Mace, sound cannons, sniper guns pointed at unarmed civilians, journalists being shot with rubber bullets, journalists being arrested for covering the protests, attack dogs unleashed on groups including children, elder Natives getting tased and violently arrest [sic], protesters marked with numbers and kept in dog kennels after arrest.... (Wood)

Statements by individuals define the violence as well. Loreal Black Shawl, identified as a descendent of the Oglala Lakota and Northern Arapaho tribes and Army veteran, is quoted as saying, "We are there because we are tired of seeing the water protectors being treated as non-humans" (Mele). Brian Trautman, an Army veteran and national board member of Veterans for Peace, wrote, "many of the veterans who joined VSSR wanted to intervene in and stop long-standing U.S. imperial policy of waging war for resources against vulnerable peoples. They understood that this was not something strictly happening abroad; it was also happening at home. They recognized that the violence against the water protectors was an expression of rampant U.S. militarism and structural white supremacy" (Trautman).

The discussion of violent tactics and the acknowledgement of the ideology of militarism behind it starts to redefine the former soldiers. Carillo-Rowe sees the coalitional subject as one no longer tied to the politics of location. While traditionally a soldier is tied to violence, that locational positioning is being questioned here as the veterans' groups call out violence, militarism, and policies of waging war. In this way, the veterans' identities are being removed from their former location as a soldier implementing US militaristic policies.

New identity formation, however, requires more than this, and so is seen in the coalition with indigenous peoples. In the second theme then, the veterans' groups discuss the need to protect Americans. The Veterans Stand statement begins

> We are veterans of the United States Armed Forces, including the U.S. Army, United States Marine Corps, U.S. Navy, U.S. Air Force and U.S. Coast Guard and we are calling for our fellow veterans to assemble as a peaceful, unarmed militia at the Standing Rock Indian Reservation on Dec 4-7 and defend the water protectors from assault

and intimidation at the hands of the militarized police force and DAPL security. (Wood)

Drawing the distinction between the militarized other, the statement defines veterans as the defenders. In other places, veterans are referred to as "human shields" (Mele). One Air Force veteran, Elizabeth Williams, is quoted stating, "We are prepared to put our bodies between Native elders and a privatized military force, …We've stood in the face of fire before. We feel a responsibility to use the skills we have" (Levin). Another veteran, Jake Pogue, stated, "We're not coming as fighters, but as protectors . . . . Our role in that situation would be to simply form a barrier between water protectors and the police force and try to take some of that abuse for them" (Levin). While protecting sounds more traditional to the understanding of soldier/military veteran, the coalitional alliance to protecting indigenous peoples allows a redefining to occur. They are not fighters, they are unarmed protectors.

Finally, I argue that all of this, positions the veterans' past actions, when they were soldiers, as unjust, and thus redemption, and a new self-worth, emerges through this new mission. The veterans acknowledge their past wrongs, connecting their soldier status to the militarism they condemn. The Veterans for Peace Thanksgiving statement posited, "As veterans we are aware of our legacy as military veterans as participants in the ways in which we have perpetuated injustice across the globe and against indigenous people" ("Veterans for Peace Calls"). The veterans point to their oath to serve and protect, as rationale for the current action. One veteran, Kevin Basl wrote, "Like many post-9/11 veterans, I left the military seeking redemption. Perhaps that's why, after I saw those images of police violence against water protectors, I went to Standing Rock. There, instead of helping military contractors make money, I felt like I was finally serving the people." Similar sentiments were written by Will Griffin, former Army paratrooper and now member of Veterans for Peace.

> I was in Iraq when President Bush announced the 'surge' in January 2007. I was in Afghanistan when President Obama announced the 'surge' in December 2009. But it wasn't until I visited Standing Rock in October 2016 when I actually served the American people. This time, instead of fighting for corporate interests, I was fighting for the people.

Marine Corp veteran Tyson Manker added, "(Veterans) swore an oath to the Constitution that never expires . . . . It's proven we're dedicated to country and willing to stand up (to anything), like the federal government" (Spearie 1).

These are not merely acts of personal identity transformation. The veterans' groups explicitly make the connection to enhanced self-worth, through the action of going to Standing Rock, as they call for veterans to mobilize and deploy. The Veterans Stand statement ends, "Let's stop this savage injustice being committed right here at home. If not us, who? If not now, when? Are you a hero? Are you honorable? Not if you allow this to be the United States. It's time to display that honor, courage, and commitment we claim to represent. It's time for real Patriots. Now more than ever, it's time for anyone and everyone to lead" (Wood). The author of this statement, Michael A. Wood, is quoted elsewhere arguing "If we're going to be heroes, if we're really going to be those veterans that this country praises, well, then we need to do the things that we actually said we're going to do when we took the oath to defend the Constitution from enemies foreign and domestic" (Linehan). In these statements, Wood infers that past actions have not been those of honorable heroes, but in acting truly to uphold the oath they took (to protect against domestic enemies), they can become heroes deserving of praise.

Conclusion

The veterans who deployed to Standing Rock present a unique case study of activism. While they were not the primary stakeholder in this protest, their rhetoric positioned them as directly relevant to the indigenous peoples' struggle by redefining who they were as veterans. Chavez argued that past theorizing

> explored the "ego function" within both self- and other-directed movements to suggest that the need to build one's sense of identity and self is important for activists, whether one advocates for her or his own rights or the rights of someone or something else. Examining movements where the direction is self- and other-oriented at the same time, however, challenges the "either/or" dichotomy . . . . Implicitly, coalitional politics built between mostly disparate groups are "both/and" activities. (13)

The rhetoric mobilizing veterans to Standing Rock serves dual ego identity functions (both/and). While it encourages an awareness of past and present injustices against indigenous peoples, I argue that it also, and more so, serves a self-directed function—redefining who military veterans can be if they stand for Standing Rock. Through this coalitional subjectivity, it unmakes the veterans who supported corporate interests and upheld militarism, and in their place creates heroes who serve and protect.

Works Cited

"A Significant Victory at Standing Rock." *Veterans for Peace*, 2016, www.veteransforpeace.org/our-work/position-statements/significant-victory-standing-rock. Accessed 25 May 2018.

Atkins-Sayre, Wendy. "Articulating Identity: People for the Ethical Treatment of Animals and the Animal=Human Divide." *Western Journal of Communication*, vol. 74, no. 3, 2010, pp. 309-328.

Basl, Kevin. "Why I Answered the Call for Veterans to Go to Standing Rock." *OtherWords*, 2017, https://otherwords.org/why-i-answered-the-call-for-veterans-to-go-to-standing-rock/. Accessed 25 May 2018.

Carillo Rowe, Aimee. "Moving Relations: On the Limits of Belonging." *Liminalities: A Journal of Performance Studies*, vol. 5, no. 5, 2009, pp. 1-10.

—. "Subject to Power—Feminism without Victims." *Women's Studies in Communication*, vol. 32, no. 1, 2009, pp. 12-35.

Chávez, Karma R. "Counter-Public Enclaves and Understanding the Function of Rhetoric in Social Movement Coalition-Building." *Communication Quarterly*, vol. 59, no. 1, 2011, pp. 1-18.

Gregg, Richard B. "The Ego-Function of the Rhetoric of Protest." *Philosophy & Rhetoric*, vol. 4, no. 2, 1971, pp. 71-91.

Griffin, Will. "After Two Wars, Standing Rock is the First Time I Served the American People." *Common Dreams*, 30 October 2016, www.commondreams.org/views/2016/10/30/after-two-wars-standing-rock-first-time-i-served-american-people#. Accessed 25 May 2018.

"History." *Veterans for Peace*, https://www.veteransforpeace.org/who-we-are/history. Accessed 25 May 2018.

Iaconangelo, David. "The Calvary Arrives: Veterans Bring 'Symbolic Value' and Support to Standing Rock; Veterans are Pouring into North Dakota just Days before the Monday Deadline to Vacate." *Christian Science Monitor*, 3 December 2016. Lexis-Nexis.

Levin, Sam. "Army Veterans Return to Standing Rock to Form a Human Shield against Police; A Growing Group of Military Veterans are Willing to Put their Bodies between Native American Activists and the Police Trying to Remove Them." *Guardian*, 11 February 2017. Lexis-Nexis.

Linehan, Adam. "'Where Evil Resides': Veterans 'Deploy' to Standing Rock to Engage the Enemy—The US Government." *TaskandPurpose.com*, 21 November 2016, taskandpurpose.com/where-evil-resides-veterans-deploy-to-standing-rock-to-engage-the-enemy-the-us-government. Accessed 25 May 2018.

Mele, Christopher. "Veterans to Serve as 'Human Shields' for Dakota Pipeline Protesters." *New York Times*, 29 November 2016. Lexis-Nexis.

Spearie, Steven. "Dakota Access Oil Pipeline; Local Veterans Join Protest. They Say Native Americans Have Been Disrespected." *The State Journal-Register* [Springfield, IL], Il news sec., 8 December 2016, p. 1. Lexis-Nexis.

Stewart, Charles J. "Championing the Rights of Others and Challenging Evil: The Ego Function in the Rhetoric of Other-Directed Social Movements." *Southern Communication Journal*, vol. 64, no. 2, 1999, pp. 91-105. doi: 10.1080/10417949909373125

Trautman, Brian. "US Veterans on the Line at Standing Rock...Still Fighting for Democracy." *CityWatch*, 12 December 2016, citywatchla.com/index.php/2016-01-01-13-17-00/important-reads/12272-us-veterans-on-the-line-at-standing-rock-still-fighting-for-demcracy. Accessed 25 May 2018.

Veterans for Peace Thanksgiving statement: "Veterans for Peace Calls for Solidarity with Standing Rock this Thanksgiving." *Veterans for Peace*, 2016, www.veteransforpeace.org/our-work/position-statements/veterans-peace-calls-solidarity-standing-rock-thanksgiving. Accessed 25 May 2018.

Veterans for Peace position statement: "Veterans for Peace Statement in Support of the Pipeline Resistance at Standing Rock." *Veterans for Peace*, 9 September 2016, www.veteransforpeace.org/our-work/position-statements/veterans-peace-statement-support--pipeline-resistance-standing-rock. Accessed 25 May 2018.

"Who We Are." *Veterans for Peace*, www.veteransforpeace.org/who-we-are. Accessed 25 May 2018.

Wood, Michael, Jr. "Veterans for Standing Rock #NoDAPL." 2016. www.gofundme.com/veterans-for-standing-rock-nodapl. Accessed 25 May 2018.

Reinventing *Yin-Yang* to Teach Rhetoric to Women

Hui Wu

As complimentary forces or energies corresponding to each other being balanced within a course of order, the Chinese concept of *yin-yang* has prompted rhetoric scholars to question established dichotomies in the Western analytical framework. Using it as an indigenous methodology, scholars engage polarized opposites in ongoing intellectual investigations to strengthen the notion of balanced methodology (Mao, W53; Chen, "Beyond" and "Introduction"). So far, *yin-yang* has been verified as a perspective, a methodology, an approach, or an interpretive framework to advance theories and methods (Chen, "Beyond" and "Introduction"; Mao, 2009; Fang and Faure, 35, 320-333). However, *yin-yang* has yet to be systematically conceptualized in its own right as a key component of Chinese indigenous rhetorical theory (Wu, "Yin-Yang"). In fact, China's first treatise on rhetoric, *Guiguzi* (pronounced as *Gwaygootze*), weaves *yin-yang* intrinsically into the fabric of rhetorical theory with its own definition and functionality. A contemporary of Aristotle (384-322 BCE), the alleged author, Guiguzi (Master of the Ghost Valley), recommends persuaders to uphold the *Dao* through the use of *yin-yang* to develop themselves into sages of rhetoric who represent the highest level of judicious intellect, wisdom, and morality (Wu, "Redrawing" 84-85, 90-94, 100-102).

Although not taught specifically to female persuaders, Guiguzi's *yin-yang* rhetoric could originally be practiced by both genders. Later, the *yin-yang* concept was manipulated philosophically by Dong Zhongshu (董仲舒179-104 BCE) to create gender hierarchy. In his treatise, *Chun Qiu Fan Lu* (秋繁露 *Luxuriant Gems of the Spring and Autumn*) Dong integrates *yin-yang* into Confucianism, not to guide rhetorical performance as Guiguzi had done, but to form a new philosophy of nature and the human.¹ In a new rhetorical genre similar to Western expository writing, Dong is able to not only explicate concepts in Confucian classics to form his own theory on state governance, but also redefine *yin-yang* into a hierarchical relationship that subordinated women (Wang, "Dong Zhongshu's Transformation," 209 and *Images* 163-164). He labels the sun, superiors, and males as *yang*, and the moon, subordinates, and females as *yin*, with *yang* having authority over *yin* (Wang, "Dong Zhongshu's Transformation," 215-216). Dong's prescription of *yin-yang* has perpetuated unequal gender stratification in Chinese society at large and still influences the Chinese conceptualization of gender relations today. In other words, while Guiguzi established *yin-yang* as the foundational philosophy in the rhetorical tradition, Dong reshaped the concept into signifiers of gender hierarchy with the female as the subordinate.

Given the prevailing tradition surrounding *yin-yang*, we may wonder how Chinese women receive the *yin-yang* concept in terms of perception of gender and rhetorical practice. Has *yin-yang* been formally taught to women? If so, who has taught it and in what ways? If *yin-yang* indeed is the foundation of Chinese rhetoric (Wu, "Yin-Yang"), how do *yin-yang* forces impel, mediate, or enrich rhetorical women's processes of persuasion, particularly in addressing gender relations? Most importantly, if we accept that rhetoric is the ability to see the available means of persuasion to seek and demonstrate probable truth (Aristotle, 1356a 1), how do Chinese women understand *yin-yang* and reinvent it to discipline and guide their rhetorical practice in order to seek and illuminate truth about gender?² To answer these questions, this study draws upon the *yin-yang* philosophy of rhetoric in *Guiguzi* to offer a rhetorical reading of Ban Zhao's *Lessons for Women*, the first women's book in China, and her intellectual impact on other so-called "women's classics" to argue that these books should be read as rhetorical instruction grounded on an reinvented concept of *yin-yang*. My proposition aims to reveal the roles women teachers have played in reconstructing gender relations to broker power and space for women, while helping understand women's historic contributions to Chinese rhetoric, particularly their roles of shaping and modeling *yin-yang* rhetorical practice.

---

1. The author of the book remains controversial. But most scholars have accepted the authenticity of the author and the text (Queen, 5).

2. Chapter and passage numbers, instead of page numbers, in Aristotle's *On Rhetoric* and *Guiguzi* are used for consistent reference regardless of translated editions.

Yin-Yang as the Foundation for Chinese Rhetoric in *Guiguzi*

Guiguzi presents *yin* and *yang* as interactive interdependent flexible energies while transforming their metaphysical nature into a philosophical power that regulates, specifically, the process of persuasion and communication (I.1, III.1). The *yin-yang* forces are intertwined and correlated as well as interact with and transform each other to move and balance rhetorical acts and respond to constantly changing situations. They are action and inaction simultaneously, and accordingly, flexible, adjustable, and responsive at the disposal of the sage of rhetoric (*Guiguzi*, I.1.). Guiguzi's *yin-yang* philosophy guides and controls rhetorical moves and purposes; it determines if a speech or a communication act succeeds or fails. It constitutes the superb quality and characteristics of an exemplary persuader, or a sage of rhetoric as Guiguzi perceives, all for the purpose of persuading the single-person audience in a private setting (Garrett, "Classical"; Wu, "Redrawing" 12-15). The ultimate goal of persuasion is upholding the *Dao* through *yin-yang* to illuminate truth, justice, morality, and propriety (Wu and Swearingen, 515-516).

Guiguzi lays down the philosophical foundation of his rhetorical theory by illustrating the relationship between *yin-yang* and rhetorical motions (*Guiguzi*, I.1.1-I.1.6, III.1). On this foundation, "*yin* and *yang* are in harmony," and "the beginning and the ending are working together to set on a course" (*Guiguzi*, I.1.5). Guiguzi recommends that all persuaders develop themselves into sages of rhetoric who can understand when and how to deploy rhetorical strategies through *yin-yang*. Yet, all persuaders are not sages of rhetoric. Persuaders, to Guiguzi, are individuals who talk to convince others and extend assistance (*Guiguzi*, II.9.1), while sages possess sensibility and wisdom to follow the way of *yin*; insensible persons follow the way of *yang* (*Guiguzi*, II.10.4). They know that "all speeches in the *yang* category begin with lofty topics, while those dealing with *yin* references rely on low and small matters" (*Guiguzi*, I.1.6). Low and small matters, however, are not petty gossips or backstabbing; they may be trivial daily matters that the rhetor utilizes to establish his/her persona for persuasion. Sages of rhetoric, Guiguzi conceptualizes, know answers to all issues, foresee the development of all things, and understand the human mind and ways of thinking.

During the process of persuasion, when sages of rhetoric follow the way of *yin*, they are following the *Dao* because "the *Dao* of the ancient kings was *yin*" (*Guiguzi*, II.10.4). Here *yin* may refer to wisdom and knowledge gathered from the past as well as "strategic silence and understatement when talking 'up' to a superior who may present a threat" (Swearingen, 145). Scholars have explored how the interactions of *yin-yang* strengthen the *Dao* in understanding the Chinese mind with regard to culture, ontology, cosmos, and gender (Fang; Hall and Ames, 91; Jenkins; R. Wang, "Dong Zhongshu"). In Guiguzi's theory of rhetoric, however, the *Dao* grounded on *yin-yang* is "the fundamental principle that prescribes how to progress in response to changes, how to overcome setbacks, and how to address objections" (*Guiguzi*, I.1.4). The *Dao* is also the source of "omniscient intellectual conscience" (*Guiguzi*, II.12.3, III.1.1). Guiguzi's teaching of rhetoric has influenced women teachers of rhetoric whose texts became available centuries later.

Embodying *Yin-Yang* to Teach Rhetoric to Women

A preliminary reading of the so-called classics for Chinese women reveals that the women teachers of rhetoric embody *yin-yang* to perform and teach rhetoric as sages of rhetoric to follow the *Dao* to seek truth about sexes in order to achieve equal gender relations. Writing books in different time periods, learned women, though very few, joined men to teach rhetoric. Instead of merely listening to men's teaching of Confucian virtues and *yin-yang* to subordinate women, they reshaped moral concepts and adjusted male-dominated rhetorical strategies to broker power and space for women. Four women's classics, *Lessons for Women, Women's Analects, The Doctrine for the Inner Chamber*, and *A Brief Survey of Exemplary Women* (also see Wang, *Images*, 177-194, 326-340, 372-390) developed a rhetorical genre of instruction that incorporates argument, instruction, advice, and narrative. Although they are called "women's books" in China and "conduct books" or "instruction texts" in the West (Bacabac, 159-160; Raphals, 249), they are in fact rhetorical instruction books, because they teach a women-centered philosophy of rhetoric with which they reconceptualize rhetorical terms and strategies in the dominant male tradition.

Ban Zhao (45-114 BCE) was the author of *Lessons for Women*. Known for her classical learning and writing, Ban was summoned by Emperor He of the late Han Dynasty to teach classics, poetry, and historiographies to the queen, concubines, and court ladies. Near the end of her life, Ban felt that she had yet to educate her daughters how to perform a proper gender-specific rhetoric in order to survive as wives and daughters-in-law in a severely gendered society. Although many Chinese scholars read Ban's primary concerns in her book as about women's virtues, duties, and status to meet societal expectations (Wen, Chapter 1), their reading tends to overlook her embodiment and teaching of a re-gendered *yin-yang* rhetoric that counterbalances male power. Also, reading Ban Zhao from a modern feminist perspective, we may think that her recommendation of women to humble themselves supports gender subordination. However, her encouragement of women's humility shows her keen awareness of a gendered reality and her *yin-yang* rhetorical motions to "help women exercise agency within their marital families and respect and influence" (Barabac, 169). As my reading will demonstrate, Ban teaches and preforms an embodied rhetoric that enables women to deploy *yin* to acquire the gain of *yang* (*Guiguzi*, II.10.3).

Ban's treatise reveals multifaceted *yin-yang* rhetoric that she practices and teaches, specifically through the strategy of self-degradation and teaching of female humility to broker space for rhetorical performances. The opening sentence in her book serves as an example. "I, the unworthy writer, am unsophisticated, unenlightened, and by nature unintelligent, but I am fortunate both to have received not a little favor from my scholarly father, and to have had a mother and instructresses upon whom to rely for a literary education as well as for training in good manners" (Wang, *Images* 178). Her strategy—yielding herself to traditional expectations of women and then presenting herself as a beneficiary of women's education--is what Guiguzi calls "deploying the way of *yin* to acquire the gain of *yang*" (*Guiguzi*, II.10.3). In Ban's performance, *yin* is lowering her female self, even in disparaging terms, to "yield to the inside" and "to shape situations" (*Guiguzi*, I.1.6); then when the situation shaped by *yin* naturally intersects with *yang*, she moves on to credit her parents with her own education. This recognition involves both *yin* and *yang* moves. On the one hand, she yields to the traditional expectation of the humble female through *yin*; on the other hand, she grasps the interactive moment of *yin* and *yang* to lead to an implied recognition of her as a female sage with 'literary talent" and "moral integrity" (Wang, *Images* 177). The motion of *yang* allows Ban to "reach out' and "take action" (*Guiguzi*, I.1.6). In other words, the *yin-yang* moves interact to give her authority to speak out and share wisdom. Her embodied rhetorical performance represents a *yin-yang* tactic Guiguzi recommends--embracing virtues to acquire *yin* through *yang* and adding force to acquire *yang* through *yin* (*Guiguzi*, I.1.6).

This *yin-yang* rhetorical principle is constantly and consistently exemplified in Ban's rhetorical performances because of her keen awareness of the gender hierarchy wherein women are born subordinate to men. For this reason, even after she has established herself as a highly respected saint-like teacher and even after she has brought up her son and educated him successfully to become a high-ranking officer who "has unprecedentedly received the extraordinary privilege of wearing the Gold and the Purple" (Wang, *Images* 178), Ban starts with a self-diminutive *yin* motion to say that "Being careless, and by nature stupid, I taught and trained (my children) without system" (Wang, *Images* 178). The *yin* motion allows her to acquire *yang*, with which she then presents her son's achievement as a result of her education. Although sounding self-debasing, Ban implies that she was the first woman who trained her son successfully and who was ready to establish a system of education. Her rhetorical performance involves sophisticated *yin-yang* strategies to establish authority to argue against the tradition that has excluded women from formal education. She now adds force to acquire *yang*, saying, "Yet, only to teach men and not to teach women—is that not ignoring the essential relation between them? According to the *Rites*, by the age of eight, boys begin to learn to read. At the age of fifteen, they should begin great learning. Why can't it be the principle (for girls)?"[3] (Shen, 8). She then teaches the same rhetorical strategy to young women. By humbling themselves, she believes, they can build personal reputations through *yin* to achieve *yang*, which makes their long speeches possible without causing others to detest them (Shen, Chapter 4).

Once she has established her authority, she re-genders the *yin-yang* concept against Dong's unequal *yin-yang* gender positions. First, Ban argues, "The Way of man and wife is intimately connected with *yin* and *yang* to lead to the full achievement of omniscient intellectual conscience (*shen ming* 神明)" (Shen, 7). Her illustration of *yin-yang* in relation to *shen ming* is the same as Guiguzi's (*Guiguzi*, II.12.3, III.1.1). This *yin* motion allows her to redefine the concept of *yin-yang* to argue that "*Yin* and *yang* are of different natures, so are different deeds (*xing* 行) of men and women. The virtue of *yang* is fortitude (*gang* 刚); the virtue of *yin* is resilience (*rou* 柔)" (Shen, 9). Here she reshapes Dong's sexually unequal *yin-yang* theory into an interdependent and interactive notion of equity to endow the female with positive traits and characters. Then Ban suggests, "Should a husband be unworthy, then he possesses nothing by which to manage (*yu* 御 or serve) his wife; should a wife be unworthy, then she possesses nothing by which to serve (*shi* 事) her husband .... The purpose of these two is the same" (Shen, 7). In so doing, Ban reveals the *Dao* [truth] of gender relations and places two sexes conceptually on an equal ground.

Ban's embodiment of *yin-yang* in her rhetoric has influenced later women teachers, such as Wang Jiefu, author of *A Brief Survey of Exemplary Women* composed near the end of the Ming Dynasty (1368-1644). Following Ban's revised *yin-yang* theory, Wang clarifies spaces for men and women to perform equally different roles. Men perform duties outside; and women inside. Arguing against Confucian's *Book of Rites*, Wang believes that both boys and girls must receive education. Yet, education is more important to girls, because they are destined to educate their sons (Shen, 137). Her book records women who deliver remonstrance speeches to their husbands and sons who hold offices. Both Ban and Wang have adjusted male theories to rhetorical

---

3. All quotations of Ban in Shen's edition are my translations to show correlated lexicons in Ban and *Guiguzi*.

instruction of women through *yin-yang* moves to negotiate space wherein women can perform embodied rhetoric to govern their husbands and sons at home.

IMPLICATIONS OF *YIN-YANG* TO RHETORICAL FEMINISM

Transnational feminist studies of rhetoric, like feminist studies of rhetorical women in general, have yet to develop a nomenclature (see Hogg, 181-183, 185-188). This study shows *yin-yang*, an indigenous rhetorical concept, enables us to rename Ban's book rhetorically, giving us hope that persistent studies of women's rhetoric will eventually generate systematic terms and concepts for a rhetorical feminism, because we are convinced that a woman "is nearly naturalized at the scene of rhetoric" (Glenn, 1-2). My study also contributes to the continuous recovery of women rhetoricians. Ban's rhetorical teaching and performance show that women participated in philosophical dialogues about *yin-yang* and employed it in their rhetoric. This rhetorical reading places Ban Zhao equally with established males in Chinese rhetoric--Confucius, Zhuangzi, Guiguzi, Hanfeizi, Dong Zhongshu, among others (Lu, *Rhetoric* and "Theory"; Mao; *Guiguzi*; Lyon; Liu and You). Finally, using *yin-yang* as an integral part of Chinese indigenous rhetorical theory to read Chinese women's books can prevent us from relying on existing, mostly Western interpretive analytical terms, to name other women's rhetorics. Instead of inheriting available frameworks and terms mostly created by Western men, rhetorical feminists can reexamine indigenous rhetorical terminologies and focus on some critical questions in their investigations. How do rhetorical women accomplish their goals? What philosophy guides them? What alternative terms, or nomenclature, embedded in their treatises and performances can we discover and systemize? My *yin-yang* reading of Ban Zhao can hopefully serve as a model for further re-gendering and un-gendering women's rhetoric to develop feminist inquiries into more responsive, inclusive, innovative meaning-making endeavors.

WORKS CITED

Aristotle. *On Rhetoric*. Translated by George Kennedy. 2nd ed., New York: Oxford UP, 2007.

Bacabac, Florence E. "Reviewing Conduct Books as Feminist Rhetorical Devices for Agency Reforms." *Peitho Journal*, vol.21, no. 1, 2018. http://peitho.cwshrc.org/files/2018/10/11_Bacabac_Reviewing-Conduct-Books_21.1_Final.pdf

Chen, Guo-Ming. "Beyond the Dichotomy of Communication Studies." *Asian Journal of Communication*, vol. 9, no. 4, 2009, pp. 398-411.

—-. "Introduction to Key Concepts in Understanding Chinese." *China Media Research*, vol. 7, no. 4, 2011, pp.1-12.

Fang, Tony. "Yin Yang: A New Perspective on Culture." *Management and Organization Review*, vol. 8, no.1, 2011, pp. 25-50.

Fang, Tony and Guy Olivier Faure. "Chinese Communication Characteristics: a Yin Yang Perspective." *International Journal of Intercultural Relations*, vol. 35, 2011, pp.320-333.

Garrett, Mary. "Classical Chinese Conceptions of Argumentation and Persuasion." *Argument and Advocacy*, vol. 29, no. 3, 1993, pp.105-115.

Glenn, Cheryl. *Rhetorical Feminism and This Thing Called Hope*. Carbondale, IL: Southern Illinois UP, 2018.

Guiguzi, China's First Treatise on Rhetoric: A Critical Translation and Commentary. Translated by Hui Wu with commentaries by Hui. Wu and C. Jan. Swearingen. Carbondale, IL: Southern Illinois UP, 2016.

Hall, David and Roger Ames. *Thinking from the Han: Self, Truth, and transcendence in Chinese and Western Culture*. Albany, New York: State of New York UP, 1998.

Hogg, Charlotte. "What's (Not) in a Name: Considerations and Consequences of the Field's Nomenclature." *Peitho Journal*, vol. 19, no. 2, 2017, pp. 181-208. http://peitho.cwshrc.org/files/2017/03/Hogg_Whats-in-a-Name_Final.pdf

Jenkins, McKay. "China and the United States: a Yin-Yang Environmental Relationship." *Southern Review*, vol. 98, no. 4, 2013, pp.574-585.

Liu, Yichun and Xiaoye You. "Reading the Heavenly Mandate: Dong Zhongshu's Rhetoric of the Way (Dao)." *Ancient Non-Greek Rhetorics*. Edited by Carol Lipson and Roberta Binkley, West Lafayette: Parlor, 2009, pp. 153-175.

Lu, Xing. *Rhetoric in Ancient China Fifth to Third Century B.C. E.: A Comparison with Classical Greek Rhetoric*. Columbia, SC: U of South Carolina P, 1998.

—. "The Theory of Persuasion in Han Fei Tzs and Its Impact on Chinese Communication Behaviors." *The Howard Journal of Communication*, vol. 5, no. 1&2, fall 1993 and winter 1994, pp.108-122.

Lyon, Arabella. "Writing an Empire: Cross-Talk on Authority, Act, and Relationships with the Other in the *Analects, Daodejing*, and *HanFeizi*," *College English*, vol. 72, no. 4, 2010, pp. 350-366.

Mao, LuMing. "Returning to Yin and Yang: From Terms of Opposites to Interdependence-in-Difference. *College Composition and Communication*, vol. 60, no 4, pp.W45-W56. 2009.

Queen, Sarah. *From Chronicle to Canon: the Hermeneutics of the Spring and Autumn According to Tung Chung-shu*. New York: Cambridge UP, 1996.

Raphals, Lisa. *Sharing the Light: Representations of Women and Virtue in Early China*. Albany, NY: State U of New York P, 1998.

Shen, Zhukun. *Tuhui nusishu baihua jie [Four Women's Books with Illustrations and Commentaries]*. 2nd Ed. Beijing: Zhongguo Huaqiao Chubanshe [China Overseas Press], 2012.

Swearingen, C. Jan. "Under Western Eyes: a Comparison of Guigucian Rhetoric with the Pre-Socratics, Plato, and Aristotle." *Guiguzi, China's First Treatise on Rhetoric: A Critical Translation and Commentary*. Translated by Hui Wu with commentaries by Hui Wu and C. Jan Swearingen. Carbondale, IL: Southern Illinois UP, 2016, pp.113-152.

Wang, Robin. "Dong Zhongshu's Transformation of Yin-Yang Theory and Contesting of Gender Identity. *Philosophy East and West*, vol. 55, no. 2, 2015, pp. 209-231.

—, editor. *Images of Women in Chinese Thought and Culture*. Indianapolis, IN: Hackett, 2003.

Wen, Xinzi. Editor. *Nusishu Pindu Quanji*. [*Commentaries on Four Women's Classics*]. Beijing: Central Broadcasting and TV Education P, 2013.

Wu, Hui. "Redrawing the Map of Rhetoric." *Guiguzi, China's First Treatise on Rhetoric: A Critical Translation and Commentary*. Translated by Hui Wu with commentaries by Hui. Wu and C. Jan. Swearingen. Carbondale, IL: Southern Illinois UP, 2016, pp. 1-31.

—. "*Yin-Yang* as the Philosophical Foundation of Chinese Rhetoric." *China Media Research*, Vol. 14, no 4, 2018. pp. 46-55.

Wu, Hui and C. Jan. Swearingen. "Interality as a Key to Deciphering *Guiguzi*, a Challenge to Critics." *Canadian Journal of Communication*, vol. 41, no. 3, 2016, pp. 503-519.

Rethinking the Oxymoron: Situating Campbell's "Rhetoric of Women's Liberation" in Waves of Feminist Rhetorical Practices

Rachel Chapman Daugherty

This year's Rhetoric Society of America conference celebrates 50 years of rhetorical theory and scholarship in which the study of feminist rhetorics has significantly impacted our field's expansion and revision. Many feminist rhetoricians mark the emergence of our subfield with Karlyn Kohrs Campbell's 1973 analysis "The Rhetoric of Women's Liberation: An Oxymoron," in which Campbell identifies the axes of substance and style as interdependent rhetorical categories that illustrate how the rhetoric of women's liberation is a distinctive rhetorical genre. Campbell found that women's liberation rhetorics were inherently plural, emphasizing that "whatever liberation is, it will be something different for each woman as liberty is something different for each person" (86). Campbell's original oxymoron demonstrated that rhetorical frameworks for analyzing social movement rhetorics did not capture the plurality of women's liberation rhetorics, but her substance-style framework was later challenged by feminist rhetoricians who criticized Campbell's theory as limited to white and liberal women's rhetorical practices (Dow and Tonn; Reid-Brinkley). In response, I argue that Campbell's substance-style method is sociohistorically situated within the rhetorical practices of Second Wave feminist activism and deserves an update to capture the plural rhetorical practices of contemporary feminist and intersectional rhetorics.[1]

---

1. Jennifer Baumgardner argues that feminism is currently in its Fourth Wave starting in 2008, in which Third Wave feminist concepts are practiced through net-

In this paper, I treat Campbell's method of substance-style as a dynamic framework for feminist rhetorical analysis that demands expansion to account for current feminist sociohistorical contexts. I argue that situating Campbell's method within feminist waves can account for rhetorical changes between waves of feminist activism and trace the growth of feminist rhetorical analysis alongside expansions of feminist theory. I offer the 2017 Women's March on Washington "Guiding Vision and Definition of Principles" statement (the official policy platform released online nine days before the January 21, 2017 marches) as a case study for analyzing the alignment between intersectional substance and style in contemporary feminist social movement rhetorics. Through my analysis of the definitional argument in the Guiding Vision," I will demonstrate how updating Campbell's framework to attend to intersectionality can reclaim the substance-style method of analyzing rhetorics of women's liberation. In the next section, I outline how analyzing the intersectional feminist substance and style of the Women's March "Guiding Vision" can create a rhetorical profile of the waves of feminist rhetoric.

Substance and Style in Intersectional Activism

Although Campbell created a starting point for understanding how women's movements demonstrated their rhetorical practices, the intersectional focus of contemporary feminist movements complicates Campbell's conclusions of the "interrelationship between the personal and the political [that] is central to a conception of women's liberation as a genre of rhetoric" (Campbell 84). Kimberlé Crenshaw's introduction of intersectionality in 1989 revealed that these personal and political interrelationships must also consider the multidimensionality of marginalized women's experiences across identity categories. Crenshaw's analysis of discrimination along race and gender lines demonstrated the importance of plural axes of analysis for understanding how intersectionality is responsive to and reflective of rhetorical contexts, leading her to expand descriptions of intersectionality from a concept to an "analytic sensibility" (Cho, Crenshaw, and McCall). I believe by reading intersectionality into Campbell's substance-style method, we can create a feminist rhetorical framework for analyzing the substance and style of intersectional arguments in rhetorical situations. By updating Campbell's method to specifically focus on the plural identities of race, class, gender, and sexuality, rhetoricians can track the evolution of public feminist thought through the rhetoric of women's liberation.

---

worked activism. For more discussion, see Baumgardner (250-252).

Crenshaw's definition of intersectionality and characterization of its analytic sensibility allow us to map these concepts onto Campbell's interdependent categories of substance and style. How might Campbell's substance-style method help us determine arguments for defining "women" and "feminism" in a policy platform like the "Guiding Vision"? I argue that tracing the named exigencies for these feminist rhetorical arguments alongside their sociohistorical contexts can illustrate what Campbell describes as the "dialectic between discourses that deal with public, structural problems and the particularly significant statements of personal experience and feeling" (85). In the following section, I demonstrate how feminist rhetoricians can map the intersectional rhetorical practices through an analysis of the intersectional substance and style of the Women's March "Guiding Vision."

A "Guiding Vision" for American Feminism

The "Guiding Vision and Definition of Principles" served as the definitional argument for shared action in the Women's March coalition by defining the ideology of march participants, articulating shared exigencies for protest, and recommending social and political changes. Coalitions and social movement organizations often create definitional arguments to clarify goals and constitute membership. Definitional arguments are especially important for women's constituencies because defining "women" is a political process and responsive to the sociohistorical context of that movement (Feree and Mueller 580). As Women's March national co-chairs Bob Bland and Carmen Perez stated, they framed intersectional feminism as the direct response to the sociohistorical context of Trump's election:

> Bland: It was intentional, especially because our new president-elect was attacking a lot of these communities with his—some of his racist rhetoric around Mexicans and building a wall.
> Perez: And I'm Mexican-American myself. Linda Sarsour, one of our national co-chairs, is Muslim American. We need to have courageous conversations. Sometimes, we — we don't speak about religion and politics and race because we don't want to offend anyone. But how are we going to learn? ("Women's March leaders")

The "Guiding Vision" articulated the coalition's goals for their mobilization as "bringing together people of all genders, races, cultures, political affiliations and backgrounds" and "recognizing that women have intersecting identities and are therefore impacted by a multitude of social justice and human rights issues" (Women's March). This document therefore claims to articulate the identities and perspectives of those who marched, defining their shared exigencies within the framework of intersectional feminism.

The "Guiding Vision" links the substance and style of the Women's March social movement rhetoric by positioning intersectional feminism as exigence and response to oppressions connected through gender. Definitional arguments are integral for plural visions of feminism because they create shared exigencies for women's activism across feminist waves. By updating Campbell's substance-style method to analyze intersectionality, rhetoricians can better situate gender-based definitional arguments within the contexts of feminine style and feminist waves. In the next section, I outline key rhetorical features of the "Guiding Vision" to illustrate the substance and style of intersectional arguments in this sociohistorical context.

Defining Intersectional Activism

Campbell's identification of substance and style as interdependent rhetorical strategies of women's liberation provides a starting point for understanding women's social movement rhetorics. Updating Campbell's framework for contemporary intersectional feminism allows rhetoricians to ask: if a movement calls itself intersectional, how do their principles reflect that ideology? The "Guiding Vision and Definition of Principles" outlines intersectionality as an ideology in action, introducing the social movement's agenda to the public by defining the exigencies and goals for the march. The first page of the "Guiding Vision" contains the Overview & Purpose section of the agenda, which outlines the vision for this "woman-led movement." The Overview & Purpose section emphasizes the inclusivity of this movement that seeks to "[bring] together people of all genders, ages, races, cultures, political affiliations and backgrounds . . . to affirm our shared humanity and pronounce our bold message of resistance and self-determination" (Women's March). While broad and inclusive statements like this one can recruit members to gender-based social movements, no direct exigence is named for what or whom is being resisted, or for what paths to self-determination are being promoted through this movement.

Campbell recognized women's divisions based on experiential sources of identification as a rhetorical problem, arguing that persuasive campaigns seeking to connect women would need to define "sisterhood" and promote connections of women's shared experiences (79). The "Guiding Vision" reflects this move to connect members based on shared gender experience by stating, "women have intersecting identities, and are therefore impacted by a multitude of social justice and human rights issues" and representing intersectionality as Crenshaw defined it in 1989. However, intersectionality as a framework for understanding or analysis is not clarified in the remainder of the "Guiding Vision." When we remember that Campbell argues that women's liberation rhetoric works from a place where it needs to create its audience to survive, then the lack of theoretical and practical clarification about intersectionality makes it a difficult framework for public audiences to grasp through the "Guiding Vision." The Women's March adopted an intersectional ideology in order to constitute an inclusive feminist coalition, but they leave their understanding of intersectionality implicit in their "Guiding Vision," potentially obfuscating this important feminist framework for their intended audience.

Women's liberation rhetoric constitutes an audience by making the personal political, connecting women's interests to specific exigencies in order to argue for change. After the Overview & Purpose section, the #WHYWEMARCH section names a legacy of 27 women "revolutionary leaders who paved the way for us to march," many of whom are women who have fought publicly for intersectional feminist concerns, and their activist legacies become the march's exigencies through this section (Women's March). #WHYWEMARCH redefines the march's exigence in by omitting reference to the march's initial resistance to Trump's election, including the quick evolution of Facebook posts from Theresa Shook of Hawaii and Bob Bland (who became one of the Women's March national co-chairs) calling for a march the day after Trump's inauguration. The "Guiding Vision" was initially released on the Women's March Facebook page as the first major communication between march organizers and members, so the omission of the coalition's initial exigence disconnects the "Guiding Vision" from the networked connections formed on social media that recruited members to this movement. Instead of connecting coalition members, the "Guiding Vision" disconnected the shared threat of Trump from their intersectional vision for change.

We can also view the rhetorical differences between Second Wave and intersectional feminism through the establishment of a "party line" in this definitional argument. Campbell argued that in women's liberation rhetoric, "each must decide whether, and if so which, action is suitable for her" (79), showing that the substance-style intersections in Second Wave women's liberation rhetorics encouraged individual dissent within coalitional solidarity. In the intersectional feminist framework of the "Guiding Vision," the substance and style of the Values & Principles section promotes this document as representative and reflective of Women's March participants. The lengthy bullet points outlining the Women's March Values & Principles repeats constitutive phrases like "we believe" and "we honor" and "we declare," as well as the feminine descriptions of "women," "mothers," "moms," sisters," and "girls" to encourage gender-based identifications between readers and the Women's March agenda. In short, "we" are intersectional feminists.

The immense scope of the Values & Principles statements demonstrates the range of contemporary feminist concerns in the United States, but many social rights activists have identified and criticized the limitations of this statement, especially in its claims for intersectionality and inclusivity. The "we believe" statement about intersecting racial oppressions initially omitted Latinx and Jewish women from inclusion, but also included Muslim women within the list of racial intersections.[2] Critics of this statement have argued that "Muslim is not a 'race' or class, it is a religion; American Muslim women are of diverse national, racial and ethnic backgrounds" (Symons), demonstrating how the Values & Principles miscategorized Muslim women's intersecting identities. Combined with the initial omission of Latinx and Jewish women, the substance of these statements limit the represented identities within the Women's March coalition. Furthermore, while people with disabilities are mentioned twice within the statement, they are subsumed under larger frameworks of the oppression of women of color and civil rights protections rather than named as another intersection of identity as disability rights activists have argued for. No disability rights organization are named under the list of contributors to the platform (Ladau). Thus, while this definitional document claims to lay out the values and mission of the Women's March, the lack of internal consistency and messy categorizations facilitated confusion and lack of understanding about how intersections work in relation to contextualized oppressions.

---

2. After the first release of the "Guiding Vision," the Women's March national organizers revised the racial oppression statement to include Latinx and Jewish women. The initial omission of Jewish women signaled the first of many challenges with anti-Semitism for the Women's March organizers post-2017 march, causing internal divisions questioning the limits of intersectionality in the Women's March values. National co-chairs Tamika Mallory and Linda Sarsour "allegedly praised Nation of Islam's Louis Farrakhan during a conference call with leaders of the group's state chapters, despite his abysmal record of anti-Semitism, homophobia, transphobia and sexism" (Abacarian). Mallory's long-standing ties with Farrakhan had already been scrutinized by Women's March members as incongruent with the Women's March Unity Principles, causing members of this intersectional coalition to express concern and distrust in the Women's March leadership. Sarsour denounced Farrakhan in a 2019 statement, attempting to ease coalitional divisions and reintroduce unity to the organization. Mallory stated that she disagreed with many of Farrakhan's statements, but did not condemn him (Friedman).

Alignment between Intersectional Substance and Style

Considering that the "Guiding Vision" statement baldly articulates participants' beliefs, the ideological stakes of this document are high. Using Campbell's practices of aligning substance and style, we can see how the redefinition of exigencies for the Women's March created disjunctures between potential marchers and the belief statements listed in the "Guiding Vision." The stylistic choice of "we believe" statements positions these values as universal within march participants, since the substance of the Overview claims to include a plurality of identities and political affiliations in march membership. Unfortunately, the stylistic miscategorizations of intersectional identities limit the potential plurality of gender-based identifications in this "woman-led" movement. While the Values & Principles may have been intended to foster identification between members, the selective highlighting of intersectional oppressions without accompanying attention to context creates dissonance between the interdependent categories of substance and style in this definitional argument. This lack of intersectional contextualization created disidentifications among march members who did not draw consistent connections from their personal exigence for participation to the redefinitions of exigence in this document.

We can also see how the substance of intersectionality as an analytic sensibility for recognizing oppressions was only partially enacted in this definitional argument. The intersectional vision of the Women's March assumed some knowledge of intersectionality for participants, putting forward a vision for women's and feminist activism without attending to the substance of intersectional theory, especially for understanding intersectionality as affecting everybody. As Cindy Griffin and Karma Chávez argue,

> [I]ntegrating an intersectional approach to the study of communication requires that scholars recognize that each individual stands and swims in the intersections of race/gender/sex/sexuality/ability/economic means and more. No individual is outside this paradigm, however much our scholarship has tried to deny this, or to suggest that only some are 'intersectional bodies.' (19)

Those wanting to protest Trump's misogynistic leadership may have expected the Women's March to prioritize concerns based on that exigence, but the "Guiding Vision" statement did not open up a space for education about the redefined framework of intersectionality as a principle, resulting in multiple isolating effects for disparate groups. While the formation of the Women's March was led by this "Guiding Vision," the statement was not delivered as a mandate for participation. However, the style of the statement *assumed* agreement and understanding of intersectional feminist values, rhetorically positioning the statement as representative of women's concerns while substantively representing intersectional ideologies.

The dissonance between substance and style in the "Guiding Vision" demonstrates that many women and feminists are developing understandings of intersectionality, but explanations of the exigencies and contexts for these intersecting oppressions are vital for identifying with intersectional feminist goals. These dissonances reveal that the current sociohistorical context of women's liberation rhetoric and feminist activism is not unified, but instead in a process of growth and education about intersectionality. I argue that situating the "Guiding Vision" as a definitional argument for intersectional feminism demonstrates attempts to enact contemporary intersectional feminist values in public activism. This rhetorical analysis of intersectional substance and style in intersectional feminist arguments reveals that more education on intersectionality is needed to recruit members and foster identification between women to belong to an intersectional movement.

Conclusion

I offer this analysis as an example of feminist rhetorical contextualization of our theories and analytical frameworks within the evolution of feminist waves. The critiques of Campbell's substance-style framework for women's liberation rhetorics read her method as static, rather than dynamically adaptable for growth in the ways that feminism has grown since 1973. Feminist rhetorical scholars can instead acknowledge the potential growth of our methods alongside our growing awareness of feminist rhetorics to analyze how arguments about intersectionality attempt to claim representation of women's beliefs while they attempt to constitute them as an audience.

Rhetorical scholars must attend to sociohistorical context in their analyses in order to determine the significance and meaning behind discursive interactions, and in the same vein, must also recognize how our theoretical frameworks for analysis are situated within these contexts. Campbell's substance-style theory was conceived during the Second Wave of feminism and the inception of feminist rhetoric, and therefore reflects Second Wave sociohistorical reading of women's liberation rhetoric. This is the inherent value of updating Campbell's substance-style theory: by attending to the context and exigence of arguments for women's liberation, we can better understand the ideological underpinnings through the substance and style of their rhetoric. With Campbell's method, we can trace the evolution of women's arguments for liberation across feminist waves, crafting clear connections across the academic-public divide, and in more immediate contexts. In closing, I encourage feminist rhetoricians to reclaim Campbell's framework as an analytical method for women's and feminist rhetorics in contemporary activist arguments. By collecting data on and analyzing women's and feminist rhetorical practices with Campbell's updated substance-style theory, I believe that we can take one step closer to detailing the discursive features of intersectional women's liberation rhetoric.

Works Cited

Abacarian, Robin. "Column: Can You Admire Louis Farrakhan and Still Advance the Cause of Women? Maybe So. Life is Full of Contradictions." *Los Angeles Times*, 4 Jan. 2019, https://www.latimes.com/local/abcarian/la-me-abcarian-womens-march-20190104-story.html.

Baumgardner, Jennifer. "Is There a Fourth Wave? Does It Matter?" *F'em!: Goo Goo, GaGa, and Some Thoughts on Balls*. Seal Press, 2011, pp. 243-252.

Campbell, Karlyn Kohrs. "The Rhetoric of Women's Liberation: An Oxymoron." *Quarterly Journal of Speech*, vol. 29, no. 1, 1973, pp. 74-86.

Chávez, Karma R., and Cindy L. Griffin. "Introduction." *Standing in the Intersection: Feminist Voices, Feminist Practices in Communication Studies*, edited by Karma R. Chávez and Cindy L. Griffin. State University of New York Press, 2012, pp. 1-30.

Crenshaw, Kimberlé. "Demarginalizing the Intersection of Race and Sex: A Black Feminist Critique of Antidiscrimination Doctrine, Feminist Theory and Antiracist Politics." *University of Chicago Legal Forum*, vol. 1989, no. 1, pp. 139-167.

Dow, Bonnie J. and Mari Boor Tonn. "'Feminine Style' and Political Judgement in the Rhetoric of Ann Richards." *Quarterly Journal of Speech*, vol. 79, 1993, pp. 286-302.

Ferree, Myra Marx and Carol McClurg Mueller. "Feminism and the Women's Movement: A Global Perspective." *The Blackwell Companion to Social Movements*, edited by David A. Snow, Sarah A. Soule, and Haspeter Kriesi, Blackwell Publishing Limited, 2004, pp. 576-607.

Freidman, Gabe. "Tamika Mallory Fails to Condemn Farrakhan's Anti-Semitism in Testy Exchange with Meghan McCain on 'The View.'" *Jewish Telegraph Agency*, 14 Jan. 2019, https://www.jta.org/quick-reads.

Stockman, Farah. "Women's March on Washington Opens Contentious Dialogues about Race." *New York Times*, 9 Jan. 2017, https://mobile.nytimes.com/2017/01/09/us/womens-march-on-washington-opens-contentious-dialogues-about-race.html.

"Women's March leaders aim for solidarity against misogyny." *PBS Newshour*, 20 Jan. 2017. http://www.pbs.org/newshour/bb/womens-march-leaders-aim-solidarity-misogyny/.

Women's March on Washington. "Guiding Vision and Definition of Principles." 12 Jan. 2017. PDF.

The Biopolitics of Counter-Attunement: A Marxist-Foucauldian Critical Agency

Catherine Chaput

Rhetoric permeates space, affecting hegemonic and counter-hegemonic activities as individuals become more or less unconsciously attuned to the ubiquitous contours of their placement in the world. In Thomas Rickert's words, such ambient rhetoric orients subjects through a "worldly rhetoricity, an affectability in how the world comes to be" (9). Agency emerges from the ability to fold into and take cues from this process. Much as Kenneth Burke instructs speakers on the significance of audience identification, Rickert signals the importance of connecting with the pervasive tenor of the environments we inhabit. Taking his lead from phenomenology, he views rhetorical attunement as an embodied and intuited sensibility and, vis-a-vis Heidegger's lectures on Aristotle, establishes pathos as the conduit for recognizing oneself within this larger spatial, psychic, and material being-in-the-world (14). From this perspective, pathos constitutes not just feelings, which are often fleeting, but the deep-seated moods and dispositions that guide our worldly practices. When we dwell in this *topos*, we find ourselves and become attuned to "what the environment affords" through its "dispersal and diffusion of agency" (15). Opening ourselves to this ambient rhetoric allows access to agentive powers and possibilities. As a hermeneutic, ambient rhetoric adds much to our rhetorical analyses. Indeed, I teach Rickert's chapter on Microsoft's start up music and have found inspiration in his theorization of the *chora* as a space of indeterminate possibility. This paper, however, pushes back against ambient rhetoric for its less developed sensibilities toward earlier materialist rhetorics.

Rickert's introduction offers an aside to such theories through references to Dana Cloud (informed by Marx) and Ron Greene (indebted to Foucault). It is difficult, he says, to get to his notion of ambient rhetoric from such perspectives because they prioritize human subjects wielding discursive agency, a communicative model that has lost traction in the digital age. Yet, these traditions, ones in which I locate myself, have neither homogenous nor complete frameworks for understanding agentive human beings. The open political question of how life, language, and power intermingle is perhaps nowhere more animated than in the biopolitical arena forged by Foucault and populated by autonomist Marxists, among others. The division of such scholarship from ambient rhetoric not only furthers a myopic and stagnant sense of these materialisms, it also misses potential collaborations between the different areas of inquiry.

Take, for instance, the role of ambient music in Rickert's rhetorical theory. A term coined by Brian Eno, ambient music prompts different "levels of attention," facilitates movement between background concepts and foregrounded ones, and creates a felt sense for potential within a "nonexistent place" (Rickert 28). Using this framework, Eno composed the Microsoft startup music to positively dispose users to what might, on occasion, become a frustrating computer-user experience. Automatically playing when a person turns on his or her computer, this music functions as ambient rhetoric inasmuch as it "persuades us prior to symbolicity"; it "situates us differently in the world, evoking other ways of being" (Rickert 33). To the extent that we allow ourselves to dwell in its affordances, we will be better enabled to navigate the computer-human experience. According to Rickert, this process "is not just a form of communication between entities but an ontological manifestation of their dynamic entanglement" (111). The music sweeps through the environment and its objects, reconstituting the computer and the listener as a human-machine dyad with its own capacities.

There is an analogue here in Marx's theory of commodity production in which workers are transformed through their experience behind the factory door. Occupying this restricted space, colliding with its machinery, and transferring value into the objects of production, human beings become entangled with the materiality of their environment. In his chapter on "The Working Day," Marx lingers on the long hours spent toiling on the factory floor, on the humans contorted into the machines, on the proposed diets that sustain the mere reproductive capacity of these workers, and on the material filth of these spaces, including the noises and smells they emit. This enormous chapter, lying at the center of *Capital*, challenges the theoretically-oriented reader with page after page of empirical data—the sights, sounds, smells, tastes, and experiences of the capitalist mode of production. Swept up in the sheer breadth of stories, the reader progressively occupies the prevailing sentiment of industrial subjects as he or she sees the parent feeding his seven-year-old son who worked at the "machine, for he could not leave it or stop it" (357); tastes the bread that contains "human perspiration mixed with the discharge of abscesses, cobwebs, dead cockroaches, and putrid German yeast" (359); and hears the guilty of manslaughter verdict for the railroad workers who, after a fifty-hour shift without breaks, caused a massive derailment when "their brains stopped thinking [and] their eyes stopped seeing" (363). The chapter draws one into these spaces and forces an extended ontological comingling; it slows a reader down and orients him or her differently, creating an imaginary space of possibility. One cannot properly appreciate Marx without dwelling purposefully within such uncomfortable material spaces, ones that this tradition highlights in its focus on lived experiences.

That capitalist culture must be studied for both its affordances and its limitations is, in fact, among the hallmark contributions of Theodor Adorno. The son of a wealthy wine merchant who would no doubt appreciate the extended *terroir* metaphor that bookends Rickert's *Ambient Rhetoric*, Adorno offers a traditional materialist counterpart to Brian Eno. From his youth through his adulthood, Adorno was captivated by music. So much so that after earning his doctorate, he moved from his home in Frankfurt, Germany, to Vienna, Austria, in hopes of establishing himself within what he imagined to be a vibrant Schönberg circle of fellow thinkers. Unable to find this likeminded community, his sojourn into life as a concert pianist was short lived. Nevertheless, Adorno continued to study and write about music. As part of the Rockefeller-funded Radio Project, he theorized radio's spatialization of musical performances. Still in its infancy, radio broadcast live in-studio performances, bringing classical music to the masses. Electromagnetic waves transmitted the performance along with an ever-present broadcast hum that Adorno called the "hear stripe" to signal its spatial reproduction through airwaves and communication apparatuses (*Essays*, 219). He discovered that music's high and low frequencies were lost through radio transmission and surmised that this "compression of [music's] dynamic range" prevents the tension of extremes to be properly felt (*Essays*, 259). For him, it is "only if the sound is 'larger' than the individual so as to enable him to 'enter' the door of the sound as he would enter the door of a cathedral that he may become aware of the possibility of merging with the totality" (*Essays*, 256). Importantly, this is not a seamless flow of identification, but a cohabitation of nonidentity within a totality that can be glimpsed but not fully known. By reducing the musical range and shrinking its spatial possibilities, radio replaces the active, if at times uncomfortable and confrontational, experience of entering into the vast, overwhelming universe of difference with the more passive experience of identification.

Like Eno and others in the ambient music movement, Adorno understands sound as producing a space of possibility—it creates its own *kairos*; unlike them, he grounds possibility in being with difference and emphasizes the intellectual labor required of its audience. Incapable of dramatic contrasts that thwart listener expectations, radio music produces ersatz experiences that equate feeling with surrender into "the sonorous flow of sequences" (*Philosophy*, 14). Such self-surrender folds subject into object through a process of homogenous identification whereas live music (because of its larger acoustic range) holds the possibility of experiencing the world through difference: "the man who surrenders to tears in music that no longer resembles him at the same time allows the stream of what he himself is not—what was damned up in the world of things—to flow back into him" (*Philosophy* 99). This musical experience demands that listeners grapple with those excluded, alienated, abject parts of being-in-the-world in the same way that Marx requires his readers to spend extended time in the workplaces of those laboring within industrial factories so foreign to much of his readership. Building on the Marxist dialectic that declares the unity of opposites, Adorno privileges an understanding of the subject that simultaneously includes and is separate from human and non-human others. It is not, therefore, the process of musical dwelling to which Adorno objects, but radio's uniform habituation. Alternatively, he seeks experiences that place nonidentity at the forefront and thus produce different dispositions through what he calls "corporeal shocks and traumas" (*Currents*, 23).

Grafting Freud onto Marx, Adorno tends to focus on the psychological aspects of materiality even as he cracks open the door for the kind of physiological constitution of subjectivity discussed within certain threads of new materialism such as Alex Weheliye's important 2014 book, *Habeas Viscus*. By shifting the focus of biopolitics from habeas corpus to habeas viscus, Weheliye emphasizes the particularities of the fleshly body instead of the collective norms and institutional exceptions of the political body. In doing so, he highlights two points: first, subjects are never self-present, coherent, and fully agentive, and, second, subjects come to be through bodily engagement with the material, symbolic, and psychic worlds. The myriad, entangled components of our subjectivity emerge, he says, "in the dominion of the ideological and physiological" (24). In his conception, the ability to modulate affectability must be located in the "reinvention of the human at the juncture of the cultural and biological feedback loop" (25). Borrowing from black feminist studies, he explores how sociological conceptions of subjectivity (race, gender, sexuality, and class, for instance) become "anchored in the human neurochemical system" (27). This socio-biological environment structures the range of possibilities for those felt experiences so crucial to Adorno's cultural theory and its constitution of human potentiality. In place of the historical narrative in which human beings begin as instinct–riddled animals (zoe) and evolve into political animals (bios) by taming those instincts with rational deliberative practices, Weheliye offers an iterative and recursive relationship between instincts and rationality in which human beings participate in the constitution of their own fleshly, animal selves by way of symbolic and material practices. So conceived, human history is the history of differently constituted instincts.

Extending Marx's claim that the social dynamics of capitalism are invisibly inscribed into commodities, Weheliye suggests that fleshly bodies equally present themselves as hieroglyphics. The networked assemblages that govern our individual practices "etch abstract forces of power onto human physiology" (50). Not merely passive recipients of the material productions that limit and delimit our being-in-the-world, we are its producers. Consequently, the animal core around which subjectivity builds its human identity "carries the potential for manumission" (130). Freedom from one set of instincts requires the production of a new set of fleshly foundations. Although Weheliye's text critiques Foucault on several counts, the idea that biopolitial change requires differently constituted bodies—ones whose psychological and physiological impulses move against the ambient rhythms of our environments—is not one of those grievances. In fact, as Foucault illustrates in his work on *parrhesia*, human freedom cannot be separated from somatic practices and purposeful engagement with built environments. For him, truth emerges through an oppositional mode of being that interrupts, antagonizes, and redirects the flows of being that drown out alternatives. This practice, what he calls an "ontology of ourselves," positively mobilizes disciplinary technologies in order to cultivate a critical revolutionary will tethered to the space of undefined possibility ("What is Revolution?" 95).

While many view Foucault's work on care of the self as a return to humanism, one dangerously close to neoliberal individualism, this reading seems incompatible with the critical austerity emphasized in his final public lectures. In these lectures, care of the self involves the "search, practice, and experience through which the subject carries out the necessary transformations on himself in order to have access to truth" (*Hermeneutics*, 15). Such a subject voluntarily submits to rigorous physical and mental exercises designed to assess, mobilize, and orient bodily impulses. A lifelong vocation, this "self-subjectivation" (*Hermeneutics*, 214) includes exercises in concentration, restraint, and physical endurance designed to produce new fleshly instincts. An individual practices turning away from expected, desired, automated responses until this ability to act contrary becomes perpetually "available and can be resorted to whenever the opportunity arises" (*Courage*,

231). Availability is housed in the body: its potential lies "in our sinews. We must have it in such a way that we can actualize it immediately and without delay" (*Courage*, 326). Cultivating a new set of instincts, those individuals who practice an oppositional care of the self become agents of truth willing to disrupt the ambient structures that regulate their environment.

These *ethopoetic* activities set the stage for what Foucault views as a militant philosophy—a lifestyle intended to be a catalyst for social change. Exemplifying such militancy, the Cynics, he notes, lead a philosophical life, but do so by embodying their founding principles in such extreme form that their everyday life transforms into a life of transgression. In addition to knowing the truth and acting justly, the Cynics commit to altering "the value of the currency" (*Courage*, 227). Although variously interpreted, Foucault explains this duty as the principle of shifting social convention. He says that "the forms and habits which usually stamp existence and give it its features must be replaced by the effigy of the principles traditionally accepted by philosophy" (*Courage*, 244). As the living representative of that effigy, the Cynical lifestyle marks the traditional life as counterfeit. Of course, the demand that one revalue the currency calls up another meaning: the pathways that carry energetic charges. Moving through human and nonhuman matter, currents guide life energy along particular routes that can be redirected, increased and decreased, opened and closed, all by way of interruption. Thus, the Cynics revalue their embodied passions and their automated responses so as to serve as points of refraction that redirect the larger sociocultural and political currents. Attuned differently, such individuals hold the possibility for interrupting dominant flows of being and thus forging new and yet unknown futures.

Offering a glimpse into how a Marxist-Foucauldian framework might intersect with new materialist perspectives, this paper calls for dwelling, with our differences, in these nodes of intersection. Such a position avoids dichotomizing old and new materialisms: in the expanded materialist world, it seems counter-intuitive to ignore the multiple, recursive, co-presences of earlier materialisms. On the contrary, this position asserts that possibilities proliferate within intersectional frameworks. It suspects that the collision of multiple materialisms produces many rhetorical pathways toward thinking human and nonhuman subjectivity, reflecting on the entanglement between history and biology, tracking the forces of vitality, and forging modes of political engagement.

Works Cited

Adorno, Theodor. *Currents of Music*. Ed. Robert Hullot-Kentor. Polity Press, 2009.
—. *Essays on Music*. Ed. Richard Leppert. Trans. Susan Gillespie. U of California P, 2002.
—. *Philosophy of New Music*. Trans. Robert Hullot-Kentor. U of Minnesota P, 2006.
—. "On Subject and Object" *Critical Modes: Interventions and Catchwords*. Trans. Henry Pickford. Columbia UPs, 1998. 245-258.
Foucault, Michel. *The Courage of Truth: Lectures at the Collège de France, 1983-84*. Ed. F. Gross. Trans. Graham Burchell. Palgrave Macmillan, 2011.
—. *The Hermeneutics of the Subject: Lectures at the Collège de France, 1981-1982*. Ed. Frédéric Gross. Trans. Graham Burchell. Palgrave Macmillan, 2005.
—. "What Is Revolution?" *The Politics of Truth*. Semiotext(e), 2007. 83-95.
Marx, Karl. *Capital: Volume I*. Trans. Ben Fowkes. Penguin, 1990.
Rickert, Thomas. *Ambient Rhetoric: The Attunements of Rhetorical Being*. U of Pittsburgh P, 2013.
Weheliye, Alex. *Habeas Viscus: Racializing Assemblages, Biopolitics, and Black Feminist Theories of the Human*. Duke UP, 2014.

The Invention and Reinvention of the Outsider Persona: Jackson, Trump, and Anti-Establishment Ethos

Jacob W. Justice

On March 15, 2017, the recently inaugurated President Donald J. Trump did what no twenty-first century president had done before: he visited Andrew Jackson's plantation, the Hermitage. Commemorating what would have been the seventh president's 250th birthday, Trump laid a wreath on Jackson's tomb and delivered a brief speech espousing the virtues of the "people's president." In his address, Trump declared himself a "big fan" of Jackson's, and praised Old Hickory for having "confronted and defied an arrogant elite" before asking the audience of 400 people: "Does that sound familiar to you?" (Trump, "Remarks"; Meyer and Ebert). Throughout the address, Trump meandered from his prepared remarks to point out perceived parallels between himself and Jackson, noting with giddy enthusiasm that political elites reviled both his own victory and that of Jackson's. Trump concluded his tribute as though he were addressing Andrew Jackson directly, promising that his administration would "build on your legacy" (Trump, "Remarks").

Presidents have long used and abused public memories of their predecessors for persuasive purposes (Kiewe 253). Nonetheless, Trump's embrace of Jackson is remarkable, coming at a time when Jackson's record has been increasingly scorned, particularly for his role as "an unapologetic defender of slavery" and the "main architect" of the Trail of Tears (Meacham 7). Even as modern Democrats have distanced themselves from their party's Jacksonian roots, Trump has elevated Jackson to a unique "rhetorical presence in the Trump White House" (Suebsaeng; Krieg). Trump's attempts to analogize himself to Jackson are notable not because these comparisons are accurate, but rather because such comparisons represent a concerted effort to invent a specific rhetorical persona. An overlooked similarity is that "much like Trump, Jackson was an elite member of society" and famous for his wealth but somehow able to build a public image as a "defender of the common man" (Cheathem). I argue that the outsider persona debuted by Jackson and reinvented by Trump deserves further critical analysis. Such attention will not only bring a degree of clarity to the sources of Trump's appeal, but will also help rhetorical scholars understand how the outsider/establishment dualism continues to animate American politics.

Trump's victory presents a conundrum to rhetorical scholars: how did Trump secure such a fervent core of followers despite breaking every rule of American politics? Since Trump's election, political analysts have struggled to explain the fierce loyalty of core Trump supporters (Struyk). Although debate persists about which factors were most influential in causing Trump's victory, "top political operatives" agree that the "seemingly unbreakable bond with his core supporters, no matter how provocative his words or deeds" was an essential variable (Lauter). I argue that Trump's outsider persona was crucial to fostering a durable bond between Trump and his base. In a Gallup poll conducted during the 2016 Republican primaries, Trump supporters identified "Trump's status as a nonpolitician and an outsider" as the key variable "that drives their support" for him, rather than "his positions on issues or specific policies" (Newport and Saad). Focus groups have shown that Trump's status as "the anti-elite candidate . . . made him more or less immune to criticism from the mainstream parties or the mainstream media" in the eyes of his supporters (Guo). Trump's outsider persona was also critical in minimizing the fallout from controversies that would have been fatal for other candidates, creating a situation where criticism from establishment figures only reinforced his popularity and strengthened "his authenticity as an outsider" (Newport and Saad).

Richard C. Fording and Sanford F. Schram argued that the unshakeable loyalty of Trump supporters remains an "understudied topic," and called for further exploration into why

> Trump's base was so loyal to him during and after the campaign in spite of his profligate lying, reliance on outlandish conspiracy theories, constant name-calling and demonizing of his opponents, and his continual smearing of various 'out groups' who he sought to denigrate for political effect. (674)

Echoing this sentiment, Denise M. Bostdorff recognized a basic puzzle of the Trump presidency concerns the fact that, somehow, "enough voters in the right states were willing to take a chance on an outsider with no political experience—a billionaire with a track record in obvious contradiction to his populist claims—as the means toward political transformation" (698). Trump's ability to maintain "such a stubbornly loyal political base" remains "one of the most puzzling, enduring and intriguing questions about the Trump presidential phenomenon" (Malcolm). To explain Trump's appeal, our attention must turn to rhetoric, and more specifically, Trump's ability to invent a populist "outsider persona" that insulated him from political attacks while allowing him to cultivate a passionate and loyal following of voters who were unpersuaded by arguments delivered by more credentialed, "establishment" figures.

I argue that the populist outsider persona remains one of the most resonant inventional resources available in American politics. Rhetorical scholars have acknowledged the existence of an outsider persona, but have yet to elaborate the recurring characteristics that constitute it (Gibson and Heyse 245; Serazio). In what follows I describe the features of the populist outsider persona adopted by Jackson and Trump. I develop this argument in three parts. First, I theorize the qualities of the outsider persona. Second, I examine Trump's 2016 Republican National Convention address, explaining how it constructed and enacted an outsider persona. Third, I explain the findings of this essay, which shed light on the underlying sources of Trump's political appeal and add clarity to discussions of similar outsider figures.

Purity, Nostalgia and Decisiveness in the Outsider Persona

In arguing that Trump's rhetoric constructed an outsider persona, I extend previous rhetorical scholarship on persona. Persona has been defined as "a role or roles that a rhetor takes on for strategic purposes" (Campbell and Burkholder 21; Ware and Linkugel). From the age of Jackson to the age of Trump, members of the public have "relied on preferred constructions of a persona to make decisions about character in leadership" (Mahaffey 501). When analyzing rhetorical personae, it is crucial to recognize that "what is believed to be true" about a candidate "often displaces the truth itself," as Lynn Hudson Parsons observed about the Jackson-Adams race of 1828 (110). I focus primarily upon the populist outsider persona, a variant of the outsider archetype that I argue was adopted by Jackson and Trump. A diverse cast of historical figures such as Andrew Jackson, Abraham Lincoln (Donald), Barry Goldwater (Kamarck), Ronald Reagan (Zelizer), Bill Clinton (Ifill), and even Barack Obama (Foer) have been described as outsiders. At the same time, labels such as "anti-establishment" and "outsider" are "both politically useful and empirically unverifiable" (Serazio 191). The loose use of these labels points to the need to define such a persona more clearly to avoid flattening the distinctions between various manifestations of the outsider persona.

I argue that the populist outsider persona, as debuted by Jackson and reinvented by Trump, contains three distinguishing characteristics. First, the outsider is framed as untainted by the corruption that audiences understand to be endemic to the current political order. In crafting such a Manichean dichotomy between the "the pure people" and "the corrupt elite" (Mudde and Rovira Kaltwasser 43; Duffy; Maddux), the rhetor adopts what Lee terms the "populist argumentative frame" (355). After it was used to great effect by Jackson, this image of the "outsider, separated from the intrigues of Washington, became the model for many presidential campaigns well into the twenty-first century" (Parsons 195). Second, the outsider is associated with nostalgic longing for a romanticized past, locating "political victory in the resurrection of a simpler idealized history" (Lee 358). This nostalgic theme is manifest in the rhetoric of both Jackson and Trump. In Jackson's anti-corruption pledge to "cleanse the Augean stable" (an allusion to a Greek myth involving Hercules), one can hear echoes of Trump's promises to "drain the swamp" and "Make America Great Again" (Bromwich). Third, the outsider is understood to be a "man of action" (reflecting the gendered nature of this persona) capable of confronting entrenched interests on behalf of "the people." Capitalizing on popular demand for decisive leadership, outsiders draw "upon anti-intellectualism and a sense of urgency" to craft for themselves "an image of a man of action, rather than words, who is not afraid to take difficult and quick decisions, even against 'expert' advice" (Mudde and Rovira Kaltwasser 64). In the next section, I detail the enactment of the outsider persona in Donald Trump's 2016 address at the Republican National Convention.

THE OUTSIDER PERSONA IN TRUMP'S 2016 REPUBLICAN NATIONAL CONVENTION ADDRESS

On July 21, 2016, Donald Trump formally accepted the nomination for president at the Republican National Convention (RNC) in Cleveland, Ohio. Trump's RNC speech is a fitting case study of his larger campaign for three reasons. First, Trump's RNC speech "brought special emphasis to the core messages of his presidential campaign" (Balz, "Grim Portrait"). Second, nomination acceptance speeches "consistently provide interesting insights into the speakers, their parties, and their perceptions about the audience" (Vigil 345). Third, the speech occurred at a particularly crucial juncture of Trump's presidential bid, "was without question the most important Trump has ever delivered" (Balz, "Grim Portrait"), and a "make-or-break moment" for a campaign riddled with controversies (Balz, "Trump's Acceptance Speech"). In what follows, I explain how Trump enacted all three components of the outsider persona in his acceptance speech.

Trump's RNC address began with a dystopian (and often evidence-free) vision of a country in existential crisis, suffering from rampant crime, terrorism, illegal immigration, financial insecurity, poverty, and crumbling infrastructure, thanks to the malpractice of politicians. Turning to foreign policy, Trump described a nation emasculated abroad due to the Obama administration's weakness and Hillary Clinton's tenure as Secretary of State. After painting this grim picture of terminal decline, Trump began to stake out a vision for how he would address these crises, albeit in very vague terms. In doing so, Trump enacted the first characteristic of the populist outsider persona by emphasizing his own purity and adopting the populist argumentative frame. Distinguishing himself from an ineffective and incompetent political establishment, Trump asserted that "the problems we face now—poverty and violence at home, war and destruction abroad—will last only as long as we continue relying on the same politicians who created them" (Trump, "2016 RNC").

In the next section of the speech, Trump continued to differentiate himself from corrupt and inept political elites. Appealing to Americans who felt abandoned by the political establishment, Trump declared "I AM YOUR VOICE" (Trump, "2016 RNC"). This statement allowed Trump to "portray himself as a clean actor, who is able to be the voice of the 'man in the street' since there are no intermediaries between him and 'the people'" (Mudde and Rovira Kaltwasser 44). To support his claim to immunity from special-interest influence, Trump recounted his experiences consoling "crying mothers who have lost their children because our politicians put their personal agendas before the national good," stating plainly that "I have no patience for injustice, no tolerance for government incompetence, no sympathy for leaders who fail their citizens" (Trump, "2016 RNC").

Later in the acceptance address, Trump elaborated upon the nostalgic themes that were central to his overall campaign, enacting the second characteristic of the populist outsider persona. Trump made a host of pledges aimed at restoring the nation's former glory. Excoriating Bill and Hillary Clinton for their support of past trade agreements, Trump vowed "to bring our jobs back to Ohio and to America" (Trump, "2016 RNC"). Trump argued his administration would protect "the great miners and steel workers of our country," figures who symbolize a bygone era of widespread blue-collar manufacturing jobs. Appealing to a desire for national renewal, Trump's speech concluded by reinforcing these nostalgic themes, ending with his signature slogans:

> To all Americans tonight, in all our cities and towns, I make this promise: We Will Make America Strong Again.
>
> We Will Make America Proud Again.
>
> We Will Make America Safe Again.
>
> And We Will Make America Great Again.

Trump's nostalgic appeals were laced with both racism and sexism, "mobilizing supporters to be outraged . . . in defense of white cultural worlds that, in this formulation, are perceived to be under constant attack" and in the process defining "white male workers as the virtuous majority whom Trump claims to represent" (Maskovsky 435).

Importantly, Trump presented himself as the singular person capable of delivering such a national restoration, enacting the third characteristic of the populist outsider persona. In perhaps the most infamous line of the address, Trump proclaimed that "nobody knows the system better than me, which is why I alone can fix it. I have seen firsthand how the system is rigged against our citizens" (Trump, "2016 RNC"). This statement is crucial to the speech's persona-building functions, as Trump appealed to his "business acumen to construct" his "status as a *political* outsider" (Mudde and Rovira Kaltwasser 71). In this passage, Trump "defined himself as a bedrock figure in American culture: the figure who faces danger alone, who follows his own code of conduct . . . he is the man who uses his great wealth to protect the powerless from evil" (Greenfield). By creating an image of America engulfed in elite-inflicted crises, Trump illustrated the need for decisive style of leadership that only outsiders possess.

Trump's RNC address enacted all three characteristics of the populist outsider persona: immunity to corruption, nostalgic longing, and decisiveness. In doing so, Trump presented the American Dream as being threatened by the selfish decisions of incompetent politicians, inviting the audience to put faith in a fearless and cunning outsider. Although the speech was unlikely to persuade any Americans outside of his political camp, Trump tailored his appeals to manipulate the fears and anxieties of his core supporters.

Conclusion

Several important implications stem from this analysis. First, I have illustrated the power of the populist outsider persona to produce faithful devotion to the outsider and radical skepticism towards insiders. When effectively constructed, the populist outsider persona offers a potent means to overcome the barriers traditionally encountered by politically inexperienced or unconventional candidates. The populist outsider persona insulates the candidate from criticism by rendering the arguments of establishment figures epistemologically suspect in the eyes of loyal supporters via "the rhetorical production of skepticism toward concentrated power and institutional structures of governance" (Lee 362). Trump's harsh depiction of the political establishment—complicit in the country's decline or even actively seeking to stoke national chaos and destruction—encouraged the audience to overlook issues with his temperament and lack of experience. By participating in the co-construction of an outsider persona with their followers, Jackson and Trump reinforced the "terministic screens" of their audiences, creating a "device that unifies all those who share the same enemy" (Burke 51). This persona helped build identification between speaker and audience by juxtaposing the virtues of the outsider against the wickedness of the insider, creating "a rhetorical Vile beast to be slain" or "a negation to be negated" (Griffin 464). Trump's efforts to create an outsider persona were no doubt assisted by the country's hyper-polarization and the tendency of conservatives to consume partisan news media sources (Jamieson and Cappella).

The explanation for Trump's appeal that I have forwarded here is particularly important because it accounts for alternative interpretations. After Trump's victory, "a heated debate broke out among political commentators over the source of Donald Trump's support. Was it driven primarily by economic anxiety, as the early conventional wisdom often argued, or more by racism and other cultural factors?" (Casselman). The argument developed here about Trump's use of the populist outsider persona can be used to incorporate both perspectives. The first aspect of the persona responded to widespread frustration with the political establishment and a feeling that elites had forgotten the economic plight of ordinary people, recurring themes of populist discourse. The second aspect of the persona, the rhetorical longing for an idealized past, drew on cultural fears about loss of white dominance and simple racism. Trump's call to return the country to a mythic past had great resonance, "especially for older white men" who fondly remembered an era when "American society was less diverse" (Inglehart and Norris 16). In the populist outsider rhetoric of both Jackson and Trump, one can discern "the equation of toughness, maleness, and whiteness" (Kazin 21). The populist outsider persona therefore accounts for both of the seemingly contradictory economic and cultural explanations of Trump's appeal.

A second contribution is to clarify the meaning of the term "outsider," which is frequently and uncritically lobbed in political debates to describe a vast range of figures. For the term "outsider" to have any meaning, the anti-establishment rhetoric of Jackson and Trump must be distinguished from the likes of Obama, Reagan, and others who utilized somewhat similar themes.

The populist outsider persona that I have theorized here contributes to this goal by distinguishing between outsiders within the political system and the populist outsider outside of that system altogether. The populist outsider persona requires adoption of the populist argumentative frame by presenting a narrative featuring ordinary Americans pitted against an unaccountable class of elites. However, the outsider rhetoric of Jackson and Trump can be distinguished from that of Reagan and Obama and others inside the political system based on the call to invest faith in a decisive "man of action." Future rhetorical research should focus on other manifestations of the outsider persona, such as the progressive outsider persona (adopted by Elizabeth Warren and Bernie Sanders) that expresses skepticism towards elites (defined in economic and not purely cultural terms) but is future-oriented (as opposed to predominantly nostalgic) and advocates for community-based solutions rather than presenting the outsider as a messianic figure capable of single-handedly fixing the nation's problems. Such analyses will be necessary now more than ever as non-traditional political candidates and populist movements continue to surge around the world.

Works Cited

Balz, Dan. "Trump's Acceptance Speech Thursday Shaping Up to be a Make-Or-Break Moment." *The Washington Post*, 21 July 2016, p. A09.

—. "Trump's RNC: Grim Portrait of America, Law-And-Order Message for Disaffected." *Chicago Tribune*, 21 July 2016, www.chicagotribune.com/news/nation-world/politics/ct-analysis-republican-national-convention-20160721-story.html.

Bromwich, Jonah Engel. "The Wild Inauguration of Andrew Jackson, Trump's Populist Predecessor." *The New York Times*, 20 Jan. 2017, www.nytimes.com/2017/01/20/us/politics/donald-trump-andrew-jackson.html?_r=0

Bostdorff, Denise M. "Obama, Trump, and Reflections on the Rhetoric of Political Change." *Rhetoric & Public Affairs*, vol. 20, no. 4, 2017, pp. 695–706.

Burke, Kenneth. *Language as Symbolic Action*. University of California Press, 1966.

Campbell, Karlyn Kohrs, and Thomas R. Burkholder. *Critiques of Contemporary Rhetoric*. 2nd ed., Wadsworth Publishing Company, 1997.

Casselman, Ben. "Stop Saying Trump's Win Had Nothing to do with Economics." *FiveThirtyEight*, 9 Jan. 2017, www.fivethirtyeight.com/features/stop-saying-trumps-win-had-nothing-to-do-with-economics/.

Cheathem, Mark R. "Donald Trump: A Modern-Day Andrew Jackson?" *Jacksonian America*, 26 Oct. 2015, www.jacksonianamerica.com/2015/10/26/donald-trump-a-modern-day-andrew-jackson/.

Donald, David Herbert. "The Outsider From Illinois." *The New York Times*, 12 Feb. 1996, www.nytimes.com/1996/02/12/opinion/the-outsider-from-illinois.html.

Duffy, Cat. "States' Rights Vs. Women's Rights: The Use of the Populist Argumentative Frame in Anti-Abortion Rhetoric." *International Journal of Communication*, vol. 9, 2015, pp. 3494–3501.

Foer, Franklin. "What's Wrong with the Democrats?" *The Atlantic*, July/Aug. 2017, www.theatlantic.com/magazine/archive/2017/07/whats-wrong-with-the-democrats/528696/.

Fording, Richard C., and Sanford F. Schram. "The Cognitive and Emotional Sources of Trump Support: The Case of Low-Information Voters." *New Political Science*, vol. 39, no. 4, 2017, pp. 670-686.

Gibson, Katie L., and Amy L. Heyse. "'The Difference Between a Hockey Mom and a Pit Bull': Sarah Palin's Faux Maternal Persona and Performance of Hegemonic Masculinity at the 2008 Republican National Convention." *Communication Quarterly*, vol. 58, no. 3, 2010, pp. 235-256.

Greenfield, Jeff. "Donald Trump's Caesar Moment." *Politico*, 22 July 2016, www.politico.com/magazine/story/2016/07/2016-donald-trump-rnc-convention-speech-reaction-214086

Griffin, Leland M. "A Dramatistic Theory of the Rhetoric of Movements." *Critical Responses to Kenneth Burke*, edited by William H. Rueckert, University of Minnesota Press, 1969, pp. 456-478.

Guo, Jeff. "The Real Reasons Donald Trump's so Popular — for People Totally Confused by it." *The Washington Post*, 12 Dec. 2015, www.washingtonpost.com/news/wonk/wp/2015/12/12/the-four-basic-reasons-that-explain-why-donald-trump-actually-is-so-popular/?utm_term=.5d4481308c01

Ifill, Gwen. "The 1992 Campaign: The Democrats; Touring in Midwest, Clinton Plays Up an Outsider Image." *The New York Times*, 25 Oct. 1992, www.nytimes.com/1992/10/25/us/1992-campaign-democrats-touring-midwest-clinton-plays-up-outsider-image.html

Inglehart, Ronald F., and Pippa Norris. "Trump, Brexit, and the Rise of Populism: Economic Have-Nots and Cultural Backlash." *Harvard Kennedy School Faculty Research Working Paper Series*, Aug. 2016, www.hks.harvard.edu/publications/trump-brexit-and-rise-populism-economic-have-nots-and-cultural-backlash. Accessed 7 Jan. 2018.

Jamieson, Kathleen H., and Joseph N. Cappella. *Echo Chamber: Rush Limbaugh and the Conservative Media Establishment*. Oxford University Press, 2008.

Kamarck, Elaine. "Donald Trump? Meet Barry Goldwater." *The Brookings Institution*, 30 Mar. 2016, www.brookings.edu/blog/fixgov/2016/03/30/donald-trump-meet-barry-goldwater/.

Kazin, Michael. *The Populist Persuasion: An American History*. BasicBooks, 1995.

Kiewe, Amos. "Framing Memory through Eulogy: Ronald Reagan's Long Good-Bye." *Framing Public Memory*, edited by Kendall R. Phillips, University of Alabama Press, 2004, 248-266.

Krieg, Gregory. "Obama Tried to Take Andrew Jackson Off the $20. Now Trump is Visiting His Grave." *CNN*, 16 Mar. 2017, www.cnn.com/2017/03/14/politics/donald-trump-andrew-jackson-nashville-visit/index.html.

Lauter, David. "Even Elite Campaign Aides Still Aren't Sure Why Donald Trump Succeeded." *Los Angeles Times*, 2 Dec. 2016, www.latimes.com/politics/la-na-pol-campaign-aides-harvard-20161202-story.html.

Lee, Michael J. "The Populist Chameleon: The People's Party, Huey Long, George Wallace, and the Populist Argumentative Frame." *Quarterly Journal of Speech*, vol. 92, no. 4, 2006, pp. 355-378.

Maddux, Kristy. "Fundamentalist Fool or Populist Paragon? William Jennings Bryan and the Campaign Against Evolutionary Theory." *Rhetoric & Public Affairs*, vol. 16, no. 3, 2013, pp. 489–520.

Mahaffey, Jerome Dean. "Converting Tories to Whigs: Religion and Imagined Authorship in Thomas Paine's *Common Sense*." *Southern Communication Journal*, vol. 75, no. 5, 2010, pp. 488-504.

Malcolm, Andrew. "Inside the Mystery of Donald Trump's Stubbornly Loyal Political Base." *Miami Herald*, 6 Nov. 2018, www.miamiherald.com/article221164105.html.

Maskovsky, Jeff. "Toward the Anthropology of White Nationalist Postracialism." *HAU: Journal of Ethnographic Theory*, vol. 7, no. 1, 2017, pp. 433-440, www.haujournal.org/index.php/hau/article/view/hau7.1.030/2710.

Meacham, Jon. "A Lasting Political Influence." *Time Magazine, Special Edition, Andrew Jackson: An American Populist*, 21 July 2017, pp. 4-9.

Meyer, Holly, and Joel Ebert. "Trump Tours The Hermitage, Lays Wreath on Andrew Jackson's Tomb." *The Tennessean*, 15 Mar. 2017, www.tennessean.com/story/news/politics/2017/03/15/trump-arrives-hermitage-historic-visit-andrew-jacksons-home/99164802/.

Mudde, Cas, and Cristóbal Rovira Kaltwasser. *Populism: A Very Short Introduction*. Oxford University Press, 2017.

Newport, Frank, and Lydia Saad. "Trump Support Built on Outsider Status, Business Experience." *Gallup*, 4 Mar. 2016, news.gallup.com/poll/189773/trump-support-built-outsider-status-business-experience.aspx.

Parsons, Lynn Hudson. *The Birth of Modern Politics: Andrew Jackson, John Quincy Adams, and the Election of 1828*. Oxford University Press, 2009.

Serazio, Michael. "Encoding the Paranoid Style in American Politics: 'Anti-Establishment' Discourse and Power in Contemporary Spin." *Critical Studies in Media Communication*, vol. 33, vol. 2, 2016, pp. 181-194.

Struyk, Ryan. "6 in 10 People who Approve of Trump Say They'll Never, Ever, Ever Stop Approving." *CNN*, 17 Aug. 2017, www.cnn.com/2017/08/17/politics/trump-approvers-never-stop-approving-poll/index.html.

Suebsaeng, Asawin. "Steve Bannon Pushed Trump to Go Full Andrew Jackson." *The Daily Beast*, 17 Mar. 2017, www.thedailybeast.com/steve-bannon-pushed-trump-to-go-full-andrew-jackson.

Trump, Donald J. "Full Text: Donald Trump 2016 RNC Draft Speech Transcript." *Politico*, 21 July 2016, www.politico.com/story/2016/07/full-transcript-donald-trump-nomination-acceptance-speech-at-rnc-225974.

Trump, Donald J. "Remarks by the President on 250th Anniversary of the Birth of President Andrew Jackson." *The White House Office of Press Secretary*, 15 Mar.

2017,www.whitehouse.gov/the-press-office/2017/03/15/remarks-president-250th-anniversary-birth-president-andrew-jackson.

Vigil, Tammy R. *Connecting with Constituents: Identification Building and Blocking in Contemporary National Convention Addresses*. Lexington Books, 2015.

Ware, B.L., and Wil A. Linkugel. "The Rhetorical *Persona*: Marcus Garvey as Black Moses." *Communication Monographs*, vol. 49, no. 1, 1982, pp. 50-62.

Zelizer, Julian E. "This is Reagan's Party." *The Atlantic*, 3 Feb. 2016, www.theatlantic.com/politics/archive/2016/02/this-is-reagans-party/459603/.

Contributors

Kristian Bjørkdahl is a postdoctoral fellow and head of teaching at the Centre for Development and the Environment at the University of Oslo, Norway. He does research on American pragmatism, the idea of Nordic exceptionalism, the rhetoric of solidarity, the organization of science communication, the cultural history of meat, and more. He is co-editor of several books, including *Rhetorical Animals: Boundaries of the Human in the Study of Persuasion* (with Alex C. Parrish) and *Pandemics, Publics, and Politics: Staging Responses to Public Health Crises* (w/Benedicte Carlsen). He is co-editor of a Norwegian-language rhetoric magazine, *Kairos*.

David Blakesley is the Campbell Chair in Technical Communication and Professor of English at Clemson University, as well as a Fellow of RSA. He is also the founder and CEO of Parlor Press, a leading publisher in rhetoric, composition, and digital culture, and the editor of *KB Journal*. He writes about visual and digital rhetorics, Kenneth Burke, rhetoric, and film.

Leah Ceccarelli is a professor in the Department of Communication and director of the Science, Technology, and Society Studies interdisciplinary graduate certificate program at the University of Washington, Seattle. Her research focuses on the rhetoric of science. She is a recipient of the National Communication Association's Douglas W. Ehninger Distinguished Rhetorical Scholar Award, as well as other awards for two of her articles, and each of her two books. She serves on the editorial boards of five journals, and co-edits a book series on Transdisciplinary Rhetoric sponsored by the Rhetoric Society of America and Penn State University Press.

Catherine Chaput is an associate professor of English at the University of Nevada, Reno, where she teaches courses in rhetorical theory and criticism, argumentation, and core humanities. Her research focuses on the relationships among rhetoric, affect, and political economy as they manifest within particular social, cultural, and political sites. She is the author of two monographs and multiple articles and book chapters.

Rachel Chapman Daugherty is a Visiting Senior Lecturer and Assistant Director of First-Year Composition at Texas Woman's University, where she teaches courses in writing and rhetoric. Her dissertation, "Constructing Feminist Coalitions: Activist Arguments for Membership and Memory in the Women's March Archives," examines digital archives of the 2017 Women's March and reveals how intersectional feminist activists build coalitions by constructing archives to positively frame coalitional memory. Her research focuses on coalition-building practices in activist and educational contexts, as well as feminist pedagogy and writing program administration. Her essays have appeared in *Peitho* and *Innovative Higher Education*.

Richard Leo Enos is Emeritus Piper Professor (State of Texas) and past Holder of the Lillian Radford Chair of Rhetoric and Composition at Texas Christian University. His research area is classical rhetoric. He is a Past President of the Rhetoric Society of America, RSA Fellow, recipient of the RSA George Yoos Distinguished Service Award and the RSA Cheryl Geisler Mentorship Award.

Joseph Good is a PhD candidate at the University of Maryland, where he teaches academic and professional writing. His research focuses on rhetoric and public policy, analyzing the endemic issues of democratic representation.

Heidi E. Hamilton is a professor in and chair of the Communication and Theatre department at Emporia State University. Her work is primarily in the area of foreign policy rhetoric, social movement persuasion, and political argumentation, including those issues involving gender. Her work has appeared in *Gender and Political Communication in America: Rhetoric, Representation, and Display* (Lexington); *Media Depictions of Brides, Wives, and Mothers* (Lexington); and *Controversia: An International Journal of Debate and Democratic Renewal*.

Michelle Iten is an assistant professor of English at Virginia Military Institute, where she teaches the history and theories of rhetoric, civic discourse, argument, and rhetorical style.

Jacob Justice is a postdoctoral teaching associate at Northeastern University, where he teaches public speaking. His essays have appeared in *Rhetoric & Public Affairs* and *Argumentation & Advocacy*.

Zornitsa D. Keremidchieva is Assistant Professor of Communication Studies at the University of Minnesota. Her scholarship advances feminist and other critical perspectives on the cultural and political dimensions of governance. Her publications have appeared in journals such as the *Quarterly Journal of Speech, Women's History Review, Feminist Media Studies, Women & Language, Journal of Argumentation in Context, Argumentation & Advocacy, The WAC Journal*, and *Advances in the History of Rhetoric*; and in edited collections such as *Globalizing Intercultural Communication, Networking Argument, Sage Handbook of Gender and Communication, The Sage Handbook of Rhetorical Studies*, and the published proceedings of ISSA.

Jens E. Kjeldsen is a professor of rhetoric and visual communication at University of Bergen, Norway. His main research interests are visual rhetoric and argumentation, political rhetoric, ethos and credibility, speech-making and speech writing, and rhetorical theory and research methods. He is currently developing work in the fields of rhetorical reception studies and rhetorical working through. Kjeldsen is co-founder and immediate past president of the Rhetoric Society of Europe. His work has appeared in journals such as *Argumentation, Argumentation and Advocacy,* and *Rhetorica Scandinavica*. Among his publications are *Rhetorical Audience Studies and Reception of Rhetoric* (Ed. Palgrave 2018).

A. Abby Knoblauch is an associate professor of English at Kansas State University, where she teaches everything from first-year writing to graduate seminars on rhetorical theory. Her recent work focuses on embodied rhetorics, fat rhetorics, and composition pedagogy. She has published work in a variety of venues, including CCC, Composition Studies, and a number of edited collections. In her free time, she wrangles her two terribly behaved but deeply loved rescue dogs, and attempts to perfect her homemade bagel recipe.

Laura Leavitt is an independent writer and teacher.

Andrea Abernethy Lunsford is the Louise Hewlett Nixon Professor of English, Emerita, at Stanford University. The Director of Stanford's Program in Writing and Rhetoric from 2000 to 2013 and the founder of Stanford's Hume Center for Writing and Speaking, she developed undergraduate and graduate writing programs at the University of British Columbia and at The Ohio State University, where she also founded The Center for the Study and Teaching of Writing. She is the editor, author or co-author of twenty-three books, including *Essays on Classical Rhetoric and Modern Discourse, Singular Texts/Plural Authors, Reclaiming Rhetorica, Everything's an Argument, The Everyday Writer,* and *Everyone's an Author*. Her awards include the MLA's Mina Shaughnessy Prize, the Conference on College Composition and Communication's Exemplar Award. and the Richard Braddock Award for best article in *College Composition and Communication*.

Paul Lynch is an associate professor at Saint Louis University, where he directs the Prison Education Program. Recent work has appeared in *College English, Contagion,* and *Rhetoric Society Quarterly*.

Carolyn R. Miller is SAS Institute Distinguished Professor of Rhetoric and Technical Communication, Emerita, at North Carolina State University, where she taught from 1973 to 2015. She is a former president of the Rhetoric Society of America, former editor of *Rhetoric Society Quarterly*, and an RSA Fellow. She has published in genre studies, rhetorical theory, and rhetoric of science and technology.

Roxanne Mountford is Professor of English at the University of Oklahoma, where she serves as chair and writing program administrator and teaches courses in the teaching of writing and in rhetorical criticism. Her books include *The Gendered Pulpit: Preaching in American Protestant Spaces*, *Women's Ways of Making It in Rhetoric and Composition* (with Michelle Ballif and Diane Davis) and *Rhetoric and Writing Studies in the New Century: Historiography, Pedagogy, and Politics* (edited with Cheryl Glenn). Her recent work on rhetorical education has appeared in the journals *Rhetoric Society Quarterly* and *Argumentation*.

James J. Murphy is Emeritus Professor of Rhetoric at the University of California, Davis. His books include *Rhetoric in the Middle Ages: A History of Rhetorical Theory from St. Augustine to the Renaissance*, *Quntilian on the Teaching of Speaking and Writing*, *Demosthenes' On the Crown*, *Renaissance Eloquence*, and *A Short History of Writing Instruction from Ancient Greece to Contemporary America*. In 1983, he founded Hermagoras Press, a leading publisher of titles in rhetoric and its history. He is a Fellow of the Rhetoric Society of America.

Jacqueline Jones Royster is Professor of English in the School of Literature, Media, and Communication at Georgia Tech. Her research centers on rhetorical studies, literacy studies, women's studies, cultural studies, areas in which she has authored and co-authored numerous articles and book chapters. She is the author or co-author of *Southern Horrors and Other Writings: The Anti-Lynching Campaign of Ida B. Wells-Barnett* (1997), *Traces of a Stream: Literacy and Social Change among African American Women* (2000), *Profiles of Ohio Women*, 1803–2003 (2003), and *Feminist Rhetorical Studies: New Horizons in Rhetoric, Composition, and Literacy Studies* (2012).

Jack Selzer is the author or coauthor or editor or coeditor of many books, including *Understanding Scientific Prose* (1994), *Kenneth Burke in Greenwich Village* (1997), *Rhetorical Bodies* (1999), *Kenneth Burke in the 1930s* (2007), *1977: The Cultural Year in Composition* (2008), and *The War of Words* by Kenneth Burke (2018). He is a former president of the Rhetoric Society of America and an RSA Fellow.

Shelley Sizemore is Director of Community Partnerships in the Office of Civic and Community Engagement at Wake Forest University. She is a doctoral candidate at the University of North Carolina-Greensboro in educational leadership and cultural foundations. She has previously co-authored a chapter in the book *Truth in the Public Sphere* (2016).

Ryan Skinnell is an associate professor of rhetoric and writing at San José State University. He is author or editor of five books, including *Reinventing (with) Theory in Rhetoric and Writing Studies* (Utah State, 2019) and *Faking the News: What Rhetoric Can Teach Us About Donald J. Trump* (Societas, 2018). He has also published numerous essays in academic and popular outlets on rhetoric, history, writing, and politics.

Joonna Smitherman Trapp is the Director of the Writing Program at Emory University and the WAC/WID director. Her essays have appeared in *CCC Online, Journal of the Fantastic in the Arts, Scope: An Online Journal of Film and TV Studies*, and *Dialogue: A Journal for Writing Specialists*. She was the co-editor of *JAEPL* (Journal of the Assembly for Expanded Perspectives on Learning) for eight years.

David Stock is Associate Professor of English at Brigham Young University, where he teaches undergraduate and graduate courses in writing and rhetoric and co-directs the Research and Writing Center. His research interests include rhetorical education, research methods in writing studies, and writing center studies. He edited *The Memoir of Ednah Shepard Thomas* (WAC Clearinghouse) and has published in *Rhetoric Society Quarterly, WLN: A Journal of Writing Center Scholarship, Praxis: A Writing Center Journal*, and other venues.

Dave Tell is Professor of Communication Studies and Co-Director of the Institute for Digital Research in the Humanities at the University of Kansas. He is the author of *Remembering Emmett Till* (University of Chicago Press, 2019) and a founding director of the "Emmett Till Memory Project." He is the inaugural Public Humanities Officer for the Rhetoric Society of America.

Victor J. Vitanza is Professor Emeritus in the Department of English at Clemson Universityh. He was the founding director of Clemson's Rhetorics, Communication, and Information Design program from 2005 to 2019. He is the Director of the journal PRE/TEXT. His books included *Negation, Subjectivity, and The History of Rhetoric, Sexual Violence in Western Thought and Writing: Chaste Rape*, and *Chaste Cinematics*. He is a Fellow of RSA.

Ron Von Burg is an associate professor of Communication at Wake Forest University. His essays have appeared in *Critical Studies in Media Communication, Southern Communication Journal*, and *Argumentation and Advocacy*.

Scott Welsh is Associate Professor and Interim Chair in the Department of Communication at Appalachian State University in Boone, North Carolina. His work explores rhetorical practice in the context of democratic politics. He is the author of *The Rhetorical Surface of Democracy: How Deliberative Ideals Undermine Democratic Politics*.

Ben Wetherbee is Assistant Professor of Interdisciplinary Studies and English at the University of Science and Arts of Oklahoma, where he serves as Coordinator of Writing. His scholarship, which focuses on rhetorical theory and history, writing pedagogy, and film theory, has appeared in the *Journal of Multimodal Rhetorics*, *Present Tense*, the *Journal of Contemporary Rhetoric*, and the *Henry James Review*, among other journals and collections.

Elizabethada A. Wright is a professor at the University of Minnesota Duluth, where she teaches in the writing studies program with a focus on feminist rhetorical theory and serves as the president of the University Education Association-Duluth. She is also on the graduate faculty at the University of Minnesota Twin Cities. Her essays have appeared in *Rhetoric Review*, *Rhetoric Society Quarterly*, and *Linguistic Research*. In 2020, she won the Robert A. Miller College English Association Memorial Prize for best essay in the *CEA Critic*.

Hui Wu is Professor of English and Chair of the Department of Literature and Languages at the University of Texas at Tyler. Her research espouses history of rhetoric and composition, comparative rhetoric, and feminist rhetorics, and composition studies. Her books include *Once Iron Girls: Essays on Gender by Post-Mao Chinese Literary Women* (Lexington 2010), *Reading and Writing about Disciplines* (Fountainhead 2015), and *Guiguzi, China's First Treatise on Rhetoric: A Translation and Commentary* (with Jan Swearingen Southern Illinois UP 2016).

Richard E. Young is Emeritus Professor of English and Rhetoric at Carnegie Mellon University and former Head of the Department of English. Prior to that he was a member of the Center for Research on Language and Language Behavior and Head of the Department of Humanities at The University of Michigan. His principal area of research has been invention in rhetoric. While at Carnegie Mellon he presided over the development of the PhD in Rhetoric and the Masters in Professional Writing. He is one of the founders of the Rhetoric Society of America.

David Zarefsky is Owen L. Coon Professor Emeritus of Argumentation and Debate, and Professor Emeritus of Communication Studies, Northwestern University, where he taught courses in argumentation and in American public discourse. He is a Fellow and past president of the Rhetoric Society of America. His most recent book is *Lyndon Johnson, Vietnam, and the Presidency: The Speech of March 31, 1968*, forthcoming from Texas A&M University Press (2021).

www.ingramcontent.com/pod-product-compliance
Lightning Source LLC
Chambersburg PA
CBHW032213230426

43672CB00011B/2541